Prophet's Daughter

Prophet's Daughter

The Life and Legacy of
Bahíyyih Khánum,
Outstanding Heroine of the
Bahá'í Faith

Janet A. Khan

Bahá'í
PUBLISHING
Wilmette, Illinois

Bahá'í Publishing, 415 Linden Avenue, Wilmette, IL 60091-2844
Copyright © 2005 by the National Spiritual Assembly of the Bahá'ís of the
United States
All rights reserved. Published 2005
Printed in the United States of America on acid-free paper ∞

08   07   06   05   4   3   2

Library of Congress Cataloging-in-Publication Data
Khan, Janet A. (Janet Adrienne), 1940-
    Prophet's daughter : the life and legacy of Bahíyyih Khánum : outstanding
    heroine of the Bahá'í faith / Janet A. Khan.
        p. cm.
    Includes bibliographical references and index.
    ISBN 10: 1-931847-14-2 (alk. paper) ∞
    ISBN 13: 978-1-931847-14-8 (alk. paper) ∞
        1. Bahâyyih, Khânum. 2. Bahais—Biography. 3. Bahai Faith. I. Title.

BP395.B33K47 2005
297.9'3'092—dc22
[B]
                                                                2005041150

Cover design by Robert A. Reddy
Book design by Suni D. Hannan
Cover photo courtesy of Edit Kálmán

For Peter,
With abiding gratitude

Contents

Chapter 5:
Her Role during Shoghi Effendi's Absences

Chapter 6:
The Glorious Companion of Shoghi Effendi

Chapter 7:
The Hill of God Is Stirred

A Note to the Reader

The system of transliterating Persian and Arabic terms followed in this book is one of several that are currently in use. It has been chosen because Shoghi Effendi, Guardian of the Bahá'í Faith, advocated its use for the sake of consistency.

However, place names and other terms that have familiar, well-established English equivalents (e.g., Baghdad, Tehran, Sulaimaniya) appear in their familiar form unless they occur as part of a quotation that employs the Bahá'í system (e.g., Baghdád, Ṭihrán, Sulaymáníyyih). The same is true for honorific titles (sultan, shah, mullah), which appear in the familiar form unless they occur as part of a quotation or part of a proper name that is translated according to the Bahá'í system (e.g., Sulṭán 'Abdu'l-'Azíz, Mullá Ḥusayn).

Preface

This book is about an extraordinary but little-known woman, Bahíyyih Khánum, who transcended the limitations of a cultural background notorious for its blind fanaticism, its narrow outlook, and its uncompromising refusal to accommodate the forces of modernity. Her story is a testimony to the power of the human spirit to triumph over adversity. The record of her life and achievements provides reassurance and hope to all who are apprehensive about humanity's ability to overcome the powers of ignorance and repression that trouble the world today.

Born in Persia (now known as Iran*) in the middle of the nineteenth century, she was the daughter of Mírzá Husayn-'Alí (1817–92), known as Bahá'u'lláh, the Prophet-Founder of the Bahá'í Faith. Bahá'u'lláh's courageous and forthright presentation of teachings on emancipation, unity, and harmony attracted hatred and relentless persecution in the countries of the Middle East. As a result, Bahíyyih Khánum endured imprisonment or house arrest for six decades.

Events of her life described in this book, and passages within it that are quoted from the Bahá'í writings, are best understood with a basic knowledge of the Bahá'í Faith. It is appropriate, therefore, to briefly discuss the circumstances surrounding the origin of the Bahá'í Faith and the developments in the functioning of the Bahá'í community after Bahá'u'lláh's passing.† Some features of the religion's history need to be considered in the light of the Persian culture in which it arose.

---

* Persia officially adopted the name Iran in 1935. References in the Bahá'í writings use both terms; hence the two terms are used interchangeably in this work.

† For references concerning details of the history and teachings of the Bahá'í Faith, please refer to the basic reading list that appears at the end of this volume.

A distinctive feature of that culture in the nineteenth century was a certain refinement of speech and courtesy of expression that called for the use of elaborate titles and forms of address. This style of expression may be unfamiliar or strange to Westerners brought up with a tradition of precise, unadorned speech and a preference for informality in addressing others. In nineteenth-century Persian culture, to refer to individuals of stature in society by their given names, or even to address them directly, was regarded as an unacceptable form of familiarity. Consequently, we find use of the title Bahá'u'lláh, meaning "the Glory of God," and other designations such as "the Blessed Beauty" or "the Abhá Beauty" in referring to Him. The title 'Abdu'l-Bahá, meaning "the Servant of the Glory," is used for His eldest son and designated successor in authority, as is the term "the Master."

Followers of Bahá'u'lláh are honored through their designation as "servants" if male, and as "handmaidens" or "maidservants" if female. These titles signify the recognition of their commitment to conform their conduct to the religion's precepts. For some readers, the use of such terms could well initially elicit a negative impression—the image of gullible devotees offering passive obedience and subservience to self-deluded, charismatic religious figures who have propounded extravagant claims to divine authority. However, further investigation and careful scrutiny reveal that such an image is far removed from the Bahá'í way of life, with its emphasis on the dignity and freedom of the individual, the fostering of aspiration, the development of the intellectual powers of all people, and the preservation of personal initiative within the broad limits of social cohesion.

Another element that might puzzle Western readers is the use of certain images of nature in the Bahá'í writings. For example, the tree appears in the Bahá'í writings as a powerful symbol, with terms such as "the Divine Lote-Tree" being used to refer to Bahá'u'lláh. Its connotations of strength, endurance, flexibility, and benefit to all are particularly appealing to those sensitized to the wonder and beauty of the natural world. The male members of Bahá'u'lláh's family are designated as "branches," with 'Abdu'l-Bahá being identified as "the Most Great Branch." The females of the family are honored with the appellation of "leaves," and the term "Greatest Holy Leaf" appears in many places in this book in reference to Bahíyyih Khánum.

The Bahá'í world view is that the development of humanity is evolutionary and purposeful, proceeding from the dawn of recorded history, through the present day, to a future of world unity and the flourishing of a world civilization for many thousands of years to come. The constructive interaction of the forces of religion and science provides both the motivation and the means for this process. Religion provides enlightened values and a code of behavior that promotes a creative and unified society. Science provides an ever-deepening understanding of the operation of the universe and gives rise to new technology, including energy sources, communications facilities, and means of transportation. These new technologies, in turn, advance the evolution of society.

The entire evolutionary process arises from the continuing interaction between God and humanity. The divine will, Bahá'ís believe, is conveyed to humanity through a series of Messengers of God, Who have appeared in the past, some hundreds of years apart, and will continue to come at intervals of a thousand or more years in the future. This process is described in the Bahá'í writings as one of progressive revelation, and the Messengers are known as Manifestations of God. Their messages, when examined in their pure form as given by the Manifestation, are very similar in their fundamental spiritual values but significantly different in the social laws applicable to the period in which the Manifestation appears.

The period of thousands of years of recorded history during which Manifestations of God have come to humanity is known in the

Bahá'í Faith as the Cycle of Prophecy. Its distinguishing feature is that each Manifestation of God, during His particular Dispensation, foreshadowed the coming of another Manifestation—either as the return of the Messenger setting out the prophecy or as a distinct religious entity Who would bring teachings to unify humanity and provide the foundation for world civilization over a vast period designated as the Cycle of Fulfillment. Thus all of the great religions extant in the world today contain, in their pristine form, the expectation of the coming of a Promised One.

The most arresting feature of the Bahá'í Faith is the belief that Bahá'u'lláh is the Manifestation of God Who fulfills the prophesied coming of this Promised One, and that the turmoil of the present time is associated with the transition to the long anticipated unification of the peoples of the world. Those who are able to resist the natural tendency to dismiss summarily such an extraordinary claim will seek evidence to support or disprove it. They will carefully scrutinize not only His fulfillment of specific elements of prophetic expectation, but also beyond that, the record of His life, the caliber of His teachings, and the extent to which the application of His teachings is eradicating the many deeply entrenched barriers to unity. Those who carefully investigate His claim ultimately reach a conclusion that transcends rational analysis to attain the level of spiritual conviction.

The Dispensation of Bahá'u'lláh is anticipated to endure no less than one thousand years. It is divided into three ages: the Heroic Age, the Formative Age, and the Golden Age.

The Heroic Age began in 1844. It was inaugurated in Persia by the declaration of Siyyid 'Alí-Muḥammad, known as the Báb ("Gate"), that He was the bearer of a message from God which concluded the Prophetic Cycle and foreshadowed the imminent advent of the Promised One. Such statements resonated within the souls of thousands of people in Persia, rapidly attracting large-scale support but causing consternation to a firmly rooted religious establishment that held both government and people within its clutches. The early history of the Bahá'í Faith is drenched with the blood of some twenty thousand martyrs, with the thirst for vengeance unquenched by the martyrdom of the Báb in 1850.

Bahá'u'lláh, to Whom the followers of the Báb turned for leadership after the Báb's martyrdom, was imprisoned in an underground dungeon in Tehran in 1852 and exiled to Baghdad very soon thereafter. These traumatic events marked the beginning of the suffering of Bahíyyih Khánum, then a small child, described in some detail in this book. Bahá'u'lláh's declaration of His mission in 1863 brought the full force of ecclesiastical opposition upon Him and His followers. He remained a prisoner and an exile for the rest of His life and was transferred successively to the Ottoman cities of Constantinople (Istanbul) and Adrianople (Edirne). Finally, He and His family were incarcerated in the notorious prison city of Acre on the Mediterranean coast. He passed away in 1892, and His remains were interred at Bahjí, on the outskirts of this city. The Bahá'í World Center is located in the twin cities of Haifa and Acre in what is now the State of Israel. The repression and persecution of the Bahá'ís by Muslim clerics continues to the present day and is fueled by the false accusation that the location of the Bahá'í World Center in Israel is an expression of partisan involvement in the political tensions of the region. Appeals to reason, pointing out that Bahá'u'lláh came to Acre involuntarily, as a prisoner in the time of the Ottoman Turkish domain here, are fruitless in the face of blind religious fanaticism.

Unique to the Bahá'í Faith are its provisions to prevent the enduring schisms that have grievously diminished the strength and cohesion of the Prophetic Cycle religions as a consequence of disagreements over authority and organization after the passing of the Manifestation. These provisions are contained in the Covenant of

Bahá'u'lláh, which sets out explicitly in writing the arrangements for authority and organization after the passing of Bahá'u'lláh. They focus primarily on 'Abdu'l-Bahá, the eldest son of Bahá'u'lláh, who was appointed Center of Bahá'u'lláh's Covenant and the authorized interpreter of the Bahá'í writings. Although 'Abdu'l-Bahá appears in this book in a role supplementary to that of his sister, Bahíyyih Khánum, his wisdom and strength of character are apparent. 'Abdu'l-Bahá's passing in 1921 marked the end of the Heroic Age.

The second of the three ages in the Dispensation of Bahá'u'lláh is the Formative Age, with its distinguishing feature being the establishment throughout the world by Bahá'ís of an Administrative Order for their Faith. This system of organization and administration of the Bahá'í community is based on principles laid down by Bahá'u'lláh and further elaborated by 'Abdu'l-Bahá, in his will and testament, within his capacity as authorized interpreter of his father's writings.

The Bahá'í Faith has no priesthood and is free from the privileges, prerogatives, and rituals that are generally associated with ecclesiastical structures. The Bahá'í Administrative Order has two arms, one elected and the other appointed. The elected arm consists of individuals who are elected to serve as members of Spiritual Assemblies. These local and national bodies are endowed with the authority to administer the affairs of their Bahá'í community through the exercise of legislative, judicial, and executive powers in matters pertaining to religious practice. An internationally elected body, the Universal House of Justice, was formed in 1963 and acts as the head of the Bahá'í Faith. All Bahá'ís turn to it for guidance.

The appointive arm of the Administrative Order is composed of individuals of high standing in the community who are appointed to act in an advisory capacity to Assemblies and individuals. They offer counsel, foster adherence to the spiritual values of the religion, and call attention to those measures required to protect the Bahá'í Faith from the inadvertent corruption of its teachings with the passage of time. These individuals are designated as Counselors and Auxiliary Board members, and, along with their assistants, are organized into five boards of Counselors, one for each continental area of the world. Their work is coordinated and supervised by the International Teaching Center, which is located at the Bahá'í World Center and functions under the guidance of the Universal House of Justice.

To bring the Bahá'í administrative structure into being, 'Abdu'l-Bahá appointed his eldest grandson, Shoghi Effendi, as Guardian of the Faith. The poignancy of the relationship between Shoghi Effendi, then a young man in his early twenties, and the elderly Bahíyyih Khánum is described in this book, as is the crucial role she played in the period of transition immediately following 'Abdu'l-Bahá's passing. By discharging his functions, which included acting as the authorized interpreter of the Faith, Shoghi Effendi successfully completed his mission to expand and protect the fledgling Faith by the time of his own passing in 1957.

As the membership of the Bahá'í community grows, the influence of its Administrative Order will extend to a greater proportion of society. Bahá'ís believe that its methods of operation—with an emphasis on maintaining a careful balance between centralized and decentralized functioning, the use of democratic procedures in the election of its administrative bodies, measures to preserve indivual freedom and initiative, and safeguards for fostering cultural diversity—provide both a pattern and a nucleus for a future world society. Bahá'ís anticipate that the Formative Age will culminate, perhaps centuries into the future, with the evolution of its Administrative Order into an inclusive entity known as the World Order of Bahá'u'lláh, which will be animated by Bahá'í spiritual and administrative principles.

Inevitably, attempts have been made periodically to subvert the provisions of the Covenant of Bahá'u'lláh by those whose sense of personal superiority over others leads them to seek the individual power and authority denied them by that Covenant. The Bahá'í Faith makes no secret of the fact that, at various times in its history, a few ambitious and egotistic individuals have strenuously endeavored to violate the Bahá'í Covenant for their own ends. When efforts to persuade such individuals to cease their attempts to disrupt the Bahá'í community prove unsuccessful, the head of the Faith has no option but to designate them as Covenant-breakers and exclude them from membership in the Faith. Covenant-breakers are left free to pursue their own interests. Throughout the history of the Faith, the fruitless labors of Covenant-breakers have ultimately proven beneficial to the Bahá'í community by serving as a reminder of its commitment to building a society suffused with the spirit of equality and loving support for all of its members. Bahíyyih Khánum's personal example as an individual of high standing in the community is particularly instructive in this regard.

The third and final age of the Bahá'í Dispensation is its Golden Age, which lies hundreds of years in the future, when the transformation of human society through the influence of the Bahá'í teachings will give rise to the foundation of a world civilization having a dazzling splendor far beyond our capacity to visualize.

The Dispensation of Bahá'u'lláh will be terminated by the advent of the next Manifestation of God, Who will bring teachings that rest on the same spiritual foundation but that have social principles designed to meet the needs of that time. This process will continue in the millennia to come in the Cycle of Fulfillment and will give energy and direction to an ever-advancing civilization of incomparable magnificence.

The vital role of Bahíyyih Khánum in the early days of the Bahá'í Dispensation, when the Bahá'í Faith was beset by threats and dangers from cruel and relentless enemies, can only properly be assessed in the distant future. At that time, the significance of her actions and her example will become more clearly apparent, and the gratitude and admiration of those who contemplate the nobility of her life will be boundless.

Chapter 1 ❧

Bahíyyih Khánum, Scion of Bahá'u'lláh

Bahíyyih Khánum was the eldest daughter of Bahá'u'lláh, the Prophet and Founder of the Bahá'í Faith, a religion that had its origins in Iran in the middle of the nineteenth century. She witnessed firsthand the momentous events surrounding the birth of this new Revelation and subsequently played a major role in its emergence as an independent world religion. Bahíyyih Khánum's contribution to the development of the Bahá'í Faith is unique. Indeed, a systematic study of the exploits and achievements of this relatively unknown Persian woman is long overdue. Furthermore, the example of her life is of enduring importance, and her personal qualities have special relevance to the issues confronting contemporary society.

Role in Bahá'í History

Bahíyyih Khánum was born in Persia (modern-day Iran) in 1846. Her life spanned all but two years of the most turbulent and formative period in the history of the Bahá'í Faith, a period characterized by the exploits and the trials of the Faith's central figures and by the sufferings and sacrifices of the legion of martyrs who arose to champion the infant religion. Those who are familiar with this record will be aware of the broad outline of the life of Bahíyyih Khánum. She was not only an observer but also an active participant in many of these tumultuous happenings. Indeed, after her death in 1932, Shoghi Effendi, the Guardian of the Bahá'í Faith, stated, "In her face one could easily read the history of the Cause from its earliest days to the present moment."[1]

Born into a noble and wealthy family, Bahíyyih Khánum was two years younger than her distinguished brother 'Abdu'l-Bahá and several years older than her brother Mírzá Mihdí. Her mother was the illustrious Ásíyih K͟hánum, titled "Navváb."* The family was inevitably caught up in the vortex of events that surrounded the birth of the Bahá'í religion.

At the age of six she witnessed the sacking and plundering of her parents' property when her father was imprisoned in the Síyáh-K͟hál, the "Black Pit" of Tehran. She shared with her mother, Navváb, and her brother 'Abdu'l-Bahá the gnawing anxiety concerning whether Bahá'u'lláh would be executed. While her mother was absent, endeavoring to obtain information about the situation of her beloved husband and attempting to provide for the daily needs of the family, Bahíyyih K͟hánum alone cared for her infant brother.

When Bahá'u'lláh was released from incarceration, He and His family and a number of close associates were exiled to Baghdad in 1853. Thus began a period of exile that, for Bahíyyih K͟hánum, was to last until the end of her life and to include periods of captivity. She shared the imprisonment and banishment of Bahá'u'lláh when He was, at the behest of the Persian and Ottoman civil and ecclesiastic authorities, sent first to Baghdad, then to Constantinople, then to Adrianople, and finally to the prison city of Acre.

From her earliest days, Bahíyyih K͟hánum had an appreciation of the station of her father as a Messenger of God and a deep love and desire to serve Him and the cause He founded. At each stage of her life, she was called upon to undertake delicate and difficult missions and to demonstrate heroic qualities of character and spirit in service to that cause. She was elevated to a high rank by Bahá'u'lláh, Who also bestowed upon her the title of the Greatest Holy Leaf, a designation that members of the Bahá'í Faith often use when referring to her.

---

* An honorific implying grace, highness, majesty.

With the passing of Bahá'u'lláh in 1892, 'Abdu'l-Bahá was appointed in the will and testament of his father as the head of the Bahá'í Faith. During this period of transition and the years that followed, internal and external enemies of the religion arose to challenge 'Abdu'l-Bahá's authority and to crush the Bahá'í Faith. In the midst of this storm, Bahíyyih Khánum was the sole living member of Bahá'u'lláh's family who did not abandon 'Abdu'l-Bahá. She, together with 'Abdu'l-Bahá's wife, Munírih Khánum, and their daughters remained his only staunch and loyal supporters.

Following the death of her father, the Greatest Holy Leaf lived in the household of 'Abdu'l-Bahá. Because of the high station conferred upon her by Bahá'u'lláh and her unique qualities, she served as the head of 'Abdu'l-Bahá's household. She cultivated social relationships to shield her brother and acted as the honored hostess to the increasing numbers of pilgrims from the East and the West. In all things she was his loyal partner and trusted confidant. Finally, when the sultanate was overthrown in 1908 and all political and religious prisoners of the Ottoman state were freed, 'Abdu'l-Bahá was able to embark on his historic travels to the Western world. During his two-year absence from the Holy Land, 'Abdu'l-Bahá left the running of the affairs of the Cause in the hands of Bahíyyih Khánum. She was, according to Shoghi Effendi, 'Abdu'l-Bahá's "competent deputy, His representative and vicegerent, with none to equal her."[2]

The death of 'Abdu'l-Bahá in 1921 was a crushing blow to the Greatest Holy Leaf. Despite her great sense of loss, she made the necessary arrangements for his funeral, safeguarded his will and testament, and announced that, according to the provisions of his will, Shoghi Effendi, the grandson of 'Abdu'l-Bahá, was appointed as the Guardian of the Bahá'í Faith.

At the time of his appointment, Shoghi Effendi was a student at Oxford University. On his return to the Holy Land, he became aware of the responsibility that he was called upon to shoulder. Overwhelmed by the magnitude of the task, he embarked on a period of preparation and reflection that involved an extended sojourn in Switzerland. Before his departure he left "the affairs of the Cause both at home and abroad, under the supervision of the Holy Family and the headship of the Greatest Leaf."[3]

In her capacity as acting head of the Bahá'í Faith, Bahíyyih Khánum rallied its members in support of the newly appointed Guardian and encouraged the expansion and consolidation of the religion throughout the world. Until the very end of her life, she remained, in Shoghi Effendi's words, his "chief sustainer," his "most affectionate comforter," the "joy and inspiration" of his life.[4]

The Greatest Holy Leaf's role in Bahá'í history is unparalleled in religious history. To assess this role, it is necessary to take into consideration the constraints under which women in the Middle East lived in the nineteenth and early twentieth centuries. Women in the Islamic world were largely invisible. They enjoyed few rights and had no status in the community. They were veiled and led a cloistered existence separated from all men except the members of their immediate family. Deprived of the opportunity for education and confined to the home, they tended to be illiterate. They were not permitted to participate in public affairs and had no role in religion. In addition, the historical record of the era contains few references to women, since it was considered unethical and improper for historians, who were mostly male, to invade the privacy of women by inquiring into their lives.

While the sources of information about Bahíyyih Khánum are scattered and sometimes sparse, it is particularly significant that Bahá'u'lláh Himself chose to withdraw "the veil of concealment" from His daughter, thereby opening the way for historians to study her life, to rescue her from invisibility, to appreciate her role in society, and to assess her contribution to history.[5]

Rank and Station

Bahíyyih Khánum occupies a unique position in the Bahá'í Faith. Bahá'u'lláh elevated her to an exalted rank and called her to a unique station. He addresses her in the following words: "We have elevated thee to the rank of one of the most distinguished among thy sex, and granted thee . . . a station such as none other woman hath surpassed. Thus have We preferred thee and raised thee above the rest, as a sign of grace from Him Who is the Lord of the throne on high and earth below."[6]

The Greatest Holy Leaf thus ranks "as foremost among the members of her sex in the Bahá'í Dispensation." Her high station is not, however, confined solely to the realm of women. Indeed, after the passing of 'Abdu'l-Bahá, Shoghi Effendi referred to Bahíyyih Khánum as the "last remnant" of Bahá'u'lláh's family and designated her as "its most exalted member."[7]

What is the significance of such designations? In today's world, where women are largely marginalized by traditional ecclesiastical structures and deprived of positions of authority, what lessons can be drawn concerning the role of women in religion? What are the implications of rank and the approaches to leadership within a faith community?

Outstanding Heroine and Archetype

Descriptions of the spiritual and personal qualities of Bahíyyih Khánum in the writings of the Bahá'í Faith are numerous. They provide insight into her unique station, illustrate her outstanding contribution to the development of the religion, and outline possible implications for contemporary society. The Greatest Holy Leaf is described as "the outstanding heroine of the Bahá'í Dispensation" and as "the Last Survivor of a Glorious and Heroic Age." She is also designated as the "archetype of the people of Bahá,"* whose "heavenly ways" are, according to the Guardian, "a model" for members of the religion to emulate, and her "celestial attributes" are "their prototype and their guide."[8]

Throughout the ages, heroic figures, saints and philosophers, kings and generals, artists and politicians, revolutionaries and terrorists, and even rock stars have served to inspire and guide the behavior of women and men. Held up as the embodiments of certain ideals and values that are prized by the society that honors them, their lives have been taken as models of right behavior, and their exploits are the stuff from which myths and dreams are made.

Archetypes likewise play an important role in the life of the individual and in religious history. The primary dictionary definition provided for "archetype" is "the original pattern or model from which copies are made; a prototype." More specialized meanings include "a coin of standard weight by which others are adjusted" and "an assumed ideal pattern of the fundamental structure of each great division of organized beings, of which the various species are considered as modifications." In literary criticism, the term conveys the notion of "a primordial image, character, or pattern that recurs throughout literature and thought consistently enough to be considered a universal concept or situation."[9]

Most religions have identified an archetypal female figure who epitomizes the female ideal of the religion and serves to motivate the women believers. While the archetypal figure is, more usually, associated with the female virtues of purity, virginity, and motherhood, there are also examples of women who transcend their cul-

---

* "People of Bahá" refers to the followers of Bahá'u'lláh—i.e., the Bahá'ís.

tural traditions. The history of religion records how women of capacity such as Deborah, the judge and prophetess who secured the Israelites' victory aver the Canaanites; Mary Magdalene, who restored the confidence of the disciples after the crucifixion; and the redoubtable Joan of Arc arose, under conditions of great difficulty and necessity, to perform remarkable services in the name of religion.[10]

How, then, to understand the significance of Bahíyyih Khánum's designation as "the archetype of the people of Bahá"? To what extent does she conform to existing archetypal patterns? What is the link between the ideals and values she embodied and the direction of social evolution? When examined in detail, it would appear that the Greatest Holy Leaf is neither simply a mother-earth type nor the typical mythical hero and martyr. Furthermore, while female archetypal figures generally serve to inspire and motivate women, the Greatest Holy Leaf's station as the "archetype of the people of Bahá" is unique among religious traditions. She is clearly designated as a model for all "people," women and men alike.

Bahíyyih Khánum's qualities have, by definition, relevance to both women and men. Both sexes derive inspiration from the example of her life and model their behavior on her qualities. This, then, calls for a reexamination of the qualities that are traditionally regarded as masculine and those that are regarded as feminine. It also requires a redefinition of the concept of heroism.

Given the public persona and notoriety that is usually associated with contemporary heroes and heroines, it is extraordinary to consider Bahíyyih Khánum's designation by Shoghi Effendi as the "outstanding heroine of the Bahá'í Dispensation" and as the "archetype of the people of Bahá." She grew up in a culture where, traditionally, women are invisible. For most of her life she was subject to many of the restrictions that characterized the existence of women in Muslim countries. To a large extent, she lived "behind the curtain," in virtual separation from men, although in the household of Bahá'u'lláh, those believers who were close to Him did come into contact with the female members of His family.[11] She not only led a life of confinement, but, owing to the customs of the time and the respect for the privacy to which women were entitled, her exploits were largely unrecorded by the oriental historians of the Bahá'í Faith.

Explorations

In the chapters that follow we will examine in detail the Greatest Holy Leaf's participation in the major events associated with the birth and early spread of the Bahá'í Faith. We will also explore the significance of her exploits, the implications of her unique station, and the importance of her example in an attempt to gain a deeper appreciation of her enduring legacy.

Chapter 2 🐦

Bahá'u'lláh's Precious Daughter

To understand Bahíyyih Khánum's contribution to the development of the Bahá'í community it is necessary to examine her role in the events that transpired during the lifetimes of her father, Bahá'u'lláh, of her brother 'Abdu'l-Bahá, and of her great-nephew Shoghi Effendi. Central to this examination are the unique relationships she enjoyed with each of these figures.

In this chapter we will examine the relationship of the Greatest Holy Leaf to Bahá'u'lláh and explore her participation in some of the turbulent events that shaped the Heroic Age of the Bahá'í Faith, an age associated with the ministries of the Prophet Bahá'u'lláh and His Forerunner, the Báb. While the historical record is incomplete—indeed Shoghi Effendi has asserted that the details of her participation were largely unrecorded by historians of the period—he has provided a broad framework that enables us to gain some insight into the nature of her service. To this broad outline we add the observations of Bahíyyih Khánum herself, drawn from the oral accounts she gave to Bahá'í pilgrims who were privileged to come into her presence in the latter part of her life. The appendix provides a detailed description of the sources used in the process of piecing together the story of her contribution to the rise and establishment of the Bahá'í Faith.

Her Relationship with Bahá'u'lláh

Bahíyyih Khánum is the beloved daughter of Bahá'u'lláh. Her deep love and affection for her father, her passionate concern for His well-being and safety, and her inconsolable distress at the time of His passing are attested to in the letters of Shoghi Effendi. Her relationship with her father was unique, far transcending the usual father-daughter relationship. She was, in the words of the Guardian, "united with the Spirit of her almighty Father" by a "mystic bond." It is evident that, from a very early age, she had a clear understanding of her father's station as the Manifestation of God for the age. Her life was wholly dedicated to serving Him and to promoting the new Revelation He introduced.[1]

Bahíyyih Khánum explains the nature of the relations between Bahá'u'lláh and the members of His family, observing that

> After his declaration we all regarded him as one far above us, and tacitly gave him a corresponding position in our demeanor towards him. He was never called upon to consider, or take part in, any worldly matters. We felt no claim upon him because of family relationship—no more than that of his other followers. When we had but two rooms for all, one was set apart for him. The best of everything was always given to him. He would take it and then return it to us and do without. He slept upon the floor because his people had no beds, although he would have been furnished one had he wished it.[2]

The writings of Bahá'u'lláh set out the uniqueness of His relationship with His daughter and disclose the dual aspects of that bond. For example, on the physical plane the Greatest Holy Leaf is described as "a leaf that hath sprung from this preexistent Root," and the tenderness of the father's love for His daughter is conveyed in the following testimony: "How sweet thy presence before Me; how sweet to gaze upon thy face, to bestow upon thee My loving-kindness, to favour thee with My tender care, to make mention of thee in this, My Tablet—a Tablet which I have ordained as a token of My hidden and manifest grace unto thee."[3]

Beyond the ties of physical relationship, Bahá'u'lláh underlines a transcendent purpose for her physical being, a purpose that relates to her recognition of His station as Manifestation of God and the fulfillment of her purpose in life. He states, "We have created thine eyes to behold the light of My countenance, thine ears to hearken unto the melody of My words, thy body to pay homage before My throne. Do thou render thanks unto God, thy Lord, the Lord of all the world." Bahá'u'lláh likewise expresses pleasure at the manner in which she exemplified the spiritual qualities embodied by the Manifestation of God when He states, "I can well inhale from thee the fragrance of My love and the sweet-smelling savour wafting from the raiment of My Name, the Most Holy, the Most Luminous." As a testimony to Bahíyyih Khánum's outstanding qualities, Bahá'u'lláh bestows upon her a unique spiritual station, elevating her to "the rank of one of the most distinguished among thy sex" and granting her "a station such as none other woman hath surpassed." He counsels her to fulfill this rank in the following manner: "Be astir upon God's Tree in conformity with thy pleasure and unloose thy tongue in praise of thy Lord amidst all mankind. Let not the things of the world grieve thee. Cling fast unto this divine Lote-Tree from which God hath graciously caused thee to spring forth. I swear by My life! It behoveth the lover to be closely joined to the loved one, and here indeed is the Best-Beloved of the world."[4]

Bahá'u'lláh's counsel was, indeed, the motivating force of her being. The Greatest Holy Leaf's very existence was centered on her recognition of the station of Bahá'u'lláh. She had a clear understanding of the importance of His Revelation and an unswerving commitment to furthering the Cause of God—with all its attendant tests and trials.

Her Unique Role during Bahá'u'lláh's Ministry

There are few historical records detailing Bahíyyih Khánum's participation in the events of the early days of the Bahá'í cause. In part, this appears to be due to the traditional reticence of Eastern historians to intrude into the privacy of the female members of Bahá'u'lláh's family. It is also probable that these historians lacked an appreciation of the role women could potentially play in activities outside of the home, including their involvement in religious matters. Nevertheless, drawing upon the letters of Shoghi Effendi and his analysis of the seminal events in the unfoldment of the Bahá'í Faith, it is possible to obtain glimpses into the significance of the role the Greatest Holy Leaf played in the events that transpired during Bahá'u'lláh's ministry.

Tehran

Following the martyrdom of the Báb in 1850, the morale of His followers declined to a low ebb. Seeking to avenge the death of their leader, some misguided and irresponsible young men attempted to kill the shah. The shah received only superficial injuries; nevertheless, the event precipitated widespread persecution of the Báb's followers. Though completely innocent, Bahá'u'lláh, because of His close association with the Báb, was immediately arrested on suspicion of His involvement in the crime.

The imprisonment of Bahá'u'lláh in 1852 in Tehran's underground dungeon known as the Síyáh-Chál (Black Pit) set in motion a chain of events that impacted the fortunes of the Bahá'í Faith and the lives of His family members. Bahíyyih Khánum was "still in her infancy" when her father was incarcerated; nevertheless, the Guardian affirms that this event marks the beginning of her unique participation in the unfoldment of the new religious movement. The Guardian writes, "From the beginning of her life, from her very childhood, she tasted sorrow's cup; she drank down the afflictions and calamities of the earliest years of the great Cause of God."[5]

When Bahá'u'lláh was taken into custody, His property was confiscated and plundered. The Greatest Holy Leaf's parents suddenly lost their earthly possessions, and, within the space of a single day, the family was plunged into poverty. Bahá'u'lláh's beloved wife Navváb and her children were turned out of their home, and she resorted to selling a few personal belongings to feed her family. Beyond the overwhelming financial difficulties, there was a "gnawing suspense that ate into the hearts" of the family members as, "at any moment" they expected to receive "the news of Bahá'u'lláh's imminent execution."[6]

Shoghi Effendi spells out the nature of her suffering and some of the spiritual lessons Bahíyyih Khánum learned from these early experiences. He states that she sank abruptly "to the state of a sufferer from unconcealed poverty" after having been "the privileged member of one of the wealthiest families in Ṭihrán." He attests that as a consequence of "the sacking and plundering of her glorious Father's wealth and holdings, she learned the bitterness of destitution and want."[7]

In her spoken chronicle, Bahíyyih Khánum graphically recalls the sudden nature of the family's change in circumstances. Her carefree childhood was overtaken by fear and anxiety. After being driven from their home, the family resided in a little house that was not far from the prison where Bahá'u'lláh was being held. Her mother had managed to save a few of her marriage treasures, which were subsequently sold so the money could be used to pay the jailers to take food to Bahá'u'lláh in prison and to meet the expenses of daily living. However, in her recollections of this period, Bahíyyih Khánum makes few comments about her personal situation, but focuses instead on depicting the appalling conditions under which Bahá'u'lláh lived, the family's apprehension that He would be executed, and her mother's efforts to alleviate the sufferings of her beloved husband.

Bahíyyih Khánum describes the conditions of her father's imprisonment in the Síyáh-Chál:

> The prison into which my father had been cast was a terrible place, seven steps below the ground; it was ankle-deep in filth, infested with horrible vermin, and of an indescribable loathsomeness. Added to this, there was no glimmer of light in that noisome place. Within its walls forty Bábís were crowded; murderers and highway robbers were also imprisoned there.
>
> My noble father was hurled into this black hole, loaded with heavy chains; five other Bábís were chained to him night and day, and here he remained for four months. Picture to yourself the horror of these conditions.
>
> Any movement caused the chains to cut deeper and deeper not only into the flesh of one, but of all who were chained together; whilst sleep or rest of any kind was not possible. No food was provided, and it was with the utmost difficulty that my mother was able to arrange to get any food or drink taken into that ghastly prison.[8]

As a child, the Greatest Holy Leaf was clearly aware of the conditions under which her father was living. She was also cognizant of the very real dangers faced not only by Bahá'u'lláh but also by the early followers of the Báb who were accused of being infidels by the exponents of religious fanaticism. She recalls how "Every morning one or more of these brave and devoted friends would be taken out to be tortured and killed in various ways of horror," and recounts how the various classes of the populace were all given opportunities to carry out barbaric methods of torture against the hapless Bábís. She describes the scene of execution—the quiet heroism of the victim, the frenzy of the mob that eagerly crowded around to witness the carnage—all to the accompaniment of "a drum [that] was loudly beaten."[9]

As can be seen from her spoken chronicle, the sound of these horrific events appears to be most vivid in her memory and to evoke the sense of anxiety that characterized this period of her life. She states,

> These horrible sounds I well remember, as we three children clung to our mother, she not knowing whether the victim was her own adored husband. She could not find out whether he was still alive or not until late at night, or very early in the morning, when she determined to venture out, in defiance of the danger to herself and to us, for neither women [n]or children were spared.
>
> How well I remember cowering in the dark, with my little brother, Mírzá Mihdí, the Purest Branch, at that time two years old, in my arms, which were not very strong, as I was only six. I was shivering with terror, for I knew of some of the horrible things that were happening, and was aware that they might have seized even my mother.
>
> So I waited and waited until she should come back. Then Mírzá Músá, my uncle, who was in hiding, would venture in to hear what tidings my mother had been able to gather.[10]

After four months, Bahá'u'lláh was released from prison following the intervention of the Russian consul. However, the Persian government decreed that He and His family were to be banished to Baghdad. The severity of this banishment was to surpass that of "the premeditated attacks and the systematic machinations of the court, the clergy, the government and the people" that Bahá'u'lláh had already experienced in Tehran. Indeed, Shoghi Effendi attests that such events constituted "the prelude to a harrowing and extensive captivity." He characterizes the impact of the decree in the following terms: "Extending over a period of more than forty years, and carrying Him successively to 'Iráq, Sulaymáníyyih, Constantinople, Adrianople and finally to the penal colony of 'Akká, this long banishment was at last ended by His death, at the age of over three score years and ten, terminating a captivity which, in its range, its duration and the diversity and severity of its afflictions, is unexampled in the history of previous Dispensations."[11]

In a prayer revealed by Bahá'u'lláh, He describes the hardships endured during the first stage of that "'terrible journey'" to Baghdad. He specifically mentions the sufferings of the "'frail-bodied men and children of tender age'" who accompanied Him on this exile and the extreme weather conditions to which they were subjected— a cold "'so intense that one cannot even speak, and ice and snow so abundant that it is impossible to move.'"[12]

Shoghi Effendi places this journey to Baghdad in the context of religious history and foreshadows its significance for the future of the Bahá'í Faith and for humankind. He writes,

This enforced and hurried departure of Bahá'u'lláh from His native land, accompanied by some of His relatives, recalls in some of its aspects, the precipitate flight of the Holy Family into Egypt; the sudden migration of Muḥammad, soon after His assumption of the prophetic office, from Mecca to Medina; the exodus of Moses, His brother and His followers from the land of their birth, in response to the Divine summons, and above all the banishment of Abraham from Ur of the Chaldees to the Promised

Land—a banishment which, in the multitudinous benefits it conferred upon so many divers peoples, faiths and nations, constitutes the nearest historical approach to the incalculable blessings destined to be vouchsafed, in this day, and in future ages, to the whole human race, in direct consequence of the exile suffered by Him Whose Cause is the flower and fruit of all previous Revelations.[13]

The exile of Bahá'u'lláh to Baghdad opened a period in which Bahíyyih Khánum, then a seven-year-old child, was to share "the imprisonment, the grief, [and] the banishment of the 'Abhá Beauty."* In her chronicle, she describes the efforts her mother made to nurse her beloved husband back to health and to make the necessary preparations for the long and arduous journey from Tehran to Baghdad. This "fearful journey," which was undertaken in the depths of winter, lasted three months. The route was over high mountains covered with deep snow, and the means of comfort were scant. The Greatest Holy Leaf recalls the sufferings the exiles experienced as they traversed the difficult terrain mounted on mules. Her father had not yet recovered from the hardships of His imprisonment. Her mother, in the final stages of pregnancy, suffered greatly as she was conveyed in a *takh-i-raván,* a type of couch attached to the back of a jolting mule. Despite her weakened condition, however, she exerted every effort to care for the family. Food was scarce, and the family did not have sufficient clothing to protect them from the biting cold. En route, the family sometimes "'encamped in wilderness places,'" though they lacked the necessary equipment. At other times they stayed in a caravansary.[14]

_____

* A reference to Bahá'u'lláh; *Abhá,* which derives from His name, means in Arabic "Most Glorious."

Baghdad

The period in Baghdad was marked by several outstanding events that affected the development of the Bahá'í Faith and the lives of Bahá'u'lláh's family members. These included the activities of Bahá'u'lláh's half-brother Mírzá Yaḥyá, whose spurious claims to the leadership of the Bábí community created a storm of disunity. His machinations precipitated Bahá'u'lláh's withdrawal to the mountains of Sulaimaniya and subsequently contributed to the further exile of Bahá'u'lláh and His immediate followers to the heart of the Ottoman Empire. Bahá'u'lláh's declaration of His mission as the Manifestation of God for this age took place immediately before His departure for Constantinople.

When the family arrived in Baghdad in 1853 Bahíyyih Khánum expanded the activities in which she engaged. The health of both of her parents was fragile. She leaves the following account in her spoken chronicle:

> Ásíyih Khánum, my dear mother, was in delicate health, her strength was diminished by the hardships she had undergone, but she always worked beyond her force.
>
> Sometimes my father himself helped in the cooking, as that hard work was too much for the dainty, refined, gentle lady. The hardships she had endured saddened the heart of her divine husband, who was also her beloved Lord. He gave this help both before his sojourn in the wilderness of Sulaymáníyyih, and after his return.[15]

In her desire to relieve her beloved parents and to assume her share of the load, the Greatest Holy Leaf began what became a lifelong practice of assisting her dear mother with the work of the household. She was her mother's loving helper, working beyond her strength in the various household tasks. She recounts the following episode:

> One day when an old lady was there, I was told to prepare the samovar—it was very heavy to carry upstairs, for my arms were not extremely strong. The old lady said: "One proof that the Bábí teaching is wonderful is that a very little girl served the samovar!"
>
> My father was amused, he used to say, "Here is the lady converted by seeing your service at the samovar!" [16]

The arrival of Mírzá Yaḥyá in Baghdad and his burning desire for power and leadership of the Bahá'í community created great difficulties for Bahá'u'lláh and His family. The Guardian characterizes Mírzá Yaḥyá as "the prime mover of mischief, the focal centre of hate." Indeed, he attests that Mírzá Yaḥyá's "plotting" and "treachery" as well as his "heedlessness and perversity" unchained a veritable "hurricane" in the city. To reduce the potential for disunity among the community of believers and to allow them to reach their own conclusions concerning whom to follow, Bahá'u'lláh determined in 1854 to withdraw from Baghdad. [17]

Before His retreat into the wilderness, Bahá'u'lláh not only commanded the believers to treat Mírzá Yaḥyá with respect but also offered His half-brother and his family the shelter and hospitality of the house in which His own family lived.

The Greatest Holy Leaf explains how, out of respect for Bahá'u'lláh's wishes, her mother and uncle, Mírzá Músá, and she, herself, endeavored to do all in their power to care for Mírzá Yaḥyá's family. Despite their ministrations, he proved to be a very difficult guest. He complained about the food and the inadequacy of their efforts to make him comfortable. He refused to share the burden of the work. What was most difficult, however, was Mírzá Yaḥyá's fear that he would be located and arrested by the government officials as a result of his purported leadership of the Bábí community. Because of his anxiety, Mírzá Yaḥyá kept the doors of the house locked and refused to permit anyone to visit. When Navváb's baby son, born soon after arrival in Baghdad, became critically ill, he would not even allow a doctor to be called. And after the infant's death, no one was permitted to come to prepare the body for burial. Rather, the baby's body was given to a stranger, who took it away for burial. The family never knew where the body was laid to rest.

Bahíyyih Khánum provides the following vivid account of these days, which were so full of sorrow. Referring to her loneliness and the anguish of her family members, she recounts,

> As for me, I led a very lonely life, and would have liked sometimes to make friends with other children. But Ṣubḥ-i-Azal [Mírzá Yaḥyá] would not permit any little friends to come to the house, neither would he let me go out!
>
> Two little girls about my own age lived in the next house. I used to peep at them; but our guest always came and shouted at me for opening the door, which he promptly locked. He was always in fear of being arrested, and cared for nothing but his own safety.
>
> We led a very difficult life at this time as well as a lonely one. He would not even allow us to go to the Hammán* to take our baths. Nobody was permitted to come to the house to help us and the work therefore was very hard.
>
> For hours every day I had to stand drawing water from a deep well in the house; the ropes were hard and rough, and the bucket was heavy. My dear mother used to help, but she was not very strong, and my arms were rather weak. Our guest never helped.

* Public bath.

My father having told us to respect and obey this tyrannical person, we tried to do so, but this respect was not easy, as our lives were made so unhappy by him.[18]

Shoghi Effendi spells out the outstanding qualities that the Greatest Holy Leaf manifested during this stage of her childhood. He states that "she bore, with complete resignation and acquiescence, uncounted ordeals. She forgot herself, did without her kin, turned aside from possessions, struck off at one blow the bonds of every worldly concern; and then, like a lovelorn moth, she circled day and night about the flame of the matchless Beauty of her Lord."[19]

After two years in Sulaimaniya, Bahá'u'lláh returned to Baghdad in 1856 and set about shaping and reviving the spiritual vitality and unity of the Bábí community. In anticipation of His return, His beloved wife and the Greatest Holy Leaf made a wonderful coat for Bahá'u'lláh. Her niece recalls, "They worked at this labour of love, using small pieces of red tirmih,* very precious stuff, which had survived, in some way, the loss of nearly all her extensive and rare wedding treasures. For six months they sewed and fitted these pieces together, and a beautiful coat was the result. Very acceptable indeed, for He came back in the coarse, rough coat of a dervish. And they had no money for buying coats at that time in Baghdad."[20]

On his return to Baghdad, Bahá'u'lláh succeeded in bringing a new spirit to the Bábí community. His fame continued to grow, and many spiritually minded people from all walks of life were attracted to investigate His message and to seek His guidance. After several years, those who were jealous of His influence and fearful of losing their power began to agitate against Him and to seek the intervention of civil and ecclesiastical authorities. Their activi-

---

* Valuable cloth, e.g., cashmere or fine wool.

ties eventually led to the exile of Bahá'u'lláh and some of His followers to Constantinople (modern-day Istanbul) and ultimately to Adrianople (now Edirne, Turkey). Before His departure from Baghdad, Bahá'u'lláh made known to some of the members of His immediate family His station as a Manifestation of God.

Shoghi Effendi has summarized the major events that took place in the ten-year period of Bahá'u'lláh's sojourn in Baghdad from 1853 to 1863. While specific details concerning Bahíyyih Khánum's involvement in these historical events are unknown, we do have the following fascinating—and indeed intriguing—glimpse into the significance of her contribution in the following extract from one of Shoghi Effendi's letters:

> And when at a later time this revered and precious member of the Holy Family, then in her teens, came to be entrusted by the guiding hand of her father with missions that no girl of her age could, or would be willing to, perform, with what spontaneous joy she seized her opportunity and acquitted herself of the task with which she had been entrusted! The delicacy and extreme gravity of such functions as she, from time to time, was called upon to fulfil, when the city of Baghdád was swept by the hurricane which the heedlessness and perversity of Mírzá Yahyá had unchained, as well as the tender solicitude which, at so early an age, she evinced during the period of Bahá'u'lláh's enforced retirement to the mountains of Sulaymáníyyih, marked her as one who was both capable of sharing the burden, and willing to make the sacrifice, which her high birth demanded.[21]

Constantinople

Bahá'u'lláh departed Baghdad in May 1863, accompanied by members of His family and twenty-six of His disciples. Because of the high respect many of the notables as well as the general population had for Bahá'u'lláh, His departure "witnessed scenes of tumultuous enthusiasm." The Guardian provides the following accounts:

> Mounted on His steed, a red roan stallion of the finest breed, the best His lovers could purchase for Him, and leaving behind Him a bowing multitude of fervent admirers, He rode forth on the first stage of a journey that was to carry Him to the city of Constantinople....
>
> ...A caravan, consisting of fifty mules, a mounted guard of ten soldiers with their officer, and seven pairs of howdahs, each pair surmounted by four parasols, was formed, and wended its way, by easy stages, and in the space of no less than a hundred and ten days, across the uplands, and through the defiles, the woods, valleys and pastures, comprising the picturesque scenery of eastern Anatolia, to the port of Sámsún, on the Black Sea.[22]

Bahá'u'lláh's arrival in August of 1863 in Constantinople, the capital of the Ottoman Empire and the seat of the Caliphate, marked the beginning of "the most momentous years of the Heroic Age of His Dispensation." The Guardian attests that "A period in which untold privations and unprecedented trials were mingled with the noblest spiritual triumphs was now commencing."[23] This period is characterized by Bahá'u'lláh's public declaration of His mission and station and the initiation of His proclamation of that mission through a series of epistles and weighty messages He addressed to the kings and rulers of the world.

The initial phase of Bahá'u'lláh's proclamation opened in Constantinople and led to the Ottoman government's immediate banishment of the exiles to Adrianople in the midst of winter. Shoghi Effendi writes, "Bahá'u'lláh, His family, and His companions, some riding in wagons, others mounted on pack animals, with their belongings piled in carts drawn by oxen, set out, accompanied by Turkish officers, on a cold December morning, amidst the weeping of the friends they were leaving behind, on their twelve-day journey, across a bleak and windswept country, to a city characterized by Bahá'u'lláh as "'the place which none entereth except such as have rebelled against the authority of the sovereign.'" Commenting on the conditions the exiles suffered, Bahá'u'lláh attests that they were expelled from Constantinople "'with an abasement with which no abasement on earth can compare.'" In one of His tablets He describes what transpired:

> When they expelled Us from thy city, they placed Us in such conveyances as the people use to carry baggage and the like. Such was the treatment We received at their hands, shouldst thou wish to know the truth. Thus were We sent away, and thus were We brought to the city which they regard as the abode of rebels. Upon our arrival, We could find no house in which to dwell, and perforce resided in a place where none would enter save the most indigent stranger. There We lodged for a time, after which, suffering increasingly from the confined space, We sought and rented houses which by reason of the extreme cold had been vacated by their occupants. Thus in the depth of winter we were constrained to make our abode in houses wherein none dwell except in the heat of summer. Neither My family, nor those who accompanied Me, had the necessary raiment to protect them from the cold in that freezing weather.[24]

The historian Nabíl records the following description of the physical hardships the exiles endured: "'A cold of such intensity prevailed that year, that nonagenarians could not recall its like. In some regions, in both Turkey and Persia, animals succumbed to its severity and perished in the snows. The upper reaches of the Euphrates, in Ma'dan-Nuqríh, were covered with ice for several days—an unprecedented phenomenon—while in Díyár-Bakr the river froze over for no less than forty days.'" One of those exiled to Adrianople recalls that, "'To obtain water from the springs, a great fire had to be lighted in their immediate neighborhood, and kept burning for a couple of hours before they thawed out.'"[25]

In later life, Bahíyyih <u>Kh</u>ánum herself provides a poignant account of what transpired immediately before the banishment of Bahá'u'lláh and His family from Constantinople and their journey to Adrianople. She recalls the "'heart-sickening suspense'" occasioned by the threats of the officials to send Bahá'u'lláh to one place, the members of His family to another, and His followers elsewhere. The journey, she said, was "'the most terrible experience of travel'" the exiles had experienced so far. She recalls, "'It was the beginning of winter, and very cold; heavy snow fell most of the time; and destitute as we were of proper clothing or food, it was a miracle that we survived it. We arrived at Adrianople all sick—even the young and strong.'" "'That winter,'" she affirms, "'was a period of intense suffering, due to cold, hunger, and, above all, to the torments of vermin, with which the house was swarming.'"[26]

Shoghi Effendi calls attention to the severe and lifelong impact of these experiences on the Greatest Holy Leaf. He confirms, "It was in this period of extreme anxiety, when the rigours of a winter of exceptional severity, coupled with the privations entailed by unhealthy housing accommodation and dire financial distress, undermined once for all her health and sapped the vitality which she had hitherto so thoroughly enjoyed."[27]

The arrival of Bahá'u'lláh and the exiles in Adrianople in December of 1863 set the scene for the next act in the unfoldment of the drama of the Bahá'í Faith. Indeed, Shoghi Effendi writes, "The curtain now rises on what is admittedly the most turbulent and critical period of the first Bahá'í century—a period that was destined to precede the most glorious phase of that ministry, the proclamation of His Message to the world and its rulers."[28]

Adrianople

The sojourn in Adrianople was to last five years, from 1863 to 1868. After an initial period, Bahá'u'lláh won the respect and admiration of the officials and the love of the local population. However, as His spiritual stature became increasingly apparent, it agitated His enemies—in particular, His half-brother Mírzá Yaḥyá, who began to work actively not only to challenge Bahá'u'lláh's moral leadership of the community but also to threaten His life. Bahá'u'lláh referred to the resulting period of convulsion and crisis as the "Days of Stress." In the midst of this supreme crisis He revealed a tablet that spelled out the implications of His claim to be the promised Manifestation of God for the age. He arranged for the contents of this tablet to be made known to Mírzá Yaḥyá—the one who was challenging His authority and leadership—and to the other Bábís. His refusal to acknowledge Bahá'u'lláh's station was "the signal for the open and final rupture between Bahá'u'lláh and Mírzá Yaḥyá—a rupture that marks one of the darkest dates in Bahá'í history." Bahá'u'lláh describes this event as the "most great separation." In order to allow the believers each to reach an independent decision concerning the leadership of the community, Bahá'u'lláh withdrew from contact with all the believers, except for the members of His immediate family, for a period of several months. At the end of this time, all but a handful of the believers accepted the station of Bahá'u'lláh and gave Him their allegiance.[29]

The severity of the crisis, according to Shoghi Effendi, "brought incalculable sorrow to Bahá'u'lláh, visibly aged Him, and inflicted, through its repercussions, the heaviest blow ever sustained by Him in His lifetime." Nevertheless, He did not shirk from initiating the next stage in the proclamation of His mission. As Shoghi Effendi indicates,

> Though He Himself was bent with sorrow, and still suffered from the effects of the attempt on His life, and though He was well aware a further banishment was probably impending, yet, undaunted by the blow which His Cause had sustained, and the perils with which it was encompassed, Bahá'u'lláh arose with matchless power, even before the ordeal was overpast, to proclaim the Mission with which He had been entrusted to those who, in East and West, had the reins of supreme temporal authority in their grasp. The day-star of His Revelation was, through this very Proclamation, destined to shine in its meridian glory, and His Faith manifest the plenitude of its divine power.[30]

Indeed, in the midst of this turmoil, Bahá'u'lláh revealed tablets that fully expounded the implications of His station and message. The impact of these tablets, together with the continued machinations of Mírzá Yaḥyá and his confederates, emboldened the external enemies of the Faith and set the stage for the renewed exile of Bahá'u'lláh, His family, and followers.

The members of Bahá'u'lláh's family were witnesses to the events described above. Reflecting on the period, Bahíyyih Khánum indicates that the family was very poor and always in great privation. They had, indeed, become so used to suffering that they might have lived in relative contentment had it not been for "the feeling of dread and sense of unknown danger" and the actions of Mírzá Yaḥyá. Some of the drama and horror of these years is captured in the reports of Bahíyyih Khánum. She describes the response of Mírzá Yaḥyá to Bahá'u'lláh's declaration thus:

Bahá'u'lláh at this time made a fuller Declaration of Himself as the expected "Him Whom God shall make Manifest," and Who had been heralded by the Báb. He wrote the Tablet of Declaration (Lawḥ-i-Amr), directing His amanuensis to take it to Ṣubḥ-i-Azal, who, when he had read this, became very angry and "jealous fire consumed him."

He invited Bahá'u'lláh to a feast and shared a dish with Him, one half of which he had mixed with poison. For twenty-one days Bahá'u'lláh was seriously ill from the effects of this attempt.

Incensed at this failure, Ṣubḥ-i-Azal tried another plan. He asked the bath attendant (for a bribe) to assassinate Bahá'u'lláh whilst he should be taking His bath, suggesting how easily it could be done without fear of detection.

This man was so shocked and horrified that he rushed out into the street unclothed.[31]

Bahíyyih Khánum also records the fact that Bahá'u'lláh wrote epistles to the kings and rulers while in Adrianople. She observes that "'He proclaimed now more publicly that His authority was Divine, being directly given to Him by God—*that He was the Chosen One, Whom, under various names, all the religions of the earth were awaiting.*'" She attests, "'The turmoil was great; the sacred influence radiating from Him reached a wider and still wider circle.'"[32]

She describes the disastrous outcome for the family and for the religion as a result of the interaction between the persistent machinations of Mírzá Yaḥyá and the response of the enemies of the Faith to Bahá'u'lláh's rising influence:

At this time the trouble Ṣubḥ-i-Azal caused, and the mischief he made, was so constant that the authorities lost patience, and it was decided to exile the Beloved One and His family yet again.

Ṣubḥ-i-Azal's conduct was, however, not the only cause of this further exile. Our ever-watchful enemies, fearing the great influence of Bahá'u'lláh, made use of the persistent annoyance of the traitorous half-brother as a pretext to induce the Government to banish the august prisoner to a place where no learned and important people would have access to Him.

Ṣubḥ-i-Azal's libels were amplified, and the Government officials were induced to believe them. . . .[33]

The Guardian alludes to the Greatest Holy Leaf's participation in the events that transpired in Adrianople. He describes her response to "the forces of schism," affirming that, "during the Most Great Convulsion, which in the years of 'Stress' made every heart to quake, she stood as a soaring pillar, immovable and fixed; and from the blasts of desolation that rose and blew, that Leaf of the eternal Lote-Tree did not wither."[34]

Shoghi Effendi highlights the qualities of character she demonstrated, calling attention to her staunch faith, calm demeanor, and her forgiving attitude. While the precise historical details are unknown, Shoghi Effendi suggests specific actions she took and strategies she employed in upholding Bahá'u'lláh's leadership of the community and in educating some of the believers concerning the station and authority of Bahá'u'lláh. He writes, "In captivating hearts and winning over souls, in destroying doubts and misgivings, she led the field. With the waters of her countless mercies, she brought thorny hearts to a blossoming of love from the All-Glorious, and with the influence of her pure loving-kindness, transformed the implacable, the unyielding, into impassioned lovers of the celestial Beauty's peerless Cause."[35]

The days leading up to the fateful decision to banish Bahá'u'lláh and His followers yet again was marked by a great deal of uncertainty and confusion. Rumors circulated that the exiles were to be dispersed and banished to different places or secretly put to death. Then suddenly the order was issued. Shoghi Effendi describes how "one morning, the house of Bahá'u'lláh was surrounded by soldiers, sentinels were posted at its gates, His followers were again summoned by the authorities, interrogated, and ordered to make ready for their departure." The tumult occasioned by the order reverberated both within the family and in the wider community. Bahíyyih Khánum, speaking of the event in later life, indicated that she remembered "'as though it were only yesterday, the fresh misery into which we were plunged.'" She recalled how the disconsolate friends and followers crowded into the garden of Bahá'u'lláh's house, determined to resist the separation. Telegrams were sent to the government in Constantinople to seek a reprieve. At last, on 12 August 1868, Bahá'u'lláh and His family left Adrianople for Gallipoli with a Turkish military escort. However, at the time of departure, their eventual destination was not yet known. In an endeavor to alleviate the situation and to protect His family and followers, Bahá'u'lláh requested an interview with the sultan in order to have the opportunity to prove the truth of His claim. The request was ignored. In one of His tablets, Bahá'u'lláh provides the following account of His reason for taking such a step: "Although it becometh not Him Who is the Truth to present Himself before any person, inasmuch as all have been created to obey Him, yet in view of the condition of these little children and the large number of women so far removed from their friends and countries, We have acquiesced in this matter. In spite of this nothing hath resulted."[36]

In this same tablet Bahá'u'lláh expresses His outrage at the sufferings the government inflicted on His family and companions. He challenges the sultan: "Even if this Lifegiver and World Reformer be in thine estimation guilty of sedition and strife, what crime could have been committed by a group of women, children, and suckling mothers that they should be thus afflicted with the scourge of thine anger and wrath?" He attests that "No faith or religion hath ever held children responsible." He continues with the following indictment:

> Ye have plundered and unjustly despoiled a group of people who have never rebelled in your domains, nor disobeyed your government, but rather kept to themselves and engaged day and night in remembrance of God. Later, when the order was issued to banish this Youth, all were filled with dismay. The officials in charge of My expulsion declared, however: "These others have not been charged with any offence and have not been expelled by the government. Should they desire to accompany you, no one will oppose them." These hapless souls therefore paid their own expenses, forsook all their possessions, and, contenting themselves with Our presence and placing their whole trust in God, journeyed once again with Him until the fortress of 'Akká became the prison of Bahá.[37]

Shoghi Effendi captures the gnawing uncertainty that tortured the believers at this time:

> Even in Gallipoli, where three nights were spent, no one knew what Bahá'u'lláh's destination would be. Some believed that He and His brothers would be banished to one place, and the remainder dispersed, and sent into exile. Others thought that His companions would be sent back to Persia, while still others expected their immediate extermination. The government's original order was to banish Bahá'u'lláh, Áqáy-i-Kalím* and Mírzá Muḥammad-Qulí, with a servant to 'Akká, while the rest were to proceed to Constantinople. This order, which provoked scenes

---

* Also known as Mírzá Músá.

of indescribable distress, was, however, at the insistence of Bahá'u'lláh, and by the instrumentality of 'Umar Effendi, a major appointed to accompany the exiles, revoked. It was eventually decided that all the exiles, numbering about seventy, should be banished to 'Akká.[38]

The believers were, to some degree, reassured that they were not, in the end, to be separated from Bahá'u'lláh. However, Shoghi Effendi notes that the dangers and trials confronting Bahá'u'lláh at the hour of His departure from Gallipoli were so grievous that He issued a warning to His companions. Shoghi Effendi indicates that Bahá'u'lláh "warned His companions that *'this journey will be unlike any of the previous journeys,'* and that whoever did not feel himself *'man enough to face the future'* had best *'depart to whatever place he pleaseth, and be preserved from tests, for hereafter he will find himself unable to leave'*—a warning which His companions unanimously chose to disregard."[39]

Bahá'u'lláh and His family and companions left Gallipoli on 21 August 1868 on the fourth and last journey of banishment. In the course of that journey the exiles were "thrice compelled to change ships," thereby causing added suffering to the children. Their destination was the prison-city of Acre, where the Turkish authorities sent the most hardened criminals.[40]

It is apparent that one of the outstanding challenges for the family and companions of Bahá'u'lláh during the years in Adrianople was the extreme degree of stress and anxiety occasioned by the machinations of both the internal and external enemies of the Bahá'í cause. Shoghi Effendi testifies to the impact of such tensions on the Greatest Holy Leaf. He states that "The stress and storm of that period made an abiding impression upon her mind, and she retained till the time of her death on her beauteous and angelic face evidences of its intense hardships."[41]

Acre

Bahá'u'lláh's banishment to Acre marks the opening of the last phase of His ministry. The twenty-four years He spent here until His passing in 1892 comprised over half of the total period of His ministry. This banishment, will, according to the Guardian, "go down in history as a period which witnessed a miraculous and truly revolutionizing change in the circumstances attending the life and activities of the Exile Himself." It will be remembered primarily for "the widespread recrudescence of persecution, intermittent but singularly cruel, throughout His native country and the simultaneous increase in the number of His followers, and, lastly, for an enormous extension in the range and volume of His writings."[42]

The arrival of the exiles in Acre marked the "beginning of a major crisis, characterized by bitter suffering, severe restrictions, and intense turmoil." In one of His tablets Bahá'u'lláh describes how "The officials enforce every day a new decree, and no end is in sight to their tyranny. Night and day they conceive new schemes." He also affirms that "From the foundation of the world until the present day a cruelty such as this hath neither been seen nor heard of." Indeed, the first nine years of this banishment were so critical that Bahá'u'lláh designated Acre as the "'Most Great Prison.'" In one of His tablets He refers to Acre as "the most desolate of the cities of the world, the most unsightly of them in appearance, the most detestable in climate, and the foulest in water. It is as though it were the metropolis of the owl, within whose precincts naught can be heard save the echo of its cry."[43]

The final stage of the voyage to Acre was particularly wretched. Bahíyyih Khánum provides the following graphic description:

> At length we arrived at Haifa, where we had to be carried ashore in chairs. Here we remained for a few hours. Now we

embarked again for the last bit of our sea journey. The heat . . . was overpowering. We were put into a sailing boat. There being no wind, and no shelter from the burning rays of the sun, we spent eight hours of positive misery, and at last we had reached 'Akká, the end of our journey.

The landing at this place was achieved with much difficulty; the ladies of our party were carried ashore.

All the townspeople had assembled to see the arrival of the prisoners. Having been told that we were infidels, criminals, and sowers of sedition, the attitude of the crowd was threatening. Their yelling of curses and execrations filled us with fresh misery. We were terrified of the unknown! We knew not what the fate of our party, the friends and ourselves would be.

We were taken to the old fortress of 'Akká, where we were crowded together. There was no air; a small quantity of very bad coarse bread was provided; we were unable to get fresh water to drink; our sufferings were not diminished. Then an epidemic of typhoid broke out. Nearly all became ill.

The Master appealed to the Governor, but he was at first very little inclined to relax the strict rules, which he had been directed to enforce.

The Muftí had read to the people in the Mosque a Farmán* full of false accusations.

We were described as enemies of God, and as the worst kind of criminals. The people were exhorted to shun these vile malefactors; this naturally caused the attitude of intense hatred and bitter antagonism with which we were regarded.[44]

---

* Edict.

Bahá'u'lláh records the hardships the exiles experienced on arrival in the prison. He testifies, "Upon our arrival, we were surrounded by guards and confined together, men and women, young and old alike, in the army barracks. The first night all were deprived of either food or drink, for the sentries were guarding the gate of the barracks and permitted no one to leave. No one gave a thought to the plight of these wronged ones. They even begged for water, and were refused."[45]

The Greatest Holy Leaf was among those who fell ill. In later life she recalled how, on arrival in the prison, she had been overcome by the appalling situation and fainted. When companions tried to obtain fresh water to revive her, they were not successful. They were forced to use brackish water from a pool on the dirt floor, which was used by a mat-maker to moisten his rushes. Some of this water was collected and strained and put to her lips. However, it was so foul that she again fainted. She was finally revived when some of the water was thrown in her face. She also described the heartrending effect of the lack of food and drink on the condition of the babies and children, and how, when a little food was taken to Bahá'u'lláh, He commanded that it be given to the children.[46]

The physical privations and the policy of isolating the exiles from the general population continued for some time. Bahíyyih Khánum reports that they were only permitted to leave the prison barracks three times during the first two years they were there, and then only for the briefest of time. Furthermore, there was very little money and it was not possible to find people to help with the tasks of daily living. It fell to Navváb, Bahá'u'lláh's beloved wife, and to the Greatest Holy Leaf to do much of the washing, cooking, sewing, and mending of garments for the whole family.[47]

A further implication of the strict imprisonment of the exiles was that pilgrims were unable to attain Bahá'u'lláh's presence.

Bahíyyih <u>Kh</u>ánum recounts, "When Nabíl, the historian, came to 'Akká he was unable to get into the city. He lived for some time in the cave of Elijah on Mount Carmel. Thence he used to walk (about ten miles) to a place beyond the walls of the fortress. From this point he could see the windows of those three little rooms of our prison; here he would wait and watch for the rare and much-coveted happiness of seeing the hand of Bahá'u'lláh waving from the small middle window."[48]

The sudden and tragic death in 1870 of Bahá'u'lláh's beloved son Mírzá Mihdí, who was known as the Purest Branch, added to the sorrow and tribulations of the exiles. At the age of twenty-two, while rapt in prayer as he paced the roof of the prison barracks, he accidentally fell to his death through a skylight. When Bahá'u'lláh was summoned, this precious son supplicated his father to accept his life "as a ransom for those who were prevented from attaining the presence of their Beloved" and thereby make it possible for pilgrims to attain the presence of Bahá'u'lláh. This sacrifice, so lovingly offered, was accepted. Gradually the doors of pilgrimage were opened, and pilgrims began to arrive from Persia and other parts of the world.[49]

Adding to the afflictions Bahá'u'lláh and the exiles endured was the campaign of abuse and intrigue waged by those who opposed Bahá'u'lláh's leadership. Despite His explicit warnings to His followers against retaliating against their tormentors, a number of the believers, in direct violation of His instructions, pursued and killed three of their persecutors. Their precipitous action led to Bahá'u'lláh's being taken into custody and interrogated before the governorate. It also rekindled the animosity of the local population against the exiles.[50]

With the passage of time, all elements of the population began to recognize Bahá'u'lláh's innocence, and the spirit of His teachings began to penetrate their consciousness. Shoghi Effendi refers to the

fact that "the tide of misery and abasement began to ebb, signaliz-
ing a transformation in the fortunes of the Faith." After nine years
of confinement within the walls of the prison-city, Bahá'u'lláh was
permitted to leave its gates. He ultimately transferred His residence
to the mansion at Bahjí, just beyond the northern outskirts of Acre.
Commenting on the reversal of circumstances that took place during the course of His exile in Acre, Bahá'u'lláh attests, "'The Almighty . . . hath transformed this Prison-House into the Most Exalted Paradise, the Heaven of Heavens.'" [51]

While this transformation in the circumstances of Bahá'u'lláh's
life was, indeed, remarkable, Shoghi Effendi affirms that even "more
remarkable" was the "unprecedented extension in the range of His
writings, during His exile in that Prison." This prolific period of
revelation, he states, "must rank as one of the most vitalizing and
fruitful stages in the evolution of His Faith."[52] In the Acre period,
Bahá'u'lláh continued to proclaim His mission to the kings and
rulers of the world. He revealed the Kitáb-i-Aqdas (Most Holy
Book), the repository of the major laws and ordinances of His Dispensation, and tablets that reaffirmed and supplemented the tenets
and principles underlying His Dispensation.

Towards the end of His life Bahá'u'lláh had greater freedom of
movement. Not only could He reside outside the walls of the prison-
city of Acre, but on four occasions He visited Haifa. He had won
the good pleasure of the government officials and the affection of
the local people. His religion was beginning to spread to many different parts of the world, attracting a greater diversity of its peoples.
Indeed, Shoghi Effendi states that just before the passing of
Bahá'u'lláh, the religion "had . . . begun to enjoy the sunshine of a
prosperity never previously experienced."[53]

Against this background it is interesting to reflect on the contribution of the Greatest Holy Leaf to the events that transpired during the time the exiles were in Acre. While there are few and frag-

mentary details concerning the precise role the Greatest Holy Leaf played in these events, we are left with Shoghi Effendi's testimony regarding the profound impact of that imprisonment on this heroic soul. It is evident that it was the spiritual qualities she manifested that permeated all the services she performed. Shoghi Effendi affirms that "Not until . . . she had been confined in the company of Bahá'u'lláh within the walls of the prison-city of 'Akká did she display, in the plentitude of her power and in the full abundance of her love for Him, those gifts that single her out, next to 'Abdu'l-Bahá, among the members of the Holy Family, as the brightest embodiment of that love which is born of God and of that human sympathy which few mortals are capable of evincing."[54]

The Greatest Holy Leaf's clear understanding of the importance of her father's cause and her commitment to its furtherance was the dominating force of her life. Shoghi Effendi attests that "Banishing from her mind and heart every earthly attachment, renouncing the very idea of matrimony, she, standing resolutely by the side of a Brother whom she was to aid and serve so well, arose to dedicate her life to the service of her Father's glorious Cause." Shoghi Effendi then points to a number of areas of service in which the Greatest Holy Leaf made a significant contribution during the Acre period. He also highlights certain qualities of character that were, no doubt, critical to preserving unity within the community of exiles and to interacting with governmental officials in an attempt to gradually transform their attitudes from antipathy to acceptance during the first nine years of Bahá'u'lláh's exile to the prison-city. He states, "Whether in the management of the affairs of His Household in which she excelled, or in the social relationships which she so assiduously cultivated in order to shield both Bahá'u'lláh and 'Abdu'l-Bahá, whether in the unfailing attention she paid to the everyday needs of her Father, or in the traits of generosity, of affability and kindness, which she manifested, the Greatest Holy Leaf had by that time abundantly demonstrated her worthiness to rank as one of the noblest figures intimately associated with the life-long work of Bahá'u'lláh."[55]

From the following description by Shoghi Effendi, it is possible to gain some insight into the challenge 'Abdu'l-Bahá and the Greatest Holy Leaf confronted in their dealings with local officials. He writes, "How grievous was the ingratitude, how blind the fanaticism, how persistent the malignity of the officials, their wives, and their subordinates, in return for the manifold bounties which she, in close association with her Brother, so profusely conferred upon them! Her patience, her magnanimity, her undiscriminating benevolence, far from disarming the hostility of that perverse generation, served only to inflame their rancour, to excite their jealousy, to intensify their fears." Shoghi Effendi also contrasts the state of mind of the Bahá'í exiles during the most restrictive and dangerous period of their time in Acre with the spirit of confident optimism manifested by the Greatest Holy Leaf—an optimism based on understanding the power of the Faith to achieve ultimate victory. He writes, "The gloom that had settled upon that little band of imprisoned believers, who languished in the Fortress of 'Akká contrasted with the spirit of confident hope, of deep-rooted optimism that beamed upon her serene countenance. No calamity, however intense, could obscure the brightness of her saintly face, and no agitation, no matter how severe, could disturb the composure of her gracious and dignified behaviour."[56] During the later years of Bahá'u'lláh's life, He resided in the mansion at Bahjí while 'Abdu'l-Bahá, His beloved sister Bahíyyih Khánum, and 'Abdu'l-Bahá's family continued to live within the prison-city of Acre. A number of

months before Bahá'u'lláh's passing, He intimated to 'Abdu'l-Bahá
that the close of His earthly life was approaching. Shoghi Effendi
provides the following account of events that transpired around
that time:

> On the night preceding the eleventh of S͟havvál 1309 A.H. (May
> 8, 1892) He contracted a slight fever which, though it mounted
> the following day, soon after subsided. He continued to grant
> interviews to certain of the friends and pilgrims, but it soon be-
> came evident that He was not well. . . .
>
> Six days before He passed away He summoned to His pres-
> ence, as He lay in bed leaning against one of His sons, the entire
> company of believers, including several pilgrims, who had as-
> sembled in the Mansion, for what proved to be their last audi-
> ence with Him. *"I am well pleased with you all,"* He gently and
> affectionately addressed the weeping crowd that gathered about
> Him. *"Ye have rendered many services, and been very assiduous in
> your labors. Ye have come here every morning and every evening.
> May God assist you to remain united. May He aid you to exalt the
> Cause of the Lord of being."* To the women, including members
> of His own family, gathered at His bedside, He addressed similar
> words of encouragement, definitely assuring them that in a docu-
> ment entrusted by Him to the Most Great Branch ['Abdu'l-Bahá]
> He had commended them all to His care.[57]

Shoghi Effendi recounts that Bahá'u'lláh's "fever returned in a more
acute form than before, His general condition grew steadily worse, complications ensued which at last culminated in His ascension, at the
hour of dawn, on the 2nd of D͟hi'l-Qa'dih 1309 A.H. (May 29, 1892),
eight hours after sunset, in the 75th year of His age."[58]

A niece of Bahíyyih Khánum recounts that nine days after the passing of Bahá'u'lláh, His will was read, first to the men, and then to the women of the household. The will established Bahá'u'lláh's Covenant with the believers, making clear that His son 'Abdu'l-Bahá was appointed not only as the Center of the Covenant but also as Bahá'u'lláh's successor as head of the Faith and the official interpreter of His writings. All were directed to turn to 'Abdu'l-Bahá for guidance. Despite the clear provisions of the will, within a very short time, disunity regarding its interpretation emerged within the extended family and the community. 'Abdu'l-Bahá's position and authority were challenged. When, for example, 'Abdu'l-Bahá attempted to obtain a number of tablets Bahá'u'lláh had revealed for many of His followers just before His passing, he was informed by his half-brother Mírzá Muḥammad-'Alí that the tablets did not exist. Further, none of the male members of the family were willing to assist 'Abdu'l-Bahá in the tasks that he was now called upon to perform. [59]

In letters Bahíyyih Khánum wrote soon after the passing of Bahá'u'lláh, she provides an intimate glimpse into the feelings of deep loss experienced by the members of the holy family. In a letter dated May 1892, she describes the intensity of her own bereavement and offers guidance concerning ways of coping in times of trial. She writes,

> In reality no pen can depict the poignant feeling that surges in our hearts. Every expression would prove utterly inadequate, even less than the eye of a needle, inasmuch as words and syllables are incapable of conveying the intensity of this dire suffering. They are but a tiny drop compared to an ocean. Even in the vast immensity of inner significances and expositions nothing can por-

tray this calamitous event. Moreover, the tale of how these prisoners have been consumed by the fire of bereavement is interminable. During this dark and dreadful calamity, and to this God bears me witness, our souls melted and our eyes unceasingly rained with tears.

Nevertheless, when faced with the irrevocable decree of the Almighty, the vesture that best befits us in this world is the vesture of patience and submission, and the most meritorious of all deeds is to commit our affairs into His hands and to surrender ourselves to His Will. [60]

Her anguish at the behavior of those who were attacking the Faith is also conveyed in an extract from a letter written in 1897: "Should you enquire about these bereaved ones, through the grace of the Lord and the bounties of His divine Mystery, we are all well, but our grief knows no bounds. We supplicate at the Threshold of the Eternal and Almighty Beloved that He may unlock before us the doors of delight, awaken the heedless and those deep in slumber, and grant the exponents of violation a sense of justice, so that its dust may settle down, that this dissension be wiped out, and once again we may taste the sweetness of the days of bliss." [61]

The passing of Bahá'u'lláh had a profound effect on the Greatest Holy Leaf and threatened to undermine her health. 'Abdu'l-Bahá voices his concern for the health and well-being of his sister in a tablet addressed to an Eastern believer. Describing her depleted physical condition, he makes the following heartrending disclosure: "My sister, for a considerable period, that is, from the day of Bahá'u'lláh's ascension, had grown so thin and feeble, and was in such a weakened condition from the anguish of her mourning that she was close to breakdown." 'Abdu'l-Bahá confides to this trusted believer that, while it was his sister's dearest wish to leave this world, he "could not bear to behold her in that state." Thus he enlisted the aid of his friend in arranging to accompany the Greatest Holy Leaf on a trip so that she could experience "a change of air."[62]

Bahá'u'lláh's death not only added greatly to Bahíyyih Khánum's suffering and eroded her physical strength, it also precipitated events that gave rise to her increased social isolation and firmed her resolve to confront the attacks on the Bahá'í Faith. Shoghi Effendi indicates that

> Great as had been her sufferings ever since her infancy, the anguish of mind and heart which the ascension of Bahá'u'lláh occasioned nerved her, as never before, to a resolve which no upheaval could bend and which her frail constitution belied. Amidst the dust and heat of the commotion which that faithless and rebellious company engendered she found herself constrained to dissolve ties of family relationship, to sever long-standing and intimate friendships, to discard lesser loyalties for the sake of her supreme allegiance to a Cause she had loved so dearly and had served so well.[63]

Shoghi Effendi likewise affirms that "her anguish was increased by the passing of the Abhá Beauty, and the cruelty of the disloyal added more fuel to the fires of her mourning." He characterizes the nature of her response to the faithlessness of the family members and their attacks on the Faith and the impact of this on the status of Bahíyyih Khánum. "In the midst of that storm of violation," Shoghi Effendi attests, "the countenance of that rare treasure of the Lord shone all the brighter, and throughout the Bahá'í community, her value and high rank became clearly perceived. By the vehement onslaught of the chief of violators against the sacred beliefs of the followers of the Faith, she was neither frightened nor in despair."[64]

Shoghi Effendi provides the following insights into the nature of the unique functions the Greatest Holy Leaf assumed at this crucial time of transition: "She alone of the family of Bahá'u'lláh remained to cheer the heart and reinforce the efforts of the Most Great Branch,* against Whom were solidly arrayed the almost entire company of His faithless relatives. In her arduous task she was seconded by the diligent efforts of Munírih Khánum, the Holy Mother, and those of her daughters whose age allowed them to assist in the accomplishment of that stupendous achievement with which the name of 'Abdu'l-Bahá will for ever remain associated." Shoghi Effendi calls attention to the experiences that had prepared Bahíyyih Khánum for the vital role she was about to play in defense of the Covenant: "Armed with the powers with which an intimate and long-standing companionship with Bahá'u'lláh had already equipped her, and benefiting by the magnificent example which the steadily widening range of 'Abdu'l-Bahá's activities afforded her, she was prepared to face the storm which the treacherous conduct of the Covenant-breakers† had aroused and to withstand its most damaging onslaughts." [65]

---

* 'Abdu'l-Bahá.

† The Bahá'í writings embody a Covenant that consists of explicit provisions concerning the appointment of a successor following the death of the founder and the establishment of administrative institutions to guide the affairs of the religion. Covenant-breakers are members of the religious community who publicly attempt to subvert the leadership of the religion and disrupt its unity.

Chapter 3

'Abdu'l-Bahá's Brilliant Sister

Bahíyyih <u>Kh</u>ánum's relationship with her brother 'Abdu'l-Bahá far transcended the usual deep emotional bonds that unite family members. It was a mystic and spiritual relationship of great tenderness. In his letters 'Abdu'l-Bahá addresses her as "my well-beloved and deeply spiritual sister," "my honoured and distinguished sister," and "my sister in the spirit and the companion of my heart." From a perusal of these same letters, it can be seen that 'Abdu'l-Bahá was cognizant of the high spiritual rank of the Greatest Holy Leaf. He mentions her willingness to sacrifice in service to the Bahá'í Faith, acknowledges her unswerving adherence to the Bahá'í Covenant, expresses appreciation for her loyal support, and extols her abilities, sound judgment, and qualities of character. His abiding concern for her well-being and happiness is paramount.[1]

In this chapter we will examine some of the unique contributions of the Greatest Holy Leaf, characterized by Shoghi Effendi as 'Abdu'l-Bahá's "brilliant sister," to the protection and unfoldment of the Bahá'í Faith during 'Abdu'l-Bahá's ministry. We will focus specifically on her staunch support of the Bahá'í Covenant in the years following the passing of Bahá'u'lláh, her service as 'Abdu'l-Bahá's "competent deputy, His representative and vicegerent" during his absence in the Western world, and the masterly way in which she managed the household of her beloved brother.[2]

The historical record contains few details about the actual activities of the Greatest Holy Leaf. However, the testimony of the Guardian of the Faith provides a broad framework within which to assemble the fragments that can be found. By studying the events that were taking place in the Bahá'í community during 'Abdu'l-Bahá's ministry, together with Shoghi Effendi's interpretation of their significance, and the reports of Bahá'í pilgrims from the East and the West who visited Acre and Haifa, it is possible to build up at least a partial picture of some of the contributions Bahíyyih Khánum made during this period in Bahá'í history.

Support of the Center of the Covenant

Bahá'u'lláh's will and testament, the Book of His Covenant, was written entirely in His own hand. As mentioned in chapter 2, on the ninth day after His ascension, the will was "unsealed . . . in the presence of nine witnesses chosen from amongst His companions and members of His Family; [and] read subsequently, on the afternoon of that same day, before a large company assembled in His Most Holy Tomb, including His sons, some of the Báb's kinsmen, pilgrims and resident believers." The significance of this "unique and epoch-making Document" is that it embodied within its provisions the means to "perpetuate the influence" of the Faith of Bahá'u'lláh, to "insure its integrity, safeguard it from schism, and stimulate its world-wide expansion."[3]

According to the provisions of Bahá'u'lláh's will, 'Abdu'l-Bahá was appointed as the successor to Bahá'u'lláh and as the authorized interpreter of his father's writings. Shoghi Effendi spells out the implications of this appointment, stating that 'Abdu'l-Bahá ". . . had been elevated to the high office of Center of Bahá'u'lláh's Covenant, and been made the successor of the Manifestation of God Himself—a position that was to empower Him to impart an extraordinary impetus to the international expansion of His Father's Faith, to amplify its doctrine, to beat down every barrier that would obstruct its march, and to call into being, and delineate the features of, its Administrative Order, the Child of the Covenant, and the Harbinger of that World Order whose establishment must needs signalize the advent of the Golden Age of the Bahá'í Dispensation."[4]

The newly proclaimed Covenant was a prelude to the creation of the administrative machinery that would facilitate the worldwide diffusion of the Bahá'í Faith—first to the North American continent and from there to the rest of the world. However, before such expansion could take place, "the newly born Covenant of Bahá'u'lláh" had, in the words of Shoghi Effendi, "to be baptized with a fire which was to demonstrate its solidity and proclaim its indestructibility to an unbelieving world." He underscores the severity of this test, describing it as "one of the most grievous ordeals experienced in the course of an entire century."[5]

The crisis, which was to last for four years from 1892–96, was precipitated by Mírzá Muḥammad-'Alí, a half-brother of 'Abdu'l-Bahá who was specifically named in Bahá'u'lláh's Book of the Covenant as ranking second only to 'Abdu'l-Bahá. Commenting on its underlying cause, Shoghi Effendi states, "The true ground of this crisis was the burning, the uncontrollable, the soul-festering jealousy which the admitted preeminence of 'Abdu'l-Bahá in rank, power, ability, knowledge and virtue, above all the other members of His Father's family, had aroused not only in Mírzá Muḥammad-'Alí, the archbreaker of the Covenant, but in some of his closest relatives as well." The Guardian explains that a blind envy had "been smouldering in the recesses of Mírzá Muḥammad-'Alí's heart and had been secretly inflamed by those unnumbered marks of distinction, of admiration and favor accorded to 'Abdu'l-Bahá not only by Bahá'u'lláh Himself, His companions and His followers, but by the vast number of unbelievers who had come to recognize that innate greatness which 'Abdu'l-Bahá had manifested from childhood."

Rather than being mollified by "the provisions of a Will which had elevated him to the second-highest position within the ranks of the faithful," Mírzá Muḥammad-'Alí's animosity increased "as soon as he came to realize the full implications of that Document."[6]

Shoghi Effendi provides the following description of the impact of Mírzá Muḥammad-'Alí's disaffection and the support he attracted from among the extended family and the close companions of 'Abdu'l-Bahá:

Gradually and with unyielding persistence, through lies, half-truths, calumnies and gross exaggerations, this "Prime Mover of sedition" succeeded in ranging on his side almost the entire family of Bahá'u'lláh, as well as a considerable number of those who had formed his immediate entourage. Bahá'u'lláh's two surviving wives,* His two sons, the vacillating Mírzá Ḍíyá'u'lláh and the treacherous Mírzá Badí'u'lláh, with their sister and half-sister and their husbands, one of them the infamous Siyyid 'Alí, a kinsman of the Báb, the other the crafty Mírzá Majdi'd-Dín, together with his sister and half-brothers—the children of the noble, the faithful and now deceased Áqáy-i-Kalím—all united in a determined effort to subvert the foundations of the Covenant which the newly proclaimed Will had laid. Even Mírzá Áqá Ján, who for forty years had labored as Bahá'u'lláh's amanuensis, as well as Muḥammad-Javád-i-Qasvíní, who ever since the days of Adrianople, had been engaged in transcribing the innumerable Tablets revealed by the Supreme Pen, together with his entire family, threw in their lot with the Covenant-breakers, and allowed themselves to be ensnared by their machinations.[7]

---

* The practice of polygamy was common in Islamic cultures in the Middle East. Bahá'u'lláh married three wives under this tradition. Revealed after He established the Bahá'í Faith, Bahá'u'lláh's book of laws specifies monogamy as the accepted Bahá'í practice.

It was during this period, following "the passing of Bahá'u'lláh and the fierce onslaught of the forces of disruption that followed in its wake" that the Greatest Holy Leaf, "now in the hey-day of her life, rose to the height of her great opportunity and acquitted herself worthily of her task." She became the main support of 'Abdu'l-Bahá, the appointed Center of Bahá'u'lláh's Covenant. The Guardian states that "She alone of the family of Bahá'u'lláh remained to cheer the heart and reinforce the efforts of the Most Great Branch,* against Whom were solidly arrayed the almost entire company of His faithless relatives. In her arduous task she was seconded by the diligent efforts of Munírih Khánum,† the Holy Mother, and those of her daughters whose age allowed them to assist in the accomplishment of that stupendous achievement with which the name of 'Abdu'l-Bahá will for ever remain associated."[8]

While the precise nature of Bahíyyih Khánum's activities is not known, certain inferences might be drawn from an examination of the campaign waged against 'Abdu'l-Bahá and the actions he took to curb its impact.

Those who arose to repudiate the divinely established Covenant launched a campaign of vilification against 'Abdu'l-Bahá. They not only attacked the substance of Bahá'u'lláh's will and testament, but also impugned 'Abdu'l-Bahá's character and made patently false statements about his station, his use of funds, and the way in which he functioned as head of the Faith. Shoghi Effendi details the nature of the spurious calumnies they spread abroad, not only within the Bahá'í community but also in the community at large. He writes,

To friend and stranger, believer and unbeliever alike, to officials both high and low, openly and by insinuation, verbally as well as in writing, they represented 'Abdu'l-Bahá as an ambitious, a self-

---

* 'Abdu'l-Bahá.
† The wife of 'Abdu'l-Bahá.

willed, an unprincipled and pitiless usurper, Who had deliber-
ately disregarded the testamentary instructions of His Father;
Who had, in language intentionally veiled and ambiguous, assumed a rank co-equal with the Manifestation Himself; Who in
His communications with the West was beginning to claim to be
the return of Jesus Christ, the Son of God, who had come *"in the
glory of the Father";* Who, in His letters to the Indian believers,
was proclaiming Himself as the promised S͟háh Bahrám,* and
arrogating to Himself the right to interpret the writing of His
Father, to inaugurate a new Dispensation, and to share with Him
the Most Great Infallibility, the exclusive prerogative of the hold-
ers of the prophetic office. They, furthermore, affirmed that He
had, for His private ends, fomented discord, fostered enmity and
brandished the weapon of excommunication; that He had perverted the purpose of a Testament which they alleged to be primarily concerned with the private interests of Bahá'u'lláh's family by acclaiming it as a Covenant of world importance, pre-existent, peerless and unique in the history of all religions; that He
had deprived His brothers and sisters of their lawful allowance,
and expended it on officials for His personal advancement; that
He had declined all the repeated invitations made to Him to
discuss the issues that had arisen and to compose the differences
which prevailed; that He had actually corrupted the Holy Text,†
interpolated passages written by Himself, and perverted the purpose and meaning of some of the weightiest Tablets revealed by
the pen of His Father; and finally, that the standard of rebellion
had, as a result of such conduct, been raised by the Oriental
believers, that the community of the faithful had been rent asun-
der, was rapidly declining and was doomed to extinction.[9]

---

* World savior and Promised One anticipated by the Zoroastrian religion.
† Refers to the writings of Bahá'u'lláh.

During these "four distressful years," 1892–96, 'Abdu'l-Bahá endeavored to prevent Mírzá Muḥammad-'Alí and his supporters from breaching the Covenant. The Guardian refers to 'Abdu'l-Bahá's "incessant exhortations, His earnest pleadings, the favors and kindnesses he showered upon him, the admonitions and warnings He uttered, even His voluntary withdrawal in the hope of averting the threatening storm." However, all of 'Abdu'l-Bahá's exertions were, in the end, to no avail.[10]

Given the stress of this prolonged period of crisis, one can well imagine that the actions the Greatest Holy Leaf took to "cheer the heart and reinforce the efforts" of her brother must have been a great source of solace and practical support.[11] Her calm fortitude, absolute steadfastness, reliability, and other qualities of spirit and character were, no doubt, a source of great consolation to 'Abdu'l-Bahá. Furthermore, her knowledge of the Faith, her clear understanding of the Covenant, and her unwavering support for its appointed Center were strengths that 'Abdu'l-Bahá could call upon and utilize in his efforts to protect the Bahá'í cause.

She communicated a clarity of vision to all with whom she came in contact. In this regard, her letters written during this time period are very instructive. It is clear that Bahíyyih Khánum used these communications as a vehicle to educate the believers concerning the station of 'Abdu'l-Bahá and the importance of firmness in the Bahá'í Covenant. In one such letter to a Bahá'í woman in the East, she writes,

Praise be to God that He has enabled you, His well-assured leaf, to magnify at all times the glory of His gracious countenance, has sustained your life through the remembrance of His Beauty, has suffered you to rid yourself of all attachment to any one save Him that you may continually commune with His love. He has graciously assisted you to remain faithful to His weighty and irrefutable Testament, to cling tenaciously to the hem of the robe of the Centre of the Covenant of God, the All-Bountiful, and to fix your gaze entirely upon the luminous face of "Him Whom God hath purposed," the One "Who hath branched from the pre-existent Root." In truth, a myriad praises and thanksgiving should be offered in appreciation of this outpouring of divine favours and blessings. We implore the Kingdom of our Lord, the All-Glorious, that He may continually waft upon you His vitalizing breaths, may enrapture you by the uplifting transports of His delight, may quicken you through His Holy Spirit and may grant you confirmation to serve His maidservants and His leaves.[12]

Beyond her participation in educating the believers through her correspondence, it seems probable that the Greatest Holy Leaf would also have worked actively to educate and lovingly guide the members of the extended family who were opposed to 'Abdu'l-Bahá's appointment in the years before their formal separation from the Faith. When the formal separation did occur, her unquestioning willingness to separate herself from those family members who were violating the Covenant was a mark of her clear understanding of the Covenant of Bahá'u'lláh. The severing of contact with family, especially in a culture where the main arena for women's social interaction was within the family, not only created many practical difficulties but, in addition, was a cause of deep sadness for the Greatest Holy Leaf and doubtlessly increased her feelings of isolation. Nevertheless, since the priority of her life was service to the Bahá'í cause, she willingly made this sacrifice. Her principled actions must have done much to cheer the heart of 'Abdu'l-Bahá.

While the short-term impact of this phase of the crisis precipitated by the rebellion of Mírzá Muḥammad-'Alí and his cohorts was indeed disruptive, Shoghi Effendi describes the long-term salutary effect it produced within the Bahá'í community. He affirms that "the entire episode, viewed in its proper perspective, proved to be neither more nor less than one of those periodic crises which, since the inception of the Faith of Bahá'u'lláh, and throughout a whole century, have been instrumental in weeding out its harmful elements, in fortifying its foundations, in demonstrating its resilience, and in releasing a further measure of its latent powers." Indeed, Shoghi Effendi indicates that, as a result of the successful resolution of the crisis, "the provisions of a divinely appointed Covenant had been indubitably proclaimed; . . . the purpose of the Covenant was clearly apprehended and its fundamentals had become immovably established in the hearts of the overwhelming majority of the adherents of the Faith." The way was now clear for the establishment of the Faith of Bahá'u'lláh in the West, one consequence of which would be an increase in the responsibilities falling on the willing shoulders of Bahíyyih Khánum.[13]

Rise of the Faith in the West and the Arrival of the First Western Pilgrims

One of 'Abdu'l-Bahá's primary goals as the newly appointed head of the Bahá'í Faith was to shed "the illumination of His Father's Faith upon the West." Shoghi Effendi indicates that the initial determination to embark on this process

foreshadowed an auspicious event which posterity would recognize as one of the greatest triumphs of His ministry, which in the end would confer an inestimable blessing upon the western world, and which erelong was to dispel the grief and the apprehensions that had surrounded the community of His fellow-exiles in 'Akká. The Great Republic of the West,* above all the other countries of the Occident, was singled out to be the first recipient of God's inestimable blessing, and to become the chief agent in its transmission to so many of her sister nations throughout the five continents of the earth.[14]

The first recorded public reference to the Faith of Bahá'u'lláh in North America occurred on 23 September 1893, a little over a year after His passing. A reference to the name of Bahá'u'lláh was contained in a paper written by the Reverend Henry H. Jessup, Director of Presbyterian Missionary Operations in North Syria. The paper was read by the Reverend George A. Ford of Syria at the World Parliament of Religions, held in Chicago in 1893 as part of the World's Columbian Exposition, which commemorated the four-hundredth anniversary of the discovery of America by Christopher Columbus. This seminal moment was soon followed by the arrival in the United States of an Egyptian believer who had recently embraced the Bahá'í Faith. Within a relatively short period of time a number of people were attracted to the religion and arose to consecrate their lives to its service.

By 1898 a number of new believers from North America and France expressed their intention of visiting 'Abdu'l-Bahá. A party of fifteen pilgrims set sail for the Holy Land. Because of the difficulties of travel, they came in three successive parties, with the first group reaching the prison-city of Acre on 10 December 1898. Shoghi Effendi describes 'Abdu'l-Bahá's profound influence on these first pilgrims from the West and the outstanding features of their visit:

the intimate personal contact established between the Center of Bahá'u'lláh's Covenant and the newly arisen heralds of His Rev-

---

* The United States.

elation in the West; the moving circumstances attending their visit to His Tomb and the great honor bestowed upon them of being conducted by 'Abdu'l-Bahá Himself into its innermost chamber; the spirit which, through precept and example, despite the briefness of their stay, a loving and bountiful Host so powerfully infused into them; and the passionate zeal and unyielding resolve which His inspiring exhortations, His illuminating instructions and the multiple evidences of His divine love kindled in their hearts—all these marked the opening of a new epoch in the development of the Faith in the West. . . .[15]

The impact of this first pilgrimage not only spiritually transformed the individual participants; it also provided the motivation and impetus for establishing the Faith in the Western world, as Shoghi Effendi recounts: "The return of these God-intoxicated pilgrims, some to France, others to the United States, was the signal for an outburst of systematic and sustained activity, which, as it gathered momentum, and spread its ramifications over Western Europe and the states and provinces of the North American continent, grew to so great a scale that 'Abdu'l-Bahá Himself resolved that, as soon as He should be released from His prolonged confinement in 'Akká, He would undertake a personal mission to the West."[16]

Beyond the creative impulse to the advancement of the Faith resulting from the pilgrims' visit, their presence in the Holy Land profoundly affected Bahíyyih Khánum and the members of 'Abdu'l-Bahá's family. Shoghi Effendi writes, "It was through the arrival of these pilgrims, and these alone, that the gloom which had enveloped the disconsolate members of 'Abdu'l-Bahá's family was finally dispelled. Through the agency of these successive visitors the Greatest Holy Leaf, who alone with her Brother among the members of her Father's household had to confront the rebellion of almost the entire company of her relatives and associates, found that consolation which so powerfully sustained her till the very close of her life."[17]

The accounts written by the first Western pilgrims provide both a fascinating glimpse into the response of this small band of American and European women and men to the magnetic personality of 'Abdu'l-Bahá and a precious record of his sayings and guidance. In addition, these pilgrims' accounts provide firsthand impressions of the exiles' way of life in the prison-city of Acre, and some include reference to the person and functions of the Greatest Holy Leaf.

Female pilgrims from the West had the privilege of close association with the women of 'Abdu'l-Bahá's family and the other Bahá'í women who formed part of the wider group of exiles. Male pilgrims, however, did not share this privilege. Consequently, when the Bahá'í community gathered, the Eastern women were, according to the prevailing tradition of that region, likely to be veiled. It would not have been considered proper for women from the East to appear in mixed company without a veil. The Western women were not, however, similarly constrained. They were free to associate with both men and women and were not required to wear a veil.

The initial groups of Western pilgrims that arrived in Haifa in 1898 traveled by horse-drawn coach to Acre, where 'Abdu'l-Bahá resided at that time. Canadian Bahá'í May Maxwell has left for posterity the following description of her arrival at the house of 'Abdu'l-Bahá in Acre and her first meeting with him: "We passed through a large stone doorway opening on to a square court and ascended a flight of steps which led to the apartments above. There, standing beside the window of a small room, overlooking the azure sea, we found our Beloved." [18] She states that, no sooner had they been greeted by 'Abdu'l-Bahá than the Greatest Holy Leaf, the wife of 'Abdu'l-Bahá, and his daughters arrived. She describes the welcome the pilgrims received and some of the activities in which the women of the household were involved:

they welcomed us with love and tears of joy as though we had
been parted for awhile but had returned at last to our heavenly
home, as indeed we had! They took us to our rooms, which,
alas!, they had vacated for our sakes; they gave us every comfort,
anticipated every need and surrounded us with care and attention; yet through it all shone the light of wonderful spirituality,
through these kindly human channels their divine love was poured
forth and their own lives, their own comfort, were as a handful
of dust; they themselves were utterly sacrificed and forgotten in
love and servitude to the divine threshold.[19]

Ella Goodall Cooper, another member of the first group of Western pilgrims to visit Acre, provides the following illuminating pen
portrait of the Greatest Holy Leaf. She writes,

Next to meeting the Beloved Master* Himself was the privilege
of meeting His glorious sister, Bahíyyih Khánum, known as the
Greatest Holy Leaf. Her personality is indelibly imprinted upon
my memory. Tall, slender and of noble bearing, her body gave
the impression of perfect poise between energy and tranquility,
between wiry endurance and inward composure, imparting to
the beholder a sense of security, comfort and reliance, impossible to describe.

Her beautiful face was the feminine counterpart of 'Abdu'l-
Bahá's the lines of suffering and privation softened by the
patient sweetness of the mouth; the dominating brow, bespeak-
ing intellect and will, lighted by the wonderful understanding
eyes. . . . Watching their expressive changes—as one moment they

---

* 'Abdu'l-Bahá.

darkened with sympathy or pain, the next moment sparkled with laughter and humor—only served to deepen the impression of her irresistible spiritual attraction.[20]

The Western women were greatly moved by the spirit of 'Abdu'l-Bahá's household. Mrs. Phoebe Hearst set down her impressions in letters she wrote to her friends. She prefaces her remarks by commenting on the difficulty of describing what transpired during the remarkable three days she spent in Acre. She writes, "From a material standpoint everything was very simple and plain, but the spiritual atmosphere which pervaded the place and was manifested in the lives and actions among the Believers, was truly wonderful and something I had never before experienced. One needs but to see them to know that they are a Holy people." In another letter she states, "Regarding the Household, I found them all quiet, Holy people living only for the purpose of serving in the Cause of God. They dress very plainly, but with a grace that gives a sort of grandeur to their most humble abode. The purity of their morals is evident from their calm, benign and guileless faces which characterize them as a people. To become spiritually more and more like them, and like the blessed Master is my daily supplication unto God."[21]

From the pilgrims' reports, it is evident that the women of 'Abdu'l-Bahá's household were centrally involved in many of the activities in which the pilgrims participated. May Maxwell, for example, describes how 'Abdu'l-Bahá conducted the pilgrims to the shrine of Bahá'u'lláh, and, how, as they entered, the ladies of the holy family, thickly veiled, came in through a door in the opposite corner of the building. They came forward and greeted the pilgrims tenderly. Then all proceeded to visit the shrine.

Just before their departure, the pilgrims were conducted to a room where the portraits of Bahá'u'lláh and the Báb were displayed. All were profoundly moved by the experience. Immediately after, 'Abdu'l-Bahá addressed the pilgrims with parting words of guidance. May Maxwell captures the mood of the pilgrims and the loving solicitations of the members of the holy family when the time for their departure arrived; she writes,

> When He had finished speaking we were led gently away by the members of the Holy Family, and for a moment it seemed that we were dying; but our Master never removed His compassionate gaze from our faces, until we could see Him no longer, for our tears. Then we were clasped one after the other in the arms of the Holy Family, and the hearts were wrung, and it seemed as if all the cords of life were breaking; until, as we drove away from the home of our Heavenly Father, suddenly His spirit came to us, a great strength and tranquillity filled our souls, the grief of bodily separation was turned into the joy of spiritual union.[22]

Ella Goodall Cooper also records the emotion of that parting and provides some inkling of the deep bonds of love that were established, during that first historic pilgrimage, between the Western women pilgrims and the members of 'Abdu'l-Bahá's family. She writes, "When the dreaded moment came to say goodbye, the sorrow of parting from the beloved ladies was lessened only by the hope of a future visit. The last face I remember was that of the Greatest Holy Leaf, calm, gentle, radiant, her deep understanding eyes shedding the light of the Love of God upon us, that light which only glows brighter with the passing of the years."[23]

The mutuality of the loving affection between the women of the holy family and the early believers from the West is captured in the following extract from a letter Bahíyyih Khánum wrote in 1901 to a Bahá'í in the East. The letter states,

A number of your spiritual sisters, namely the handmaidens who have embraced His Cause, have arrived here from Paris and the United States on pilgrimage. They recently reached this blessed and luminous Spot and have had the honour to prostrate themselves at His Holy Threshold and to behold the radiant face of 'Abdu'l-Bahá, the Centre of the Covenant of Almighty God—may my life be offered up as a sacrifice for His sake. We have now the pleasure of their company and commune with them in a spirit of utmost love and fellowship. They all send loving greetings and salutations to you through the language of the heart.[24]

The early expansion of the Faith in the Western world received added impetus from the creative influences these early pilgrimages released. Returning to their home territories, the pilgrims actively promoted the cause they had adopted. They inspired others to travel to distant lands to teach the Faith. Embryonic Bahá'í administrative institutions were established, and some of the most important writings of Bahá'u'lláh and tablets of 'Abdu'l-Bahá were translated into English. In addition, the Bahá'ís in America set in motion an enterprise of immense significance and breathtaking vision. Shoghi Effendi provides the following account, writing,

inspired by the example set by their fellow-disciples in 'Ishqábád, who had already commenced the construction of the first Mashríqu'l-Adhkár* of the Bahá'í world, and afire with the desire to demonstrate, in a tangible and befitting manner, the quality of their faith and devotion, the Bahá'ís of Chicago, having petitioned 'Abdu'l-Bahá for permission to erect a House of Wor-

---

* Literally "Dawning-Place of the Praise of God"; title designating a Bahá'í house of worship.

ship, and secured, in a Tablet revealed in June 1903, His ready and enthusiastic approval, arose, despite the smallness of their numbers and their limited resources, to initiate an enterprise which must rank as the greatest single contribution which the Bahá'ís of America, and indeed of the West, have as yet made to the Cause of Bahá'u'lláh.[25]

The erection of this Bahá'í House of Worship in the heart of the North American continent not only received 'Abdu'l-Bahá's encouragement, but during his travels in the West, he personally put in place its foundation stone.

Her Role during the Renewal of Incarceration

Two years after the first American pilgrims departed from the Holy Land in late 1898, the second major crisis of 'Abdu'l-Bahá's ministry erupted. The crisis was largely external in nature and "persisted, with varying degrees of intensity, during more than seven years." It was "directly attributable to the incessant intrigues and monstrous misrepresentations" of Mírzá Muḥammad-'Alí, the "Arch-Breaker of Bahá'u'lláh's Covenant and his supporters," who succeeded in arousing the suspicions of the Turkish government and in inducing them to reimpose on 'Abdu'l-Bahá the conditions of a harsh confinement. Describing the impact of these dastardly attacks on 'Abdu'l-Bahá and his family, Shoghi Effendi states that they "gravely imperiled His life, deprived Him, for a number of years, of the relative freedom He had enjoyed, plunged into anguish His family and the followers of the Faith in East and West, and exposed as never before, the degradation and infamy of His relentless adversaries."[26]

The sultan's edict ordering the incarceration of both 'Abdu'l-Bahá and the community of exiles went into effect in August 1901. Initially it was rigidly enforced and 'Abdu'l-Bahá was required to submit to prolonged interrogation by the authorities. The situation of the exiles was exacerbated by the continuing machinations of the Covenant-breakers, who, through "verbal messages, formal communications and by personal interviews . . . impressed upon these notables the necessity of immediate action." They shrewdly adapted "their arguments to the particular interests and prejudices of those whose aid they solicited." Shoghi Effendi attests that "Through misrepresentation and bribery they succeeded in inducing certain people to affix their signatures as witnesses to the documents which they had drawn up, and which they despatched, through their agents, to the Sublime Porte." The accusations they raised and the numerous reports they submitted to the sultan, whose mind was, in the words of Shoghi Effendi, "already obsessed by the fear of impending rebellion among his subjects" resulted in the appointment of a commission charged "to inquire into the matter, and report the results of its investigation."[27]

Summoned to appear before the commission on a number of occasions, 'Abdu'l-Bahá responded to the charges brought against him, exposing the absurdity of the accusations, refuting the charges, and supporting his arguments with references to the provisions of Bahá'u'lláh's testament. Nevertheless, the situation was extremely grave; rumors anticipating the dangers facing 'Abdu'l-Bahá were circulated, and reports of the demise of the community and its leader emboldened certain elements in the local population to join forces with the Covenant-breakers. Confronted with this difficult situation, 'Abdu'l-Bahá instituted a number of stringent measures to protect the Bahá'í community. Shoghi Effendi states that the crisis led 'Abdu'l-Bahá "to reduce the number of pilgrims, and even to suspend, for a time, their visits, and to issue special instructions that His mail be handled through an agent in Egypt rather than in Haifa. . . . He, moreover, directed the believers, as well as His own secretaries, to collect and remove to a place of safety all the Bahá'í writings in their possession, and, urging them to transfer their residence to Egypt, went so far as to forbid their gathering, as was their wont, in His house."[28]

The atmosphere of tension and fear and the ensuing sense of isolation the members of the exiled community felt are recorded by Shoghi Effendi. He describes how, "Even His ['Abdu'l-Bahá's] numerous friends and admirers refrained, during the most turbulent days of this period, from calling upon Him, for fear of being implicated and of incurring the suspicion of the authorities. On certain days and nights, when the outlook was at its darkest, the house in which He was living, and which had for many years been a focus of activity, was completely deserted. Spies, secretly and openly, kept watch around it, observing His every movement and restricting the freedom of His family."[29]

In broad strokes, Shoghi Effendi describes the vital nature of the Greatest Holy Leaf's contribution during this critical period. "In the days of the Commission of Investigation," he writes, "she was a staunch and trusted supporter of the peerless Branch of Bahá'u'lláh ['Abdu'l-Bahá], and a companion to Him beyond compare." Her firm conviction and sense of assurance, based on her understanding of the Covenant, and her unwavering support of the course defined by 'Abdu'l-Bahá were, no doubt, a source of strength and solace to her brother and an example to the beleaguered Bahá'í community. Indeed, a pilgrim who was in the Holy Land in 1906 reported that 'Abdu'l-Bahá was heard to say he did not know what he would do without the Greatest Holy Leaf and his wife, Munírih Khánum, so greatly did he love them, and so faithfully did they love and serve him.[30]

According to pilgrims' accounts, Bahíyyih Khánum played an important role during this period in relating to women of high rank in the wider community. Writing of the "troublous time of 1905 in 'Akká," a pilgrim recounts that a Syrian officer in the Turkish army who had always been friendly with the holy family suddenly turned against them. When his scheme to ingratiate himself with the powers in Constantinople failed, he was arrested and sent to Damascus. She reports that 'Abdu'l-Bahá had no word of censure for this false friend. On the contrary, he and Bahíyyih Khánum went at once to call upon the sorrowful wife, offering her money and every assistance.[31]

Despite the restrictions imposed on the Bahá'í community, 'Abdu'l-Bahá found ways to pursue activities that were vital to the expansion and consolidation of the Faith and the establishment of its embryonic Administrative Order. The work on the construction of the shrine of the Báb in Haifa continued unabated. The tablets 'Abdu'l-Bahá revealed to guide the believers and to respond to their questions poured forth in abundance. In addition, he set in motion a wide variety of enterprises that testified to his "inexhaustible energy, marvellous serenity and unshakeable confidence." Principal among them were the initiation of construction of the first Bahá'í House of Worship in the world in Ishqábád, preparation for the one to be built in Wilmette, Illinois, and the restoration of the house of the Báb in Shíráz.[32]

During this same period, "at an hour of grave suspense," 'Abdu'l-Bahá penned his will and testament, which Shoghi Effendi describes as "that immortal Document wherein He delineated the features of the Administrative Order which would arise after His passing, and would herald the establishment of that World Order, the advent of which the Báb had announced, and the laws and principles of which

Bahá'u'lláh had already formulated." During this period 'Abdu'l-Bahá also "reared the embryonic institutions, administrative, spiritual, and educational, of a steadily expanding Faith in Persia, the cradle of that Faith, in the Great Republic of the West, the cradle of its Administrative Order, in the Dominion of Canada, in France, in England, in Germany, in Egypt, in 'Iráq, in Russia, in India, in Burma, in Japan, and even in the remote Pacific Islands." Further, to accommodate the needs of the growing and rapidly diversifying Bahá'í community, he actively fostered "the translation, the publication and dissemination of Bahá'í literature, whose scope now included a variety of books and treatises, written in the Persian, the Arabic, the English, the Turkish, the French, the German, the Russian and Burmese languages."[33]

As circumstances permitted, "whenever there was a lull in the storm raging about Him," "pilgrims, friends and inquirers . . . representative of the Christian, the Muslim, the Jewish, the Zoroastrian, the Hindu and Buddhist Faiths" would gather at 'Abdu'l-Bahá's table.[34] A pilgrim provides the following account of her impressions of some of the challenges confronting the members of the holy family and visiting pilgrims at that time, and of the ways in which these difficulties were surmounted. She writes,

> One might easily imagine the daily life of a family of prisoners—even a Holy Family—as sad and depressing to the visitor but, strange to say, in the "Most Great Prison"* quite the reverse is the case. Although absolute regularity of living is not possible—nearly every domestic event being subject to the rise of unexpected circumstances—the calm serenity of those beautiful people is never broken. They pursue their daily tasks, render their sweet service, make their little sacrifices, teach their children—and play with

---

* Bahá'u'lláh designated Acre as the "Most Great Prison" upon His arrival there in 1868.

them, too—in short, carry on, under the most extraordinary circumstances, a perfect ideal of human family life. One never hears complaint of hard conditions, only a calm acceptance of God's Will and Wisdom in every little happening, and a sure understanding of the future blessings which will be the fruit of their present patience, blessings for all the peoples of the world.

Although each individual, from the youngest servant to the Greatest Holy Leaf, is constantly on guard, no parade is made of their watchfulness. Not even a creak of a distant door or a strange footfall escapes their attentive ears, yet the visitor is never reminded that he is the cause of anxiety. When it becomes necessary to move the whole supper table suddenly into another room to escape the observation of the Turkish callers, it is done with a quiet smile and no hint of inconvenience. How obvious and easy it would be to impress the sensitive pilgrim with their daily martyrdom and the constant strain of their precarious position. . . .

Were it not for the close proximity to the barracks and its guards, one would never realize that he was visiting a Turkish prison.

Another delight to the visitor is the discovery of their spontaneous and charming humour. They make merry over every little jest, extracting all the laughter possible from it, and encourage one another to see the bright side of all things, thus distracting their minds from the tragic side of their existence.[35]

For a time, the environment in Acre was somewhat more relaxed. Historic forces were, however, at work in the Ottoman Empire that would, in time, radically change the fortunes of both the sultan and the lives of the exiles. In the climate of increasing political unrest that prevailed in Ottoman territories, the Covenant-breakers renewed their intrigues. Alarmed, Sulṭán 'Abdu'l-Ḥamíd responded by dispatching, once again, a commission of inquiry to Acre in the winter of 1907. The commission brought with it the same documents that the earlier commission had been unable to substantiate and had consequently discarded. It began by stamping its authority on the local administration. An atmosphere of fear was generated when officials known to be friendly to 'Abdu'l-Bahá were dismissed and spies were again posted around 'Abdu'l-Bahá's house. Even the poor of Acre were afraid to approach his house, and rumors were circulated that 'Abdu'l-Bahá was to be forcibly removed to Fízán in Tripolitania, and totally cut off from the world.[36]

Throughout the monthlong stay of the commission, 'Abdu'l-Bahá consistently refused to meet or to have any dealings with them despite threats and warnings of the consequences. Shoghi Effendi describes 'Abdu'l-Bahá's demeanor at that time: "Though the perils and tribulations which had encompassed Him were now at their thickest, though the ship on which He was supposed to embark with the members of the Commission was waiting in readiness, at times in 'Akká, at times in Haifa, and the wildest rumors were being spread about Him, the serenity He had invariably maintained, ever since His incarceration had been reimposed, remained unclouded, and His confidence unshaken."[37]

Shoghi Effendi recounts the final moments of the commission's time in the Holy Land. Its members had gone to Haifa to inspect the shrine of the Báb, which was under construction.

Shortly after the inspection had been made it was suddenly observed, one day at about sunset, that the ship, which had been lying off Haifa, had weighed anchor, and was heading towards 'Akká. The news spread rapidly among an excited population that the members of the Commission had embarked upon it. It was anticipated that it would stop long enough at 'Akká to take 'Abdu'l-Bahá on board, and then proceed to its destination. Consternation and anguish seized the members of His family when informed of the approach of the ship. The few believers who were left wept with grief at their impending separation from their Master. 'Abdu'l-Bahá could be seen, at that tragic hour, pacing, alone and silent, the courtyard of His house.

. . . As dusk fell, however, it was suddenly noticed that the lights of the ship had swung round, and the vessel had changed her course. It now became evident that she was sailing direct for Constantinople. The intelligence was instantly communicated to 'Abdu'l-Bahá, Who, in the gathering darkness, was still pacing His courtyard. Some of the believers who had posted themselves at different points to watch the progress of the ship hurried to confirm the joyful tidings. One of the direst perils that had ever threatened 'Abdu'l-Bahá's precious life was, on that historic day, suddenly, providentially and definitely averted.

Soon after the precipitate and wholly unexpected sailing of that ship news was received that a bomb had exploded in the path of the Sultan while he was returning to his palace from the mosque where he had been offering his Friday prayers.

A few days after this attempt on his life the Commission submitted its report to him; but he and his government were too preoccupied to consider the matter. The case was laid aside, and when, some months later, it was again brought forward it was abruptly closed forever by an event which, once and for all, placed the Prisoner of 'Akká beyond the power of His royal enemy.[38]

The "Young Turk" Revolution broke out in 1908. The sultan was forced to promulgate the constitution, which he had earlier suspended, and to release all religious and political prisoners held under the old regime. To ensure that 'Abdu'l-Bahá was included in "the category of these prisoners," an inquiry was sent by telegram to Constantinople, "to which an affirmative reply was promptly received."[39]

This final period of incarceration was fraught with great danger and tribulations for 'Abdu'l-Bahá and the members of his family. In reviewing the outstanding features of this seven-year period, 1901–1908, Shoghi Effendi called attention to "the incessant machinations" of Muḥammad-'Alí and his "despicable supporters" and to the "agitation which their cleverly-directed campaign of misrepresentation and calumny produced in quarters directly connected with Sulṭán 'Abdu'l-Ḥamíd and his advisers." These insidious activities gave rise to "trials and investigations" and led to the reimposition of a period of rigid incarceration. They were the cause of the revival of "perils" for the exiles.[40]

The contributions of the Greatest Holy Leaf to the specific events that transpired during that troublous time are largely unrecorded. However, Shoghi Effendi leaves the following description of the outstanding qualities and attitudes of mind and character that Bahíyyih Khánum manifested and the importance of these qualities to what transpired. He attests that, "but for her sleepless vigilance, her tact, her courtesy, her extreme patience and heroic fortitude, grave complications might have ensued and the load of 'Abdu'l-Bahá's anxious care would have been considerably increased."[41]

Thus ended a forty-year-long confinement in the prison-city of Acre. At the beginning of their incarceration, 'Abdu'l-Bahá and Bahíyyih Khánum had been in their early twenties. When they were freed, they were in the evening of their lives.

Entombment of the Remains of the Báb on Mount Carmel

Within eight months of his release, 'Abdu'l-Bahá was able to achieve one of the most signal acts of his ministry—the construction of a befitting mausoleum and the interment of the remains of the Báb on Mount Carmel, more than fifty years after His martyrdom. This historic enterprise had been initiated during Bahá'u'lláh's lifetime and was completed during the most difficult period of 'Abdu'l-Bahá's incarceration. Bahá'u'lláh Himself had specified the site where the shrine of the Báb was to be built and had instructed the Bahá'ís in Iran to protect and ensure the safety of the Báb's remains.

In 1899 'Abdu'l-Bahá issued instructions for the remains of the Báb to be brought to Acre. They arrived on 31 January 1899, "fifty lunar years after the Báb's execution in Tabríz." In that same year, 'Abdu'l-Bahá laid the foundation stone of the building, and the construction was begun a few months later. In the meantime, the marble sarcophagus designed to receive the body of the Báb reached the Holy Land. It was a gift of the Bahá'ís of Rangoon, Burma. The completion of the basic structure of the shrine was to take almost ten years. In the course of its construction 'Abdu'l-Bahá was beset by "manifold problems and preoccupations" occasioned by the machinations of the Covenant-breakers and his enforced absence from Haifa due to his renewed incarceration in Acre, which limited his ability to supervise the undertaking.[42]

Given the protracted difficulties in completing the construction of the shrine and the dangers confronting 'Abdu'l-Bahá and his family at that time, it was imperative for him to conceal the casket containing the remains of the Báb until it could be interred. This casket was, therefore, entrusted to the care of the Greatest Holy Leaf. It was, for a time, hidden in the room she occupied in the house of 'Abdu'lláh-Páshá, where 'Abdu'l-Bahá and his family were living.

Years later, a woman who had the privilege of serving in 'Abdu'l-Bahá's household during this period shared some fascinating observations about the manner in which the Greatest Holy Leaf undertook this weighty responsibility. She recalls noticing that it was Bahíyyih Khánum's custom to sit on the *mandar* (upholstered bench) in her room in utter silence for hours at a time. The woman indicated that, at the time, she had wondered why the Greatest Holy Leaf acted in this way. However, years later she understood that the silent and reverential attitude she had observed was due to the presence of the remains of the Báb in the Greatest Holy Leaf's room. Doubtless, Bahíyyih Khánum was acutely cognizant of the sacred trust she had to protect, and of the vital necessity of concealing the location of the Báb's precious remains.[43]

Finally, in 1909, 'Abdu'l-Bahá brought the undertaking to a successful conclusion. The Báb's remains were, at last, laid to rest in His shrine on Mount Carmel. Shoghi Effendi recounts, on "the day of the first Naw-Rúz . . . , which He celebrated after His release from His confinement, 'Abdu'l-Bahá had the marble sarcophagus transported with great labor to the vault prepared for it, and in the evening, by the light of a single lamp, He laid within it, with His own hands . . . the wooden casket containing the sacred remains of the Báb and His companion."* 'Abdu'l-Bahá announced "this glorious victory" to the Bahá'ís in the following terms:

> The most joyful tidings is this, that the holy, the luminous body of the Báb . . . after having for sixty years been transferred from place to place, by reason of the ascendancy of the enemy, and from fear of the malevolent, and having known neither rest nor tranquility has, through the mercy of the Abhá Beauty, been ceremoniously deposited, on the day of Naw-Rúz,† within the sacred casket, in the exalted Shrine on Mt. Carmel . . . By a strange coincidence, on that same day of Naw-Rúz, a cablegram was received from Chicago, announcing that the believers in each of the American centers had elected a delegate and sent to that city . . . and definitely decided on the site and construction of the Mashríqu'l-Adhkár [House of Worship].[44]

---

* The Báb was executed with one of His followers.
† New Year's Day in the Bahá'í calendar.

'Abdu'l-Bahá's Travels in Egypt and the West

No sooner had 'Abdu'l-Bahá laid the remains of the Báb in a safe and permanent resting-place than he arose with "sublime courage, confidence and resolution" to promote the Bahá'í Cause in the Western world. He embarked upon three years of travel that took him first to Egypt, then to Europe, and later to North America. During this period, he, "with unhesitating confidence, invested His trusted and honoured sister with the responsibility of attending to the multitudinous details arising out of His protracted absence from the Holy Land." Shoghi Effendi underlines the significance of this assignment and the unique station to which Bahíyyih Khánum was called. He attests that, at the time of 'Abdu'l-Bahá's absence in the Western world, she was "His competent deputy, His representative and vicegerent, with none to equal her."[45]

To understand the importance of the role that the Greatest Holy Leaf played during this period in Bahá'í history, it is useful to reflect on the meanings of the terms used by the Guardian to characterize the nature and the quality of her contribution. She was 'Abdu'l-Bahá's "competent deputy." As her brother's "deputy," Bahíyyih Khánum was nominated and appointed to stand in for 'Abdu'l-Bahá. She was empowered to act on his behalf and take charge of the affairs of the Faith during his absence. It is clear from Shoghi Effendi's characterization that her appointment was not simply a position of courtesy and that the functions she performed were not merely ceremonial. Rather, the Guardian's choice of words constitutes an exact and accurate description of the manner in which she fulfilled her vital role. Further, the use of the term "vicegerent" provides additional insight into the nature of the functions she likely performed, since this term denotes an administrative deputy, a person appointed to perform the functions of a king or magistrate. The term is also applied to a person who is deputed by God to exercise authority in government or in religious matters and to a person who substitutes for another.[46] While the specific tasks the Greatest Holy Leaf undertook are not recorded in detail and can only be deduced by inference, it would appear that the functions she performed during the absence of 'Abdu'l-Bahá were far-reaching and included attending to the administrative and spiritual guidance of the community. She was the one who was empowered to act in his absence.

It has been reported that while 'Abdu'l-Bahá was on his travels the Greatest Holy Leaf had to deal with many affairs in the Holy Land that would have been his responsibility had he been there. Her sphere of influence was enlarged. She received both dignitaries and officials of both sexes, spoke to the pilgrims on behalf of 'Abdu'l-Bahá, inspired them, gave assistance to the poor, and offered her medical services to the sick.[47]

Just before his departure for Egypt in September 1910, 'Abdu'l-Bahá addressed a touching tablet to Bahíyyih Khánum. In it, he informs her of his impending departure and laments the separation that will ensue. He expresses his unhesitating confidence in her and entreats her to pray at the shrine of Bahá'u'lláh on his behalf for the confirmation of his efforts:

O thou my sister, my dear sister!

Divine wisdom hath decreed this temporary separation, but I long more and more to be with thee again. Patience is called for, and long-suffering, and trust in God, and the seeking of His favour. Since thou art there, my mind is completely at rest.

In recent days, I have made a plan to visit Egypt, if this is God's will. Do thou, on my behalf, lay thy head on the sacred

Threshold, and perfume brow and hair in the dust of that Door, and ask that I may be confirmed in my work; that I may, in return for His endless bounties, win, if He will, a drop out of the ocean of servitude.[48]

After spending time in Egypt, 'Abdu'l-Bahá left for Europe on 11 August 1911. He landed in Marseille, proceeded to Thonon-les-Bains, and arrived in London on 4 September 1911, where he stayed for about a month. Then he traveled on to Paris, where he stayed for a period of nine weeks. In December 1911, he returned to Egypt, where he spent the winter. He embarked on his second journey to the west on 25 March 1912, sailing via Naples to New York, where he arrived on 11 April.[49] While in New York, 'Abdu'l-Bahá addressed the following tablet to his dear sister:

O Thou Greatest and Most Merciful Holy Leaf!

I arrived in New York in the best of health, and I have been at all times thinking of thee, and supplicating fervently at the threshold of the Blessed Beauty that He may guard thee in the stronghold of His protection. We are in the utmost fellowship and joy. I hope that thou wilt be sheltered under His bountiful care.

Write to me at once about Rúḥá Khánum's* and Shoghi Effendi's condition, informing me fully and hiding nothing; this is the best way.

Convey my utmost longing to all.[50]

From the foregoing, it is apparent that 'Abdu'l-Bahá not only intended to inform his sister of the progress of his travels and the state of his health, but he also turned to her as a source of clear and straightforward information, and he used her as the chosen channel

---

* A daughter of 'Abdu'l-Bahá.

for communication between himself and the Bahá'í community in the Holy Land.

'Abdu'l-Bahá's epic tour in North America lasted eight months. It carried him from coast to coast, with many intermediate stops. On 5 December 1912, he sailed from New York for Liverpool and then traveled to London, Paris, Stuttgart, Budapest, and Vienna. Shoghi Effendi describes the impact and the significance of 'Abdu'l-Bahá's travels in the West:

> It was in the course of these epoch-making journeys and before large and representative audiences, at times exceeding a thousand people, that 'Abdu'l-Bahá expounded, with brilliant simplicity, with persuasiveness and force, and for the first time in His ministry, those basic and distinguishing principles of His Father's Faith, which together with the laws and ordinances revealed in the Kitáb-i-Aqdas* constitute the bed-rock of God's latest Revelation to mankind. The independent search after truth, unfettered by superstition or tradition; the oneness of the entire human race, the pivotal principle and fundamental doctrine of the Faith; the basic unity of all religions; the condemnation of all forms of prejudice, whether religious, racial, class or national; the harmony which must exist between religion and science; the equality of men and women, the two wings on which the bird of human kind is able to soar; the introduction of compulsory education; the adoption of a universal auxiliary language; the abolition of the extremes of wealth and poverty; the institution of a world tribunal for the adjudication of disputes between nations; the exaltation of work, performed in the spirit of service, to the rank of worship; the glorification of justice as the ruling prin-

---

* Literally "Most Holy Book," the book in which Bahá'u'lláh sets forth the charter for the future world civilization He has come to raise up.

ciple in human society, and of religion as a bulwark for the protection of all peoples and nations; and the establishment of a permanent and universal peace as the supreme goal of all mankind—these stand out as the essential elements of that Divine polity which He proclaimed to leaders of public thought as well as to the masses at large in the course of these missionary journeys. The exposition of these vitalizing truths of the Faith of Bahá'u'lláh, which He characterized as the *"spirit of the age,"* He supplemented with grave and reiterated warnings of an impending conflagration which, if the statesmen of the world should fail to avert, would set ablaze the entire continent of Europe. He, moreover, predicted, in the course of these travels, the radical changes which would take place in that continent, foreshadowed the movement of the decentralization of political power which would inevitably be set in motion, alluded to the troubles that would overtake Turkey, anticipated the persecution of the Jews on the European continent, and categorically asserted that the *"banner of the unity of mankind would be hoisted, that the tabernacle of universal peace would be raised and the world become another world."* [51]

In the following passage, Shoghi Effendi captures the profound effect 'Abdu'l-Bahá's travels had on Bahíyyih Khánum—the stimulus they provided and the utter joy and satisfaction she experienced as a result of the progress of the Faith:

> No sooner had 'Abdu'l-Bahá stepped upon the shores of the European and American continents than our beloved Khánum found herself well-nigh overwhelmed with thrilling messages, each betokening the irresistible advance of the Cause in a manner which, notwithstanding the vast range of her experience, seemed to her almost incredible. The years in which she basked in the sunshine of 'Abdu'l-Bahá's spiritual victories were, perhaps, among

the brightest and happiest of her life. Little did she dream when, as a little girl, she was running about, in the courtyard of her Father's house in Ṭihrán, in the company of Him Whose destiny was to be one day the chosen Centre of God's indestructible Covenant, that such a Brother would be capable of achieving, in realms so distant, and among races so utterly remote, so great and memorable a victory.[52]

'Abdu'l-Bahá himself expressed his excitement and, indeed, a sense of wonderment at the response to the Bahá'í Faith in the Western world. In a touching tablet addressed to the Greatest Holy Leaf, he called upon his dear sister to visit the shrine of Bahá'u'lláh and offer prayers of thanksgiving. And he even revealed a special prayer for her to say on his behalf. The tablet reads,

> O My dear sister! Praise be to God, within the sheltering grace of the Blessed Beauty, here in the lands of the West a breeze hath blown from over the rose-gardens of His bestowals, and the hearts of many people have been drawn as by a magnet to the Abhá Realm.*
>
> Whatever hath come to pass is from the confirmations of the Beloved; for otherwise, what merit had we, or what capacity? We are as a helpless babe, but fed at the breast of heavenly grace. We are no more than weak plants, but we flourish in the spring rain of His bestowals. Wherefore, as a thank-offering for these bounties, on a certain day don thy garb to visit the Shrine, the ka'bih† of our heart's desire, turn thyself toward Him on my behalf, lay down thy head on that sacred Threshold, and say:

---

* *Abhá* means, literally, "most glorious"; thus *Abhá Realm* can be taken to mean "Most Glorious Realm" or "Realm of Glory."

† A term of specific meaning in Islam. Used here more generally to denote a center of worship.

O divine Providence! O Thou forgiving Lord! Sinner though I be, I have no refuge save Thyself. All praise be Thine, that in my wanderings over mountains and plains, my toils and troubles on the seas, Thou hast answered still my cries for help, and confirmed me, and favoured me, and honoured me with service at Thy Threshold.

To a feeble ant, Thou hast given Solomon's might. Thou hast made of a gnat a lion in the thicket of Thy Mercy. Thou hast bestowed on a drop the swelling waves of the sea, Thou hast carried up a mote to the pinnacles of grace. Whatever was achieved, was made possible through Thee. Otherwise, what strength did the fragile dust possess, what power did this feeble being have?

O divine Providence! Do not seize us in our sins, but give us refuge. Do not look upon our evil ways, but grant forgiveness. Consider not our just deserts, but open wide Thy door of grace.

Thou art the Mighty, the Powerful! Thou art the Seer, the Knower![53]

On 13 June 1913 'Abdu'l-Bahá sailed from Marseille for Egypt, arriving a few days later in Port Said. Residing for the most part in Ramleh, a suburb of Alexandria, he spent almost six months in Egypt, resting and restoring his health before proceeding to Haifa. Bahíyyih Khánum and several other members of the holy family, including Shoghi Effendi, traveled to Egypt to meet 'Abdu'l-Bahá on his return from his historic journeys. Again Shoghi Effendi provides a glimpse of the feelings and emotions that she might well have been experiencing during the long-anticipated reunion between brother and sister. He writes, "The enthusiasm and joy which swelled in her breast as she greeted 'Abdu'l-Bahá on His triumphant return from the West, I will not venture to describe. She was astounded at the vitality of which He had, despite His unimaginable sufferings, proved Himself capable. She was lost in admiration at the magnitude of the forces which His utterances had released. She was filled with thankfulness to Bahá'u'lláh for having enabled her to witness the evidences of such brilliant victory for His Cause no less than for His Son."[54]

The Greatest Holy Leaf stayed in Egypt for a number of weeks. She once again assumed the management of 'Abdu'l-Bahá's household, which soon became a point of attraction for visiting Bahá'ís from many parts of the world. Indeed, a number of Western women who visited as pilgrims were privileged to reside in 'Abdu'l-Bahá's home. Included among them were Mrs. Lua Getsinger and Mrs. Isobel Fraser. After a time, the Greatest Holy Leaf returned to Haifa in order to receive the pilgrims and to supervise the activities of the community.[55]

Rúḥá Aṣdaq, a Persian pilgrim, has left a fascinating record of her impression of the holy household just before 'Abdu'l-Bahá's return to Haifa. She recounts that he had invited her family to come to the Holy Land for pilgrimage. While the pilgrims were bathed in the spirit of the shrines and derived great spiritual sustenance from their association with the Greatest Holy Leaf, their only sorrow was not to have had the opportunity to meet 'Abdu'l-Bahá. She indicates that her father was required to travel to Alexandria in Egypt and that, prior to his departure, the Greatest Holy Leaf asked to see him and spent an hour in conversation with him. It transpired that Rúḥá's father visited with 'Abdu'l-Bahá in Alexandria and, on his return, brought the joyful news that 'Abdu'l-Bahá would soon return to Haifa.

Immediately preparations were made for 'Abdu'l-Bahá's arrival, though the actual date was not known. His favorite food was prepared, clothes were sewn, and everything was made ready. The pilgrim describes the excitement that prevailed:

> The main hall of the Master's house was being prepared for His arrival. All the pilgrims and members of the household gathered there. At the joyful time, 'Abdu'l-Bahá descended from the carriage and made His way towards the house. The Greatest Holy Leaf and His daughters rushed towards Him and embraced Him. . . .
>
> After a brief rest . . . , the beloved Master emerged from His room, sat before us and addressed those present with these words, "Welcome! Welcome!". . . After a prayer (was) chanted by His daughter . . . , He said, "May ye all remain in God's care." Then the ladies, with hearts overflowing with happiness, withdrew and permitted the equally anxious and tearful men to enter the hall. Shortly we all heard the resounding and heartwarming chant of the Tablet of Ru'yá . . . which cheered our hearts. And so it was on this auspicious day, 5 December 1913, events occurred that none would ever forget: all was engraved in our hearts and minds.[56]

The pilgrim later learned that the Greatest Holy Leaf, in her private conversation with Rúhá's father before his trip to Alexandria, had asked him to request 'Abdu'l-Bahá to return sooner to Haifa "to allay the anxious hearts of the pilgrims and the members of the Holy Household." The pilgrim states that her father recalled that when he conveyed the message of Bahíyyih Khánum 'Abdu'l-Bahá had smiled and said, "'How clever her ruse.'"[57]

Household Manager and Hostess to Pilgrims

From the days of Bahá'u'lláh, the Greatest Holy Leaf undertook the management of the affairs of her father's household, a function in which Shoghi Effendi said she "excelled." From early childhood she arose to assist her mother in this task. When her mother passed away, she assumed the major responsibility for this function. She managed the practical affairs of the household, arranged for the purchase and preparation of food, met the wives of the pilgrims and officials, and ministered to the women who entered the house. She was motivated by her desire to attend to the everyday needs of Bahá'u'lláh and to leave Him free to deal with those things that only He could do. To this end, she also "assiduously cultivated" social relationships in order to shield Bahá'u'lláh from the necessity of interacting with all but those with whom He chose to interact. With the passing of Bahá'u'lláh, the Greatest Holy Leaf turned with her whole heart to support her brother 'Abdu'l-Bahá.[58]

During the ministry of 'Abdu'l-Bahá, the Greatest Holy Leaf was appointed to be in charge of his household, where she continued and expanded the functions she had assumed during her father's lifetime. One of the early pilgrims, Ella Goodall Cooper, reports that the women of the household recognized the unique spiritual station of the Greatest Holy Leaf. Her notes as a pilgrim provide insight into the nature of the Greatest Holy Leaf's leadership, underlining the fact that it was her "strong yet gentle quality of authority [that] made her naturally the head of the household group that circled about 'Abdu'l-Bahá." She observes that "Her authority, so real yet so humble, was instinctively accepted by the family of the Master, who sought her wise and loving counsel upon every occasion. In this way all cooperated to save the time and strength

of 'Abdu'l-Bahá Whose life must be given to the service of all mankind, as they well realized."[59]

In performing her functions as head of 'Abdu'l-Bahá's household
and as "the honoured hostess to a steadily increasing number of
pilgrims who thronged 'Abdu'l-Bahá's residence from both the East
and the West," the Greatest Holy Leaf not only brought to bear a
sense of organization, order, and a unifying spirit, but she also demonstrated a practicality and an ability to attend to multiple tasks
without becoming absorbed in minute details.[60]

In implementing her assigned functions the Greatest Holy Leaf
was responsible for coordinating the activities of the Bahá'í women,
both local residents as well as visiting pilgrims. An early pilgrim
provides a fascinating glimpse of the Greatest Holy Leaf's role in
this regard. She describes how

> She presided over the room called *Ladies Room* which was the
> center for all family gatherings, and where the women visitors
> were entertained. From the hour of the early morning tea, at
> which 'Abdu'l-Bahá was often present, to the last good-night,
> whispered by some weary yet grateful traveler, *Khanum* (as she
> was affectionately called) was ever in demand. During the long
> day, which began before six in the morning and rarely ended
> before eleven or twelve at night, there were frequent spontaneous
> gatherings in this general room. . . . The spiritual peace and joy
> pervading these simple meetings was a new and unbelievable ex-
> perience to us—the Western pilgrims.
>
> The chanting of the sacred tablets by the Persian ladies, at the
> request of the Greatest Holy Leaf (who had thus made them
> happy) the murmur of low voices as news . . . was imparted, the
> bubbling of the friendly samovar as tea was handed around by
> the young serving maids, and, above all, the impalpable yet vi-

brant atmosphere of love and service made these meetings attract all including the children. . . . Even the birds seemed to feel
the friendly spirit for they flew freely in and out through the
open door leading to the court which was open to the sky.[61]

Additional information about some of the functions Bahíyyih
Khánum was called upon to perform in presiding over the "Ladies
Room" is provided in another pilgrim's account. It is reported that
"The friends would come to her for names for their children, for
consultation about a forthcoming marriage and requesting her blessing on the union. She would generally inform the friends about the
development of the Cause and whatever 'Abdu'l-Bahá had said. She
was the central point for the Bahá'í women in the community in
the Holy Land."[62]

The "Ladies Room" was also a magnet for visiting pilgrims. Writing of her pilgrimage in 1921, Marie Watson reports visiting the
ladies of the household every day from four to seven in the evening.
She writes,

> On Wednesday afternoons, a "Women's Meeting" is held in
> the large central room, secluded from the masculine gaze of the
> many visitors the Master receives at all hours of the day. Bahá'í
> women living outside also attend these gatherings, where one of
> the Master's daughters reads or chants the prayers and tablets of
> Bahá'u'lláh.
>
> Tea is always served with Persian cookies and grapes. The
> Master, if He can spare the time, generally looks in to greet the
> assembly, say a few words and make them all happy.[63]

A responsibility of great trust assigned to the Greatest Holy Leaf
was that of the custodianship of the spiritual treasures of the fam-

ily. Her role was to look after the sacred writings of the Founders of the Faith, to preserve the portraits of Bahá'u'lláh and the Báb, and to ensure that the relics and historical objects associated with the early days of the Faith were collected and stored. Not only did the Greatest Holy Leaf keep and preserve these precious relics, but it was she who displayed them to the visiting female pilgrims. There are numerous accounts of Bahíyyih Khánum's escorting pilgrims into a room in 'Abdu'l-Bahá's house to view the portraits of Bahá'u'lláh and the Báb. The opportunity to view these portraits was, and continues to be, much prized by Bahá'í pilgrims to the World Center of their faith. The images have, as a matter of policy, not been reproduced and circulated within the Bahá'í community.[64]

Care of the pilgrims was an enormous task, undertaken with few resources and often in a hostile and dangerous environment. From the time of Bahá'u'lláh until the time of the exiles' release from prison during the ministry of 'Abdu'l-Bahá, female pilgrims were often accommodated within the household of the family. In later years, even after houses for visiting pilgrims were built in Haifa, the women of 'Abdu'l-Bahá's family continued to prepare all the food, arrange for its delivery to the pilgrims, and attend to the pilgrims' daily needs. The scope of this task and the spirit in which the work was undertaken are illustrated by the following firsthand observations from Marie Watson. She writes,

The Master's household numbers more than a hundred persons, not counting the children of the believers and His own grandchildren. How wonderfully significant, as an example to the world, is this living service so cheerfully given by each member of the family! There is such harmony and unity in this household, where all the machinery of every-day life is carried out without a break. Every emergency is provided for; unexpected visitors are always entertained with a composure and sincerity unbelievable unless witnessed day after day as I saw it. Where in this wide world could a parallel be found, even approximate to this? No complaint, no friction amidst a variety of temperaments and of different stations in life. It is a garden of variegated flowers growing in the utmost loveliness. . . .[65]

This same pilgrim also underlines the central role Bahíyyih Khánum played in the household: "From early morning till very late at night she is in demand, and with the assistance of the Master's daughters, she carries out every detail of this formidable household."[66]

Ella Goodall Cooper, one of the early Western pilgrims, characterizes Bahíyyih Khánum's approach to life as perfectly exemplifying an "exquisite balance between the practical and spiritual teachings." She recounts the follow episode, which dramatically captures Bahíyyih Khánum's "practical efficiency." The pilgrim writes,

One day we caught a glimpse of her in the kitchen seated on a low stool, her firm, capable hands busy with a large lamb that had just been brought in from the market. Quickly dividing it, she directed which part was to be made into broth, which part served for the evening meal, which part kept for the morrow, and which sent to those poor or incapacitated friends who are daily supplied from 'Abdu'l-Bahá's table. On the shelves were huge pans holding rice soaking in clean water to be ready for the delicious pilau (a famous Persian dish), and there were many other visible evidences of the hours of preparation necessary to provide for the material welfare of the visitors.

It was then we learned of her practical efficiency. The enormous amount of work attendant upon such entertaining with only the crudest and most primitive facilities, must be seen to be appreciated. We learned that she had organized the household affairs, and each one of the Master's daughters took her turn at directing them for a week—planning the meals and marketing, and seeing that all was cooked and served to the different groups twice each day. Without running water, with only charcoal for fuel, with no gas or electricity for lighting, only oil,—the cleaning and filling of the lamps alone consumed a large amount of time and energy.[67]

Mary Hanford Ford, an early Western pilgrim, provides another description of the operation of 'Abdu'l-Bahá's household. She highlights an approach to work that combines the spiritual and practical, and the resolution of problems in a way that preserves the dignity of the individual. She writes,

The ladies of the family are admirable housewives. They make all their own simple wearing apparel, by the aid of a sewing machine from the western world. They oversee the production of the kitchen for their many guests and are thoroughly hygienic in the cleanliness of their environment. They typify the modern saint, the conception of whom obliges us to revolutionize our entire spiritual cosmogony. A fashionable woman of the western world, as helpless as are some of these artificial dames, and so eager for spiritual culture, was caught in the gentle household without a trunk, and so handsomely garbed that she felt disgraced in the presence of the lovely simplicity that reigns there. The Greatest Holy Leaf thereupon made her a print dress with her own beautiful hands, which was a model for grace and adjustment. The western woman is still puzzling perhaps over the problem of how such profound spirituality can be associated with such excellent practical skill and sense, but in reality they are always found side by side.[68]

The pilgrims who were privileged to meet Bahíyyih Khánum were moved by her vivid recollections of the events of the early days of the Faith and inspired by their awakening consciousness of her high spiritual station. They also derived deep lessons from observing the ways in which she interacted with the believers and her general attitude towards life. Marjorie Morton, who met Bahíyyih Khánum in the evening of her life, shared the following observations. Commenting on the cultural constraints under which the women of the holy family lived, she states that the Greatest Holy Leaf accepted such restrictions "as she would inclement weather that kept her indoors." Mrs. Morton states, "she had moulded her life to the bounds of her sphere, pouring into it the resources of her own spirit, and had found scope for all her qualities." [69] She affirms that

> Her life could not be called martyrdom, for she did not recognize it as such. She was not shaken by the transports of rapture of the martyr and had no urge to raise the banner, to rush to encounter, to offer up with heroic valour. Her ardour burned with a steady flame. In the face of test and danger she neither hurried nor held back, but entered the perilous way with quiet breath. Her courage was born of her understanding faith, and it was this faith, this understanding, that carried her serene through years of incessant labour and meticulous service, and through times of waiting empty-handed, —and through the bearing of irremediable sorrow and loss. [70]

Mrs. Morton makes the following observations of the Greatest Holy Leaf, from which she draws a number of lessons for life. She writes,

> Her balance, sense of fineness and fitness and practical judgment she displayed in creating order and grace in the household, and all the elements that make for well-being she blended in an

ambience of harmony. Her strong will was never used to over-
ride and her decided opinions were never pressed upon another.
Her ways were gentle. Others might break the shell with a blow;
it was for her to unsheathe the kernel with infinite care and skill.
In her you met with no exactions, no biddance: she beckoned,
smiling, and would have no one come heavy-footed or bent to
her will. So quietly did she make her influence felt that you were
scarcely conscious of its working.[71]

The Greatest Holy Leaf derived great satisfaction from her contact with the pilgrims. She rejoiced in receiving news of the progress
of the Faith in different parts of the world and in sharing the news
with the visitors. It is also interesting to note that she corresponded
with a number of pilgrims after their visit to the Holy Land. In a
letter addressed to an Eastern Bahá'í woman, Bahíyyih Khánum
provides the following encouragement to action: "Praised be God
that after attaining the holy Threshold of the Merciful in this hallowed land, this luminous Spot, you were able to take back with
you the gift of the divine fragrance of holiness, to perfume the
nostrils of the handmaids of God, to refresh and stimulate, nay
rather revive and quicken the lifeless bodies through the potency of
His wondrous exhortations, His sublime counsels and teachings."
In conclusion, she assures the believer that she has not been forgotten and that she will say prayers for her and the other Bahá'í women
in the holy shrines.[72]

Likewise, to a Western woman who had been on pilgrimage when
the Greatest Holy Leaf was absent from the Holy Land, she wrote
to convey her sorrow at not having been present to receive her. She
encouraged the believer not to be disappointed but to follow 'Abdu'l-
Bahá's guidance to her "to go into the world and give the Glad
Tidings of the Kingdom to the people and awaken the sleeping

souls." She expressed the hope that "we soon will hear of your wonderful services in the Path of the Cause of God." She counseled the woman to trust in 'Abdu'l-Bahá, affirming, "Be sure you will be successful at the end, for He has sent you and He will surely be with you and help you always."[73]

The War Years, 1914–18

Eight months after 'Abdu'l-Bahá's return to the Holy Land from his extensive travels, World War I broke out, plunging the world into turmoil, cutting him off from the Bahá'ís outside the Holy Land, and once more casting a "shadow of danger" over his life and that of his family. Shoghi Effendi indicates that, while the war surrounded the inhabitants of the Holy Land with "severe privations and grave dangers," it led ultimately to the liberation of the Faith from the yoke of Ottoman Turkish rule. He characterizes, in the following terms, the impact of the war on the inhabitants of the Holy Land and alludes to 'Abdu'l-Bahá's efforts to mitigate the people's suffering:

The privations inflicted on the inhabitants by the gross incompetence, the shameful neglect, the cruelty and callous indifference of both the civil and military authorities, though greatly alleviated through the bountiful generosity, the foresight and the tender care of 'Abdu'l-Bahá, were aggravated by the rigors of a strict blockade. A bombardment of Haifa by the Allies was a constant threat, at one time so real that it necessitated the temporary removal of 'Abdu'l-Bahá, His family and members of the local community to the village of Abú-Sinán at the foot of the hills east of 'Akká. The Turkish Commander-in-Chief . . . even expressed his intention of crucifying . . . ['Abdu'l-Bahá] and of razing to the ground the Tomb of Bahá'u'lláh.[74]

It is clear from the writings and talks of 'Abdu'l-Bahá delivered during his travels in the West that he anticipated the outbreak of war. Indeed, it is reported that he began making preparations for war conditions even before his return to the Holy Land after his world tour. With his unerring foresight, 'Abdu'l-Bahá arranged for a number of Bahá'ís who lived in the Jordan Valley and by the shores of the Sea of Galilee to grow and store corn and other grains. Later, he spent time in Tiberias personally arranging for the shipment of the grain to Haifa and Acre. With this grain 'Abdu'l-Bahá was able to feed the poor of the area during the famine years of 1914–18. Lady Blomfield describes what transpired. She writes,

> When the British arrived in Haifa, where the blockade had caused a perilous condition for the inhabitants, it was discovered that 'Abdu'l-Bahá had saved the civilian population from starvation. Provisions which He had grown, buried in under-ground pits, and otherwise stored, had been given out to the civilians of every nation living in Haifa. 'Abdu'l-Bahá did this in a military way as an army would give rations, and deep was the gratitude of those women and children who had been saved by His power to see into the future of tragedy and woe as early as 1912, when He began the preparations for the catastrophe which was to overtake that land in 1917 and 1918. When Haifa was finally occupied by the British, reserve provisions had not yet come for the army, and someone in authority approached the Master. . . .[75]

'Abdu'l-Bahá did, indeed, have a sufficient store of corn to assist the British Army.

Several years later, the British authorities expressed their appreciation of the role 'Abdu'l-Bahá had played in "allaying the burden of suffering that had oppressed the inhabitants of the Holy Land during the dark days of that distressing conflict" by conferring a knighthood on him in 1920.[76]

The Greatest Holy Leaf played a significant role in the humanitarian activities 'Abdu'l-Bahá undertook during this period. Describing her reaction to the events that transpired and the needs of the day, Shoghi Effendi states, "Age seemed to have accentuated the tenderness of her loving heart, and to have widened still further the range of her sympathies." Shoghi Effendi attests, "The sight of appalling suffering around her," rather than overwhelming the Greatest Holy Leaf, "steeled her energies and revealed such potentialities that her most intimate associates had failed to suspect."[77]

It was Bahíyyih Khánum who was responsible for feeding the poor who gravitated to 'Abdu'l-Bahá's house. It is reported that when the poor came asking for assistance, she cooked for them, sent them rations, or supplied them when they presented themselves in person. Shoghi Effendi captures the range of her activities and the qualities she manifested during the war years:

> The outbreak of the Great War gave her yet another opportunity to reveal the true worth of her character and to release the latent energies of her heart. The residence of 'Abdu'l-Bahá in Haifa was besieged, all throughout that dreary conflict, by a concourse of famished men, women and children whom the maladministration, the cruelty and neglect of the officials of the Ottoman Government had driven to seek an alleviation of their woes. From the hand of the Greatest Holy Leaf, and out of the abundance of her heart, these hapless victims of a contemptible tyranny, received day after day unforgettable evidences of a love they had learned to envy and admire. Her words of cheer and

comfort, the food, the money, the clothing she freely dispensed, the remedies which, by a process of her own, she herself prepared and diligently applied—all these had their share in comforting the disconsolate, in restoring sight to the blind, in sheltering the orphan, in healing the sick, and in succouring the homeless and the wanderer.[78]

This crisis provided the Greatest Holy Leaf with yet another opportunity to extend the range of her services to humanity and to lend her unstinting support to the initiatives embarked upon by 'Abdu'l-Bahá. Shoghi Effendi leaves us with the following description of the particular qualities of character she manifested in performing these arduous duties and the exemplary nature of her service. He writes that "She had reached, amidst the darkness of the war days the high water-mark of her spiritual attainments. Few, if any, among the unnumbered benefactors of society whose privilege has been to allay, in various measures, the hardships and sufferings entailed by that Fierce Conflict, gave as freely and as disinterestedly as she did; few exercised that indefinable influence upon the beneficiaries of their gifts."[79]

During the years when 'Abdu'l-Bahá was cut off from the Bahá'ís around the world, he engaged in revealing tablets for them in anticipation of the war's end. Little mail reached the Holy Land, and the flow of pilgrims was interrupted. Among the first pilgrims to reach the Holy Land at the end of the war were Mrs. Corinne True and her daughter, Edna, who arrived in Haifa at the end of 1919. In later years the members of 'Abdu'l-Bahá's family described the sense of isolation they had felt and how they had longed for news of the well-being of the Bahá'ís throughout the world and the progress of the Faith. One can well imagine the excitement in 'Abdu'l-Bahá's household when, finally, letters began to arrive conveying news of the believers' safety and accounts of the activities in which they had been engaged for the advancement of the Cause.[80]

Included among the tablets revealed during the war years and dispatched after the conclusion of hostilities were the Tablets of the Divine Plan, addressed to the Bahá'ís in North America, in which 'Abdu'l-Bahá bestowed on them a world mission for the propagation of the Bahá'í Faith. Other important tablets that 'Abdu'l-Bahá revealed during this period were his Tablet to Dr. Auguste Forel and a communication addressed to the Executive Committee of the "Central Organization for a Durable Peace," which was delivered to the Hague by a special delegation. In addition to these, hundreds of tablets were forwarded to individual believers, many having been written earlier but mailed at the end of the war.

Writing about the impact of the conclusion of the war on the condition of the Faith in the Holy Land, Shoghi Effendi notes,

> The danger which, for no less than three score years and five, had threatened the lives of the Founders of the Faith and of the Center of His Covenant, was now at long last through the instrumentality of that war completely and definitely lifted. The Head of the Faith, and its twin holy Shrines, in the plain of 'Akká and on the slopes of Mt. Carmel, were henceforth to enjoy for the first time, through the substitution of a new and liberal régime for the corrupt administration of the past, a freedom from restrictions which was later expanded into a clearer recognition of the institutions of the Cause. . . .[81]

Furthermore, in addition to the respect British authorities and other people of prominence and influence accorded to 'Abdu'l-Bahá, Shoghi Effendi calls attention to "the multiplying evidences" of the recognition by "all religious communities, whether Muslim, Christian or Jewish" of 'Abdu'l-Bahá's "high and unique position." One implication of the new freedom accorded to the Bahá'í Faith in the Holy Land was the arrival of increasing numbers of pilgrims from the East and West, who were now able to visit the holy shrines in comparative ease and comfort.[82]

The final years of 'Abdu'l-Bahá's ministry were marked by a "further enhancement of the prestige" of the Faith, continuing progress in the expansion and consolidation of the Bahá'í community in both the East and the West, the shaping of the administrative institutions of the Faith, and the widening of its activities and influence. The construction of the House of Worship was completed in 'Ishqábád, and in Wilmette, Illinois, "the excavations for the Mother Temple of the West were carried out and the contract placed for the construction of the basement of the building."[83]

The contributions of Bahíyyih Khánum, 'Abdu'l-Bahá's "brilliant sister," to the unfoldment of the Faith during 'Abdu'l-Bahá's ministry are many and varied. While some of her exploits have been set down in the historical record, others have been deduced from the testimony of Shoghi Effendi. It is evident that the Greatest Holy Leaf's life was devoted to the Bahá'í Cause. She willingly grasped each new opportunity to be of service. She did not flinch in the face of danger, nor did she let age deter her from taking on new and challenging responsibilities.[84]

From the tablets of 'Abdu'l-Bahá we gain a glimpse of his deep appreciation for the Greatest Holy Leaf's constant and loving support and for the unique qualities and skills she manifested in all her activities. Addressing his "affectionate sister," 'Abdu'l-Bahá shows his tender and loving concern when He states, "In the daytime and in the night-season my thoughts ever turn to thee. Not for one moment do I cease to remember thee. My sorrow and regret concern not myself; they centre around thee. Whenever I recall thine

afflictions, tears that I cannot repress rain down from mine eyes. . . ."
Indeed, he testifies to the inadequacy of words to describe her contribution: "I do not know in what words I could describe my longing for my honoured sister. Whatever it may write, my pen falls
short."[85]

Chapter 4 🕊

The "Remnant of Bahá"

The passing of 'Abdu'l-Bahá in the early morning hours of 28 November 1921 marked "the conclusion of the Primitive, the Apostolic Age of the Faith of Bahá'u'lláh." 'Abdu'l-Bahá's illustrious sister, Bahíyyih Khánum, the Greatest Holy Leaf, the "Remnant of Bahá," thus became "the last survivor" of this "glorious and heroic age."[1]

The Greatest Holy Leaf's role in the events that transpired around the time of 'Abdu'l-Bahá's passing was absolutely crucial. Though advanced in age and shattered by the loss of her beloved brother, she transcended the limitations imposed by age, girded her strength, rallied the grieving Bahá'í community, and oriented it towards acceptance of, and support for, the newly appointed Guardian, Shoghi Effendi. Through her efforts she ensured the protection of the evolving Faith of Bahá'u'lláh and its continued advancement and consolidation. Testifying to the exemplary nature of her services and to the deep well of character and devotion from which she drew at this time, Shoghi Effendi writes, "No one could ever dream that a woman of her age, so frail in body, so sensitive of heart, so loaded with the cares of almost eighty years of incessant tribulation, could so long survive so shattering a blow. And yet, history, no less that the annals of our immortal Faith, shall record for her a share in the advancement and consolidation of the world-wide Community which the hand of 'Abdu'l-Bahá had helped to fashion, which no one among the remnants of His Family can rival." In another letter he asserts that "Future generations stand in a better position to appreciate what her significance was during the early days of the Revelation and especially after the ascension of 'Abdu'l-Bahá."[2]

In this chapter we study the events that took place at the time of the passing of 'Abdu'l-Bahá and explore some of the crucial interventions and actions Bahíyyih Khánum took to defend the Covenant and promote the Faith. In addition to examining the testimony of Shoghi Effendi, we will draw upon the reports of a number of Western pilgrims and other Bahá'ís who lived in Haifa at the time of 'Abdu'l-Bahá's passing. The Western pilgrims who were present included Dr. and Mrs. Krug from New York, Mr. and Mrs. Bosch from California, and Miss Johanna Hauff from Germany.[3] Miss Ethel Rosenberg, an English Bahá'í, and Mr. Curtis Kelsey, from the United States, were residing in the Holy Land at the time. These friends had the privilege of being treated, in many ways, like members of 'Abdu'l-Bahá's family. The pilgrims from both the East and the West were invited to remain in the Holy Land until Shoghi Effendi had returned to Haifa and the public reading of 'Abdu'l-Bahá's will and testament had taken place. They were, thus, in the position to witness firsthand the role of the Greatest Holy Leaf in the historic events that transpired during those turbulent weeks.

The Passing of 'Abdu'l-Bahá

As 'Abdu'l-Bahá's great work drew to a close, it became increasingly evident through "the dreams He dreamed, through the conversations He held, through the Tablets He revealed" that he was aware "His end was fast approaching." Shoghi Effendi captures the final few days of 'Abdu'l-Bahá's life in the following touching cameo:

Till the very last day of His earthly life 'Abdu'l-Bahá continued to shower that same love upon high and low alike, to extend that same assistance to the poor and the down-trodden, and to carry out those same duties in the service of His Father's Faith, as had been His wont from the days of His boyhood. On the Friday before His passing, despite great fatigue, He attended the noonday prayer at the mosque, and distributed afterwards alms, as was His custom, among the poor; dictated some Tablets—the last ones He revealed—; blessed the marriage of a trusted servant, which He had insisted should take place that day; attended the usual meeting of the friends in His home; felt feverish the next day, and being unable to leave the house on the following Sunday, sent all the believers to the Tomb of the Báb to attend a feast which a Parsí pilgrim was offering on the occasion of the anniversary of the Declaration of the Covenant; received with His unfailing courtesy and kindness that same afternoon, and despite growing weariness, the Muftí [interpreter of Muslim law] of Haifa, the Mayor and the Head of the Police; and inquired that night—the last of His life—before He retired after the health of every member of His household, of the pilgrims and of the friends in Haifa.[4]

On the night of his passing, it is reported that 'Abdu'l-Bahá awoke at midnight, called the Greatest Holy Leaf, and bid farewell to all. Shoghi Effendi provides the following tender and intimate details of his passing:

At 1:15 A.M. He arose, and, walking to a table in His room, drank some water, and returned to bed. Later on, He asked one of His two daughters who had remained awake to care for Him, to lift up the net curtains, complaining that He had difficulty in breathing. Some rose-water was brought to Him, of which He drank, after which He again lay down, and when offered food, distinctly remarked: *"You wish Me to take some food, and I am going?"* A minute later His spirit had winged its flight to its eternal abode, to be gathered, at long last, to the glory of His be-loved Father, and taste the joy of everlasting reunion with Him.[5]

Louise Bosch, one of the Western pilgrims, in a letter addressed to her friend Ella Cooper, describes the hours immediately follow-ing the passing of 'Abdu'l-Bahá: "We five European pilgrims were in the room together with the holy family, and the holy mother (Munírih Khánum, 'Abdu'l-Bahá's wife) held my husband's hand and the Greatest Holy Leaf held mine. After a time we went back to the Pilgrim House, leaving the holy family alone. It was still night—no moon at all. Not long afterward the dawn broke, and at last the sun rose with great effulgence over the scene of this memo-rable night. Then we went over to the holy household again. We found them nearly exhausted from excessive grief."[6]

The "Last Survivor"

The impact on Bahíyyih Khánum of the sudden passing of her much-loved brother was profound. She characterized his death as "an earthquake that shook the pillars of the world," and in an ex-tract from one of her letters she provides the following heartrending testimony:

This was the most ruinous of disasters, the most dreaded of or-deals, the most hurtful of misfortunes. It was an earthquake that shook the pillars of the world; it caused a tumult and an uproar among the dwellers of earth and heaven. This terrible separation came upon us as an inescapable trial and a dismal decree. It de-stroyed all hopes of happiness, and all joy perished. By this departure, the sparkling stars were dimmed, and the heavens of mystic meaning split apart. It set the skies on fire, it scorched the seven spheres. From this departure, sorrow enveloped all mankind, it brought pain and tears to all the peoples of the earth. The lightning bolt of it consumed the world and struck the hearts of its inhabitants, so that they put on sackcloth and poured ashes on their heads. This disaster, coming all unawares, made the morning dark, and turned bright noon to night. From our breasts rose burning sighs, and from our eyes streamed our life blood. Even the Concourse on High moaned and lamented, and their clamour rose to the highest Heaven, and the weeping denizens of the pavilions of glory, striking at their faces, raised their plaintive cries. Mourning, shedding tears, their garments rent, their heads uncovered, their feet bare, the Maids of Heaven hastened out of their lofty, immaculate chambers, and groaned and cried out.[7]

Shoghi Effendi provides additional insight into the nature of her loss and her increased sense of isolation: "The ascension of 'Abdu'l-Bahá, so tragic in its suddenness, was to her a terrible blow from the effects of which she never completely recovered. To her He, Whom she called 'Áqá,' [Master] had been a refuge in times of adversity. On Him she had been led to place her sole reliance. In Him she had found ample compensation for the bereavements she had suffered, the desertions she had witnessed, the ingratitude she had been shown by friends and kindred."[8]

Despite her advanced age, her frailty, her personal grief, and her quiet modesty, the Greatest Holy Leaf arose to play a crucial role during this extremely difficult and dangerous period.

Very soon after 'Abdu'l-Bahá's passing, the resident Bahá'ís were roused from their sleep. They gathered in the central hall of 'Abdu'l-

Bahá's house. Many were weeping, apprehensive about what would happen to the Bahá'í Cause now that 'Abdu'l-Bahá had passed away. In the memoir written about Curtis Kelsey, the young American Bahá'í invited to the Holy Land by 'Abdu'l-Bahá to install the electric lighting for the Bahá'í gardens, we find a description of Bahíyyih <u>Kh</u>ánum's actions on that fateful night:

> The Greatest Holy Leaf calmly went about comforting the grief-stricken, absorbing their pain. As Curtis watched her move from person to person, stroking a shoulder, clasping a stretched-out hand, he noticed that she exhibited the kind of strength that 'Abdu'l-Bahá radiated. Some sensed that and clung to her. Her control, her poise, her unrestrained flow of compassion assured him that the Faith would not falter. She was, at that moment, the head of the Faith that her dear brother had led so successfully for twenty-nine years, giving His all. She was a tower of strength that all would rally around for support.
>
> As he watched the Greatest Holy Leaf, her eyes caught his and she walked over to him. Since he was not crying, he wondered why she was coming towards him.
>
> "Kelsey," she said, "will you take Fujita and <u>Kh</u>usraw to 'Akká to tell the friends there of the Master's passing and then come right back?"[9]

The Greatest Holy Leaf not only provided immediate comfort and leadership to the local Bahá'í community, she was also the catalyst for notifying the worldwide Bahá'í community of 'Abdu'l-Bahá's passing and for setting in motion the practical arrangements for his funeral.

On the morning of 28 November 1921, Bahíyyih <u>Kh</u>ánum cabled to the Executive Board of the Bahá'í Temple Unity, the embryonic

National Spiritual Assembly of the Bahá'ís of the United States: "HIS HOLINESS 'ABDU'L-BAHÁ ASCENDED TO 'ABHÁ KINGDOM INFORM FRIENDS. [SIGNED] GREATEST HOLY LEAF." Similar cables announcing 'Abdu'l-Bahá's death were also sent to the Bahá'ís in the East and to government officials in Palestine. The news of 'Abdu'l-Bahá's sudden and unexpected passing, in the words of Shoghi Effendi, "spread like wildfire throughout the town, and was flashed instantly over the wires to distant parts of the globe, stunning with grief the community of the followers of Bahá'u'lláh in East and West." In response, the Guardian continues, "Messages from far and near, from high and low alike, through cablegrams and letters, poured in conveying to the members of a sorrow-stricken and disconsolate family expressions of praise, of devotion, of anguish and of sympathy."[10]

The Will and Testament of 'Abdu'l-Bahá was contained in an envelope addressed to Shoghi Effendi, his eldest grandson, who was, at the time, studying at Oxford University in England. It seems likely that the custody of the will had been entrusted to the Greatest Holy Leaf. Consequently, Bahíyyih Khánum and a few selected members of the family examined the will to determine if it contained any instructions concerning 'Abdu'l-Bahá's burial. When they found that the will did not designate a place for his interment, the decision was taken to inter 'Abdu'l-Bahá's remains in one of the rooms in the shrine of the Báb, and all the necessary preparations for the funeral were put into action.[11]

The uniqueness, scale, and solemnity of the funeral are captured by the Guardian in the following description:

As to the funeral itself, which took place on Tuesday morning— a funeral the like of which Palestine had never seen—no less than ten thousand people participated representing every class, religion and race in that country. "A great throng," bore witness at a later date, the High Commissioner [Sir Herbert Samuel] himself, "had gathered together, sorrowing for His death, but rejoicing also for His life." Sir Ronald Storrs, Governor of Jerusalem at the time, also wrote in describing the funeral: "I have never known a more united expression of regret and respect than was called forth by the utter simplicity of the ceremony."

The coffin containing the remains of 'Abdu'l-Bahá was borne to its last resting-place on the shoulders of His loved ones. The cortège which preceded it was led by the City Constabulary Force, acting as a Guard of Honor, behind which followed in order the Boy Scouts of the Muslim and Christian communities holding aloft their banners, a company of Muslim choristers chanting their verses from the Qur'án, the chiefs of the Muslim community headed by the Muftí, and a number of Christian priests, Latin, Greek and Anglican. Behind the coffin walked the members of His family, the British High Commissioner, Sir Herbert Samuel, the Governor of Jerusalem, Sir Ronald Storrs, the Governor of Phoenicia, Sir Stewart Symes, officials of the government, consuls of various countries resident in Haifa, notables of Palestine, Muslim, Jewish, Christian and Druze, Egyptians, Greeks, Turks, Arabs, Kurds, Europeans and Americans, men, women and children. The long train of mourners, amid the sobs and moans of many a grief-stricken heart, wended its slow way up the slopes of Mt. Carmel to the Mausoleum of the Báb.

Close to the eastern entrance of the Shrine, the sacred casket was placed upon a plain table, and, in the presence of that vast concourse, nine speakers, who represented the Muslim, the Jewish and Christian Faiths, and who included the Muftí of Haifa, delivered their several funeral orations. These concluded, the High Commissioner drew close to the casket, and, with bowed head fronting the Shrine, paid his last homage of farewell to 'Abdu'l-Bahá: the other officials of the Government followed his example. The coffin was then removed to one of the chambers of the Shrine, and there lowered, sadly and reverently, to its last resting-place in a vault adjoining that in which were laid the remains of the Báb.[12]

Descriptions of the triumphal funeral procession and reports of the stirring eulogies delivered by the notables were relayed to the women of the holy family, since, regrettably, they were prevented from attending 'Abdu'l-Bahá's funeral by the prevailing social and cultural traditions. One of the American pilgrims, Louise Bosch, in a letter to her friend Ella Cooper, writes that "The ladies of the holy household were very much pleased with all the speeches when they heard about them, and when they afterward read them they said, repeating the Arabic proverb, 'The virtue is quite true when it is testified to by the enemy.'"[13]

In the days immediately following the passing of 'Abdu'l-Bahá, the women of 'Abdu'l-Bahá's household were, according to local custom, visited from morning till evening by weeping Syrian, Turkish, and Arab women who came to express their condolences. On occasion, however, they were able to steal away to visit his grave in a room within the shrine of the Báb.[14]

When making his way up to the shrine on Mount Carmel, Mr. John Bosch, an American pilgrim who was present at the time, described seeing ahead of him a veiled woman who was walking slowly and painfully. Observing that she appeared to be exceedingly weary, Mr. Bosch wondered momentarily if it would be appropriate for him to attempt to help her. Out of concern and courtesy and without further hesitation, he went forward, took the woman's left arm, and assisted her up the steep hill. Suddenly, the figure swung her veil back and looked deeply into his eyes. Mr. Bosch records his startled response and sets out what happened thereafter: "I looked back into the most beautiful blue eyes. Like an angel's. It's very hard to express or define the looks of an angel. I really thought she was a young woman." Later, on his return to the Pilgrim House, Mr. Bosch was visited by one of the Persian ladies who conveyed to him the deep appreciation of the Greatest Holy Leaf for the assistance he had rendered to her.[15]

Despite her grief, the Greatest Holy Leaf, as head of 'Abdu'l-Bahá's household, took care of the multiplicity of tasks that required attention in the period immediately following 'Abdu'l-Bahá's death. The Guardian describes some of these activities: "During the week following His passing, from fifty to a hundred of the poor of Haifa were daily fed at His house, whilst on the seventh day corn was distributed in His memory to about a thousand of them irrespective of creed or race. On the fortieth day an impressive memorial feast was held in His memory, to which over six hundred of the people of Haifa, 'Akká and the surrounding parts of Palestine and Syria, including officials and notables of various religions and races, were invited. More than one hundred of the poor were also fed on that day."[16]

A Western pilgrim attests that the memorial feast was entirely arranged by the members of 'Abdu'l-Bahá's household. She describes the scene at this memorable event, which was held in 'Abdu'l-Bahá's home:

> The long tables were decorated with trailing branches of bouganvilliers (sic). Its lovely purple blooms mingled with the white narcissus, and with the large dishes of golden oranges out of the beloved Master's garden made a picture of loveliness in

those spacious lofty rooms, whose only other decoration was the gorgeous yet subdued coloring of rare Persian rugs. No useless trivial ornaments marred the extreme dignity of simplicity. . . .

After the luncheon the guests came into the large central hall, this also bare of ornament, save only for the portrait of Him they had assembled to honor and some antique Persian tapestries hung upon one wall. Before this was placed a platform from which speeches were made to the wrapt and silent throng, whose very hearts were listening.

The Governor of Phoenicia, in the course of his address, spoke the following: . . . . "Most of us here have, I think, a clear picture of Sir 'Abdu'l-Bahá 'Abbás, of His dignified figure walking thoughtfully in our streets, of His courteous and gracious manner, of His kindness, of his love for little children and flowers, of His generosity and care for the poor and suffering. So gentle was He, and so simple that, in His presence, one almost forgot that He was also a great teacher and that His writings and His conversations have been a solace and an inspiration to hundreds and thousands of people in the East and in the West. . . ."[17]

Period of Renewed Anxiety

The death of 'Abdu'l-Bahá gave rise to a deep sense of anxiety in the minds of many Bahá'ís, both in the Holy Land and throughout the world, about the future of the infant Faith. They wondered who was to succeed 'Abdu'l-Bahá. Some were apprehensive that 'Abdu'l-Bahá's half-brother Mírzá Muhammad-'Alí, who had violated the provisions of the Bahá'í Covenant after the passing of

Bahá'u'lláh, might endeavor to reassert his claim to leadership of the community. Mírzá Muḥammad-'Alí had failed to accept the appointment, set out in Bahá'u'lláh's will, of 'Abdu'l-Bahá as head of the Faith, and he had engaged in such destructive behavior that he had severed his relationship to the Bahá'í community. The details of his machinations and attacks on the Covenant have been described in an earlier chapter.

Emboldened by the sudden passing of 'Abdu'l-Bahá, Mírzá Muḥammad-'Alí seized the opportunity to renew his claims to the leadership of the Faith. Indeed, it is reported that within days of 'Abdu'l-Bahá's death, he arrived at the Master's house and sought to gain entry. An attendant conveyed news of his arrival to the Greatest Holy Leaf. Her great nephew, Rúhí Effendi, was dispatched to communicate her response: "'Our Beloved does not allow and does not like you to come in, and if you come in you will add to our sorrows.'" With this, Muḥammad-'Alí departed. However, he set about actively renewing his claim to leadership through articles in newspapers and mischievous appeals to Bahá'ís in different lands— notably Egypt, Persia, and North America—to accept him as the legitimate successor to Bahá'u'lláh.[18]

Imbued with the spirit of the Covenant, Bahíyyih Khánum assumed major responsibility for initiating actions to protect the Bahá'í Faith throughout the world from the attacks of the Covenant-breakers and to ensure the continuing unity and steadfastness of the community. Cognizant of the impending dangers, she not only forewarned the believers and alerted them to the period of testing that was ahead, but she also advised them concerning the strategy they should adopt to cope with the anticipated attacks. Her cable to the Executive Board of the Bahá'í Temple Unity, which was received on 14 December 1921, illustrates her realistic understanding of the seriousness of the situation. The cable reads, "NOW IS A PERIOD OF

GREAT TESTS. THE FRIENDS SHOULD BE FIRM AND UNITED IN DEFENDING
THE CAUSE. NAKEZEENS [Covenant-breakers] STARTING ACTIVITIES
THROUGH PRESS AND OTHER CHANNELS ALL OVER THE WORLD. SELECT
COMMITTEE OF WISE COOL HEADS TO HANDLE PRESS PROPAGANDA IN
AMERICA." In a letter written to a believer in the East some months
later, she describes how the enemies of the Faith had taken advan-
tage of 'Abdu'l-Bahá's passing to press their claims to leadership
and to attempt to destabilize the community. Thus she writes,

> And now, at such a time as this, a time of our affliction and
> deep distress, the prime mover of mischief, the centre of sedition
> [Muhammad-'Alí], thinking to profit by this eclipse of the Sun
> of the Covenant, the Moon of spiritual concord, has taken ad-
> vantage of what he sees as a rare opportunity for himself, and has
> mounted a violent revolt, and with the support of their second
> chief [Muhammad-'Alí's brother, Mírzá Badí'u'lláh], has begun
> to spread the most far-fetched and malicious accusations, and is
> busy day and night, stirring up trouble and carrying out plots
> and stratagems the details of which would take too long to enu-
> merate . . . .[19]

The period of anxiety lasted for around forty days. It ended with
the Greatest Holy Leaf's announcement of the appointment of
Shoghi Effendi as the Guardian of the Bahá'í Faith, as specified in
the Will and Testament of 'Abdu'l-Bahá.[20]

During this crucial period the Greatest Holy Leaf served as the
point of contact between the holy family and the Bahá'ís throughout the world. Individual believers and Bahá'í institutions addressed
their questions to her. Her cables and letters were perceived as life-
lines to the friends, a tangible assurance that the source of guidance
had not been severed with the ascension of 'Abdu'l-Bahá. When,

for example, the American Bahá'ís inquired if a special commemorative service was planned to mark 'Abdu'l-Bahá's passing, they received the following cabled reply: "MEMORIAL MEETING WORLD OVER JANUARY SEVEN."[21]

Bahíyyih Khánum was not only the source of immediate guidance, but more importantly, she also informed the Bahá'í world about the existence of 'Abdu'l-Bahá's will and testament and its explicit provisions concerning the direction of the Faith after his passing. Part of a cable addressed to the Temple Unity Board in Chicago reads as follows: "MASTER LEFT FULL INSTRUCTIONS IN HIS WILL AND TESTAMENT. TRANSLATION WILL BE SENT. INFORM FRIENDS. [SIGNED] GREATEST HOLY LEAF."[22]

To a Bahá'í community apprehensive about the future of their Faith, the Greatest Holy Leaf's formal announcement to the Bahá'í world about the existence of 'Abdu'l-Bahá's will was, no doubt, a source of great happiness and reassurance.

The members of the family and the pilgrims who were present in Haifa at the time were aware that 'Abdu'l-Bahá had left an envelope addressed to his eldest grandson, Shoghi Effendi, who was absent from the Holy Land. Letters written to Bahá'í friends in the United States made reference to the existence of 'Abdu'l-Bahá's will and the fact that the reading of the will was contingent upon Shoghi Effendi's return. These letters also conveyed the sense of eagerness with which the family was anticipating his return.[23]

Announcement of
Shoghi Effendi's Appointment

Shoghi Effendi was twenty-four years old at the time of 'Abdu'l-Bahá's passing. After graduating from the American University in

Beirut, he had spent two years in close association with his beloved grandfather in Haifa. He had served as translator of 'Abdu'l-Bahá's tablets and letters, had accompanied 'Abdu'l-Bahá on his visits to religious dignitaries, had witnessed his contacts with high government officials, his interactions with the poor, and the manner in which he had directed the activities of the emerging Bahá'í community.

Shoghi Effendi had left the Holy Land in the spring of 1920 to begin his studies at Oxford University in England later that year. Since his primary goal was to devote himself to translation of the Bahá'í writings into English, he had selected courses of study that would enrich his understanding of the world and would assist him to gain a greater mastery of the English language. However, his studies were interrupted with the unexpected passing of his grandfather.[24]

News of 'Abdu'l-Bahá's death was cabled to the Bahá'ís in London by the Greatest Holy Leaf on 29 November 1921. Shoghi Effendi was informed later that day. He was completely overcome by the sudden intelligence and by an overwhelming sense of loss.

At first, ill health, and later difficulty in obtaining the necessary travel documents delayed Shoghi Effendi's return to the Holy Land. He sailed from England on 16 December 1921, accompanied by his sister Rúḥangíz and Lady Blomfield, a trusted English Bahá'í who had a long association with the family of 'Abdu'l-Bahá. The ship docked in Egypt and the party traveled by train to Haifa, arriving on 29 December, one month after 'Abdu'l-Bahá's passing. In her biography of Shoghi Effendi, his widow, Ruḥíyyih Khánum, describes the scene of his arrival and his reunion with the Greatest Holy Leaf:

Many friends went to the station to bring him home; it is reported that he was so overcome on his arrival that he had to be assisted up the steps. Awaiting him in the house was the only person who could in any measure assuage his suffering—his be-loved great-aunt, the sister of 'Abdu'l-Bahá. She had already—so frail, so quiet, so modest at all times—shown herself in these past weeks to be a strong rock to which the believers clung in the midst of the tempest that had so suddenly burst upon them. The calibre of her soul, her breeding, her station, fitted her for the role she played in the Cause and in Shoghi Effendi's life during this extremely difficult and dangerous period.[25]

As mentioned earlier, the Will and Testament of 'Abdu'l-Bahá was addressed to Shoghi Effendi. While the Greatest Holy Leaf had informed the Bahá'í world about the existence of 'Abdu'l-Bahá's will, its provisions had not been disclosed, since the person to whom it was addressed was yet to open it and become informed of its provisions. A few days after Shoghi Effendi's return to Haifa, the will was read to him. It is evident that he was not at all prepared for what he learned. His reaction to his appointment as Guardian of the Bahá'í Faith, the designated successor of 'Abdu'l-Bahá, is cap-tured in the following report from his widow:

> In order to understand even a little of the effect this had on him we must remember that he himself stated on more than one occasion, not only to me, but to others who were present at the table of the Western Pilgrim House, that he had had no fore-knowledge of the existence of the Institution of Guardianship, least of all that he was appointed as Guardian; that the most he had expected was that perhaps, because he was the eldest grand-son, 'Abdu'l-Bahá might have left instructions as to how the Universal House of Justice was to be elected and he might have been designated the one to see these were carried out and act as Convenor of the gathering which would elect it.[26]

Following the reading of the will to Shoghi Effendi, its provisions were progressively communicated to the Bahá'í community and to government officials in the Holy Land. On 3 January 1922 the Will and Testament of 'Abdu'l-Bahá was "read aloud to nine men, most of them members of the family of 'Abdu'l-Bahá, and its seals, signatures and His writing throughout, in His own hand, shown to them." The Guardian instructed one of those present, a Bahá'í from Persia, to prepare a true copy of the will, which was forwarded several days later by the Greatest Holy Leaf to the Bahá'ís in Persia. On 7 January 1922, 'Abdu'l-Bahá's will was read at his house in the presence of Bahá'ís from Persia, India, Egypt, England, Italy, Germany, America, and Japan.[27]

In relation to this second meeting, Curtis Kelsey's biographer records that,

> . . . a large gathering squeezed into the central room of the Master's house to hear the Will and Testament read. The text was clear: Shoghi Effendi had been appointed Guardian of the Faith, the sole interpreter of the Revelation on Earth; the Head of a world faith that had a divine mandate to lift humanity from the quicksand of materialism to verdant heights of spirituality, to help people everywhere see and integrate into their beings the reality of the oneness of humankind, to establish a world society engineered from plans conceived by God and shared with us through Bahá'u'lláh—a stupendous undertaking. No wonder Shoghi Effendi, that sensitive soul, was shaken, forced to bed for several days, unable to eat. The weight of the world had been passed onto his shoulders, the one who wanted only to serve the Master, to be His translator, who never aspired to any leadership role in the Faith, nor ever thought of such a possibility. To this humble, radiant youth was handed the mantle of directorship of God's Cause.

Many of the people who heard the Master's Will and Testament read remained in 'Abdu'l-Bahá's house most of the day carefully going over every sentence, trying to gain some insight as to where the Faith was headed. When the meeting adjourned, Curtis remembered seeing a number of men walking out weeping. They were shedding tears of joy, for the Master, in appointing Shoghi Effendi as Guardian, had protected the future of the Cause of God.[28]

Shoghi Effendi was not present either when the will was read to the family members or when it was formally presented to the select group of Bahá'ís who were present in Haifa. Nor did he attend the public memorial gathering, which, according to local custom, took place forty days after a person's death. At this gathering, it is reported that

> The guests were most anxious to have Shoghi Effendi address them a few words and one of the friends carried this message to him; Shoghi Effendi, who was with the Greatest Holy Leaf in her room, said he was too distressed and overcome to comply with their request and instead hastily wrote a few words to be read on his behalf in which he expressed the heartfelt gratitude of himself and 'Abdu'l-Bahá's family for the presence of the Governor and the speakers who by their sincere words "have revived His sacred memory in our hearts . . . I venture to hope that we his kindred and his family may by our deeds and words, prove worthy of the glorious example he has set before us and thereby earn your esteem and your affection. May His everlasting spirit be with us all and knit us together for evermore!" He begins this message: "The shock has been too sudden and grievous for my youthful age to enable me to be present at this gathering of the loved ones of beloved 'Abdu'l-Bahá."[29]

After the will was read to the believers from around the world who had participated in 'Abdu'l-Bahá's funeral, the Greatest Holy Leaf announced to the Bahá'í world the provisions of the will and the appointment of Shoghi Effendi. On 7 January, two cables were sent to Persia that read: "MEMORIAL MEETINGS ALL OVER THE WORLD HAVE BEEN HELD. THE LORD OF ALL THE WORLDS IN HIS WILL AND TESTAMENT HAS REVEALED HIS INSTRUCTIONS. COPY WILL BE SENT. INFORM BELIEVERS," and "WILL AND TESTAMENT FORWARDED SHOGHI EFFENDI CENTRE CAUSE." On 16 January, the following cable was sent to the United States: "IN WILL SHOGHI EFFENDI APPOINTED GUARDIAN OF CAUSE AND HEAD OF HOUSE OF JUSTICE. INFORM AMERICAN FRIENDS. (SIGNED) GREATEST HOLY LEAF." Soon after the cables were sent, Shoghi Effendi selected eight passages from the Will and Testament of 'Abdu'l-Bahá and circulated them among the Bahá'ís.[30]

The news of the explicit provisions contained in the will for the appointment of Shoghi Effendi as Guardian of the Cause and expounder of the text was received with joy by the entire Bahá'í world. There were, however, a small number of individuals who saw the death of 'Abdu'l-Bahá as an opportunity to gain prominence and power within the religion. Initially, the major opposition came from Mírzá Muḥammad-'Alí and his cohorts. This disaffected half-brother of 'Abdu'l-Bahá not only attempted to reassert his claim to leadership under the provisions of Bahá'u'lláh's will—a will whose provisions he had already violated during the lifetime of 'Abdu'l-Bahá—he also created great difficulties for the Guardian by seizing custody of the shrine of Bahá'u'lláh. Ruḥíyyih Khánum writes,

> Shortly after 'Abdu'l-Bahá's ascension, this disgruntled and perfidious half-brother had filed a claim, based on Islamic law (he who pretended he still had a right to be the successor of Bahá'u'lláh!), for a portion of the estate of 'Abdu'l-Bahá which he now claimed a right to as His brother. He had sent for his son,

who had been living in America and agitating his father's claims
there, to join him in this new and direct attack on the Master
and His family. Not content with this exhibition of his true nature he applied to the civil authorities to turn over the custodianship of Bahá'u'lláh's Shrine to him on the grounds that he was
'Abdu'l-Bahá's lawful successor. The British authorities refused
on the grounds that it appeared to be a religious issue; he then
appealed to the Muslim religious head and asked the Mufti in
Akka to take formal charge of Bahá'u'lláh's Shrine; this digni-
tary, however, said he did not see how he could do this as the
Bahá'í teachings were not in conformity with Shariah law. All
other avenues having failed he sent his younger brother, Badiullah,
with some of their supporters, to visit the Shrine of Bahá'u'lláh
where, on Tuesday, 30 January, they forcibly seized the keys of
the Holy Tomb from the Bahá'í caretaker, thus asserting Muḥammad 'Alí's right to be the lawful custodian of his Father's
resting-place. This unprincipled act created such a commotion
in the Bahá'í Community that the Governor of Akka ordered the
keys to be handed over to the authorities, posted guards at the
Shrine, but went no further, refusing to return the keys to either
party. [31]

This troublesome situation was to drag on for many months,
causing great anxiety and concern for Shoghi Effendi and the Greatest Holy Leaf.

In the first months of his ministry, Shoghi Effendi held extensive
discussions with a number of experienced Bahá'ís from different
parts of the world whom he invited to the Holy Land to consult
about laying the foundations for the formation of the Universal
House of Justice. It soon emerged that a prerequisite to the formation of this institution was the election of local and national insti-

tutions in countries where Bahá'ís resided. Having arrived at this conclusion, the Guardian immediately initiated visionary actions that set in motion processes that would lead progressively to the erection of the institutions of the Administrative Order of the Faith, as set forth in the Will and Testament of 'Abdu'l-Bahá.[32]

Shoghi Effendi instructed the participants to return to their home countries and work towards the formation of Local Spiritual Assemblies and the establishment of national bodies. The two Americans present were, for example, to convey to the forthcoming national Bahá'í convention that the Executive Board of the Bahá'í Temple Unity was to become a National Spiritual Assembly with the functions of guiding the national affairs of the Bahá'í community. This embryonic national body was elected in April 1922.[33]

One of the returning participants in these seminal consultations with the Guardian reported his impression of this gathering at the American convention:

> ... our visit was at the summons of Shoghi Effendi. At Haifa we met Bahá'ís from Persia, India, Burma, Egypt, Italy, England and France. ... On arrival the impression that came strongly over me was that God is in His Heaven and all is well with the world. ... We met Shoghi Effendi, dressed entirely in black, a touching figure. Think of what he stands for today! All the complex problems of the great statesmen of the world are as child's play in comparison with the great problems of this youth, before whom are the problems of the entire world. ... No one can form any conception of his difficulties, which are overwhelming ... the Master is not gone. His spirit is present with greater intensity and power. ... In the centre of this radiation stands this youth, Shoghi Effendi. ... It is a great wisdom of God granting us the countenance of this central point of guidance to meet difficult

problems. These problems, much like ours, come to him from all parts of the world. They are met and solved by him in the most informal way. . . . The great principles laid down by Bahá'u'lláh and 'Abdu'l-Bahá now have their foundation in the external world of God's Kingdom on earth. This foundation is being laid, sure and certain, by Shoghi Effendi in Haifa today.[34]

The cumulative effects of Shoghi Effendi's grief, the challenges associated with his elevation to the rank of Guardian, so unexpectedly bestowed upon him by the provisions of 'Abdu'l-Bahá's will, and his awareness of the weight of responsibility this custodianship entailed, took a tremendous toll on the young Guardian's already depleted health and physical strength. In addition, the renewed activities of the Covenant-breakers created a condition of instability, especially in the Holy Land, as did the ambivalence of the local population to the appointment of such a young man to succeed the venerable figure of 'Abdu'l-Bahá with whom they were familiar, thereby adding to the stress of the situation.

In light of these circumstances, Shoghi Effendi decided to leave the Holy Land for a temporary period during which he hoped to pray and to rest and regain his strength and confidence before returning to his duties at the World Center of the Faith. Prior to his departure he entrusted the overall supervision of the Faith to the care of his beloved great-aunt, the Greatest Holy Leaf, "whose character, station and love for him made her at once his support and his refuge." The Guardian further specified that members of the holy family were to assist her in carrying out this heavy responsibility.[35]

The extent to which Shoghi Effendi drew upon Bahíyyih Khánum's encouragement and strength at this crucial time is evident in the following passage from a letter written at the time of her passing in 1932: "After the ascension of 'Abdu'l-Bahá to the realm of the All-Glorious, that Light of the Concourse on High enfolded me, helpless as I was, in the embrace of her love, and with incomparable pity and tenderness, persuaded, guided, and urged me on to the requirements of servitude. The very elements of this frail being were leavened with her love, refreshed by her companionship, sustained by her eternal spirit. Never for a moment will her kindnesses, her favours, pass from my memory, and as the months and the years go by, the effects of them on this mourning heart will never be diminished."[36]

The Guardian's decision to absent himself from the Holy Land was announced in the following letter written early in April 1922:

> This servant, after that grievous event and great calamity, the ascension of His Holiness 'Abdu'l-Bahá to the Abhá Kingdom, has been so stricken with grief and pain and so entangled in the troubles created by the enemies of the Cause of God, that I consider my presence here, at such a time and in such an atmosphere, is not in accordance with the fulfilment of my important and sacred duties.
>
> For this reason, unable to do otherwise, I have left for a time the affairs of the Cause both at home and abroad, under the supervision of the Holy Family and the headship of the Greatest Holy Leaf until, by the Grace of God, having gained health, strength, self-confidence and spiritual energy, and having taken into my hands, in accordance with my aim and desire, entirely and regularly the work of service I shall attain to my utmost spiritual hope and aspiration.[37]

Shoghi Effendi, accompanied by his eldest cousin, left Haifa for Europe on 5 April 1922. He returned to the Holy Land in December 1922. Refreshed and reinvigorated, he assumed the reins of the Cause and devoted himself to its expansion and consolidation throughout the world.[38]

Chapter 5 🖋

Her Role during Shoghi Effendi's Absences

Bahíyyih Khánum played a vital role in the initial stage of the Formative Age of the Bahá'í Faith, an Age associated with the rise and establishment of the Bahá'í Administrative Order, the system specified in the Bahá'í writings for the worldwide administration of the Bahá'í community. The defining charter of the Administrative Order is none other than the Will and Testament of 'Abdu'l-Bahá. Through her deep understanding of this seminal document, her undeviating adherence to its provisions, her complete and loving support for the designated Guardian, Shoghi Effendi, and her efforts to educate the members of the Faith concerning the significance of the Covenant, the Greatest Holy Leaf helped prepare the Bahá'í world for its transition from the Heroic Age to the Formative Age of the Faith.

In this chapter we will begin to examine the manifold activities Bahíyyih Khánum undertook during the period when Shoghi Effendi left "the affairs of the Cause both at home and abroad, under the supervision of the Holy Family and the headship of the Greatest Holy Leaf." In all, the Guardian was absent from the Holy Land for extended periods in three consecutive years: 1922, 1923, and 1924. The record of her contribution during these crucial times—derived from the correspondence of Shoghi Effendi, the letters of the Greatest Holy Leaf, and reports from Bahá'í pilgrims and others who had the privilege of meeting her—is necessarily incomplete. However, it does provide some insight into the exemplary quality of the services she rendered, despite the weight of advanced age and the challenging nature of the issues with which she was confronted, for the expansion and consolidation of the Faith of her father.[1]

Response to Her Appointment

Bahíyyih Khánum's appointment to the "headship" of the Bahá'í Faith, though intended as an interim arrangement, clearly was not construed as a mere ceremonial position. The mandate was all-en-compassing—including the direction of "the affairs of the Cause both at home and abroad"—and specified for the Greatest Holy Leaf the primary position within the holy family. Furthermore, it is significant to note that the mandate was not confined to the internal operation of the Bahá'í community but it also extended to the conduct of business with the world at large. This was made explicit in a letter dated 5 April 1922 from Shoghi Effendi to the representative of the government in Palestine: "As I am compelled to leave Haifa for reasons of health, I have named as my representative during my absence, the sister of 'Abdu'l-Bahá, Bahíyyih Khánum." The Guardian's letter also goes on to inform the authorities that he has appointed a committee "To assist her to conduct the affairs of the Bahá'í Movement in this country and elsewhere," and he makes it clear that the committee chairman's authority to act was dependent on the written endorsement of Bahíyyih Khánum.[2]

Immediately after Shoghi Effendi's departure, the Greatest Holy Leaf convened the consultative group designated by the Guardian and communicated to the Bahá'í world news of the provisions he had made for the administration of the Faith during his absence. She wrote to the American Bahá'í magazine *Star of the West* in April 1922, enclosing the Guardian's letter announcing his departure from the Bahá'í World Center. Her letter, written in Persian, sets out the actions she took as a result of her appointment and provides insight into the spirit with which she arose to fulfill this new and weighty responsibility. A translation of her letter reads,

> The hearts of the people of Bahá* are intensely burning by reason of the great calamity, and their longing cries are rising up to the Concourse on High and the angelic dwellers in the Abhá

---

* That is, the Bahá'ís.

Paradise,* yet, this day is the day of service, and this time the time to spread the holy Teachings far and wide; therefore must God's loved ones like unto a shining flame, rise up to serve the Cause of God with all their might and vie with one another in service. Let them, even as shooting stars, drive the disloyal out— so that in the Preserved Tablet of God, they may be recorded with that company who ever stood faithful to His Covenant and Testament.

Shoghi Effendi, the Guardian of the Cause of God, the Chosen Branch and leader of the people of Bahá, as a result of intense and unceasing grief over this great bereavement, this supreme affliction, has determined to absent himself for a short period, in an effort to rest, and to regain his health, after which he will return to the Holy Land and resume his services and obligations to the Cause of God. During his absence, in accordance with his letter herewith enclosed, this prisoner is appointed to administer the affairs of the Faith, in consultation with the members of the Holy Household.

For this reason I have temporarily made arrangements so that the persons named by Shoghi Effendi may meet and the affairs be conducted in consultation with them. It is my hope that during the period of his absence the beloved of the Lord and the handmaids of the Merciful will exert their efforts to advance the Cause and accelerate its growth. He is, verily, compassionate and merciful to His servants.[3]

Further, in a letter written in 1922, on the anniversary of Bahá'u'lláh's declaration of His mission to the "very dear friends in America, through the Editors of the *Star of the West,*" the Greatest Holy Leaf expresses, on behalf of 'Abdu'l-Bahá's family, deep ap-

---

* *Abhá* means literally "glorious"; i.e., heaven.

preciation for the condolences received from so many of the Bahá'ís. She underlines the importance of Shoghi Effendi's appointment to guide the administration of the Faith and makes the following appeal: "We hope that the friends of God, the beloved and the handmaidens of the Merciful, will pray for us, that we may be enabled to help Shoghi Effendi in every way in our power to accomplish the Mission entrusted to him." The letter is signed "Bahaeyyeh Khanum, and the Family of Abdul-Baha."[4]

Direction of the Affairs of the Cause

In the absence of the Guardian, the Greatest Holy Leaf and members of the holy family were responsible for administering the affairs of the Faith throughout the world. The appointment of the Greatest Holy Leaf to the "headship" of this group meant that she had major responsibility for directing the affairs of the Cause at home and abroad. She served as the point of contact for the believers, provided guidance and encouragement, exercised wise and mature leadership, and steadied the course of the Faith during this period of transition. She rallied the Bahá'í community through the letters she wrote to individual Bahá'ís and to the Spiritual Assemblies—embryonic local governing bodies of the Faith—in the East and the West. During this crucial period, she instilled a spirit of confidence in the believers and educated them in the provisions of the Will and Testament of 'Abdu'l-Bahá. She encouraged acceptance of, and support for, the new Guardian and implemented the policies he had set in place. She helped the believers to gain a deeper understanding of the importance of establishing Local and National Spiritual Assemblies, collaborated with the Haifa Spiritual

Assembly—a body set up to administer the affairs of the Faith in the Holy Land—fostered awareness of the importance of administrative functioning, and initiated activities to protect the Faith in the Holy Land and in other parts of the world.

Encouragement of the Bahá'ís

At a time when the Bahá'í community was negotiating the transition from the ministry of 'Abdu'l-Bahá and the close of the Heroic Age to the opening of the Formative Age, the Greatest Holy Leaf served as a living link between the two. This transition required not only the acceptance of the newly appointed Guardian as Head of the Faith but also called for an adjustment in thinking to accommodate the authority of elected Spiritual Assemblies. The Greatest Holy Leaf's skill in bridging the transition and shaping the awareness of the worldwide Bahá'í community can be seen from a study of the letters she wrote at this time.

In these letters the Greatest Holy Leaf acknowledges and identifies with the personal grief of the believers at the passing of 'Abdu'l-Bahá, and she assures them that she and the other members of the holy family not only understand their feelings but also share their sorrow. She writes,

> It is certain that the people of Bahá, who are the dwellers of the Crimson Ark and breast the seas of the Lord, and who have attained to the bounties of the Abhá realm, and who are steadfast in the Covenant—they, men and women alike, young and old alike, share with these homeless ones the anguish of our bereavement and this direst of ordeals. We could hear, with the ear of the spirit, the wailing of those lovers of Him Who was the Ravisher of hearts, those like us scorched by the fires of separation, and from our own sad hearts we would lift our cries of

sorrow to the heavens, and weeping would send up our entreaties . . . to the threshold of the luminous Beauty of God.[5]

The Greatest Holy Leaf reminds the believers that, though
'Abdu'l-Bahá has passed to the next world, his spirit is still a guiding
force. She continues, "all will understand that even though that
sacred and mysterious Being has laid aside the garment of His mortal life, even though that Bird of eternity has abandoned the cage
of this earth, still is His spirit in our midst, still is He watching over
us all from the realm of the All-Glorious, ever is He gladdening the
hearts of the beloved, and to the souls of those who are fast-rooted
in the Covenant, ever is He bringing tidings of great joy."[6]

Bahíyyih Khánum brings to the believers' attention the fact that
'Abdu'l-Bahá has trained them and instilled in them the qualities
necessary for the continued development of the Faith. To underline
her point she recalls the following words, reported to have been
spoken by the Master:

"At the time when Christ rose out of this mortal world and ascended into the Eternal Kingdom, He had twelve disciples, and
even of these, one was cast off. But because that handful of souls
stood up, and with selflessness, devotion and detachment, resolved to spread His holy Teachings and to scatter abroad the
sweet fragrances of God, disregarding the world and all its peoples,
and because they utterly lost themselves in Christ—they succeeded, by the power of the spirit, in capturing the cities of men's
hearts, so that the splendour of the one true God pervaded all
the earth, and put the darkness of ignorance to flight.

"Now when I shall depart from this world, I shall leave more
than fifty thousand blessed individuals, every one of whom is
staunch and firm as the high mountains, shining out over the

earth like sparkling stars. These are the quintessence of loyalty and fellowship and love. They are the self-sacrificing watchers over the Cause, and they are the guides to all who seek after truth. Judge from this what the future will be!"[7]

The Greatest Holy Leaf draws a lesson from 'Abdu'l-Bahá's statement, encourages the friends to take action, and expresses confidence in their ability to succeed:

> It is certain that when we act in accordance with the Teachings of the Abhá Beauty* and the counsels of 'Abdu'l-Bahá, then will this world become the Abhá Paradise, and its thorns and brambles of cruelty will change into a blossoming garden of the faithful. May we all be enabled to achieve this end.[8]

Not only does the Greatest Holy Leaf remind the believers of the training they have received from the hands of the Master, but she also calls attention to the importance of his example. She refers, for instance, to 'Abdu'l-Bahá's tireless services to the Cause and to the trials and sufferings he endured in the course of his life. She recounts, "His lot, in all his life, was to be wronged, and be subjected to toil, to pain and grief. Under these conditions, the one and only solace of His sacred heart was to hear good news of the progress of the Faith, and the proclaiming of God's Word, and the spreading of the holy Teachings, and the unity and fervour of the friends, and the staunchness of His loved ones. This news would bring smiles to His countenance; this was the joy of His precious heart."[9]

---

* An appellation referring to Bahá'u'lláh.

Aware of great spiritual truths, both from experience and from her association with her beloved father and brother, the Greatest Holy Leaf prepared the believers for the inevitability of a period of testing and schooled them concerning the means by which they might attract divine assistance. She tells the believers, "The loving counsels of 'Abdu'l-Bahá have turned the beloved of the Lord into signs and tokens of humility and lowliness. He has taught them selflessness, and freedom from material things, and detachment from the world, and has enabled them to understand the verities of Heaven." This, she affirms, is sure preparation for the tests that life brings. She writes,

> It is certain that tests and trials are inseparable from this life and a vital requirement thereof, especially for the human race and above all for those who claim to have faith and love. Only through trials can the genuine be known from the worthless, and purity from pollution, and the real from the false. The meaning of the sacred verse: "Do men think when they say 'We believe' they shall be let alone and not be put to proof?"* prevails at all times and is applicable at every breath, and fire will only bring out the brightest of the gold.
>
> So it is my hope that with lowliness and a contrite heart, with supplications and prayers, with good intentions and faithfulness, with purity of heart and adherence to the truth, with rising up to serve and with the blessings and confirmations of the Lord, we may come into a realm, and arrive at a condition, where we shall live under His overshadowing mercy, and His helping hand shall come to our aid and succour.[10]

---

* Qur'án 29:2.

On receiving news from a number of Bahá'í women associated with the operation of a Bahá'í school in the village of Sang-i-Sar, Iran, that they were being persecuted and their school had been burnt down, the Greatest Holy Leaf wrote a letter that helped the women put the episode into perspective. She began by telling these devoted believers that she and the holy family were "infinitely grieved to learn of the sufferings" they had undergone, then offered a spiritual explanation for what had happened and for the significance of their response. She writes,

> Since, however, you stood firm and steadfast and unchanging, as the arrows of tyranny came against you, and since this happened for the sake of the Blessed Beauty,* and in the pathway of the One Beloved, it behoves you to thank God and praise Him, for having singled you out for this great bounty. . . .
>
> God be praised, you have been given a drop out of that ocean of tribulations that swept across the Exalted One and the Beauty of the All-Glorious, you were granted a droplet out of the seas of calamity that engulfed 'Abdu'l-Bahá. [11]

Finally, she exhorts the women in the following terms: "Be you confident of the bestowals of the Blessed Beauty and the gifts and blessings of 'Abdu'l-Bahá." [12]

In her efforts to reinforce the believers' confidence and to encourage their efforts to manifest Bahá'í values in their daily lives, the Greatest Holy Leaf emphasized the importance of steadfastness. In one of her letters she sets out the particular importance of this virtue and describes the results that accrue to the believer:

---

* Bahá'u'lláh.

All the virtues of humankind are summed up in one word "steadfastness," if we but act according to its laws. It draws to us as by a magnet the blessings and bestowals of Heaven, if we but rise up according to the obligations it implies.

God be praised, the house of the heart is lit by the light of unswerving constancy, and the soul's lodging is bedecked with the ornament of faithfulness.

Steadfastness is a treasure that makes a man so rich as to have no need of the world or any person or any thing that is therein. Constancy is a special joy, that leads us mortals on to lofty heights, great progress, and the winning of the perfections of Heaven. All praise be to the Beloved's court, for granting this most wondrous grace to His faithful people, and to His favoured ones, this best of gifts.[13]

While orienting the Bahá'í community to an awareness of the enduring spiritual lessons inculcated by 'Abdu'l-Bahá and to the example of his life, the Greatest Holy Leaf also progressively gave attention to the need for the believers to promulgate the Faith and to begin the task of establishing its institutions. In one of her letters she writes, "Dear friends! At this critical time through which the Cause is passing the responsibility that has fallen on every individual Bahá'í is great, and his duties are pressing and manifold. . . . Now the time has come for the faithful friends of 'Abdu'l-Bahá, who have been the recipients of the Glorious Light, to shine forth even as brilliant stars. The radiance of our Faith must be such as to dispel the clouds of doubt and guide the world to the Day-spring of Truth." In yet another letter she expresses her happiness that the steadfast believers are abiding by the counsels of 'Abdu'l-Bahá and are arising to serve the Faith:

The good news that the Word of God is being raised up, and His Cause glorified, and that His friends, on fire with love for Him, are arising to spread His sweet savours abroad—is coming in steadily from every quarter of the globe.

All are firmly rooted in the Faith, steadfast, turning with complete devotion to him who is the appointed and designated Centre, the Guardian of the Cause of God, the Chosen Branch, His Eminence Shoghi Effendi; are founding Assemblies, conducting meetings, teaching most eloquently and with all their energies, presenting proofs, disseminating the doctrines of the Divine Beauty and the counsels of 'Abdu'l-Bahá. It is certain that ere long the light of these Teachings will illumine the earth and gladden the hearts of the people of Bahá.[14]

Indeed, in the following touching extract from one of her letters, she makes it known that the major source of her happiness and pleasure is to receive reports of the Bahá'ís' activities in service to the Faith. She writes, "The news of your firmness in the Covenant, of your endeavour to work in unity and harmony, and of your untiring zeal and devotion in the Path of Service, has been a source of untold joy to me. For now my sole comfort lies in the loyalty and faithfulness of the friends, and my one joy in the progress of the Cause."[15]

Education of the Bahá'í Community in the Provisions of the Covenant

To appreciate the significance of the role Bahíyyih Khánum played in educating the Bahá'í community in the provisions of the Covenant, one must understand the uniqueness of 'Abdu'l-Bahá's will and testament. This historic document, written entirely in his own handwriting, forms the blueprint of the Bahá'í Administrative Order, the charter of a future world civilization. It is unique in religious history. In addition to proclaiming the "fundamental beliefs of the followers of the Faith of Bahá'u'lláh," it "establishes the institution of the Guardianship as a hereditary office and outlines its essential functions; provides the measures for the election of the International House of Justice, defines its scope and sets forth its relationship to that Institution; prescribes the obligations, and emphasizes the responsibilities, of the Hands of the Cause of God; and extolls the virtues of the indestructible Covenant established by Bahá'u'lláh."[16]

The document also calls upon the "entire company of the followers of Bahá'u'lláh to arise unitedly to propagate His Faith, to disperse far and wide, to labor tirelessly and to follow the heroic example of the Apostles of Jesus Christ; warns them against the dangers of association with the Covenant-breakers, and bids them shield the Cause from the assaults of the insincere and the hypocrite; and counsels them to demonstrate by their conduct the universality of the Faith they have espoused, and vindicate its high principles."[17]

Bahá'ís in the East and the West embraced the Will and Testament of 'Abdu'l-Bahá and accepted its provisions. The Guardian affirms that they arose "with clear vision and inflexible determination to inaugurate the Formative Period of their Faith by laying the foundations of that world-embracing Administrative system designed to evolve into a World Order which posterity must acclaim as the promise and crowning glory of all the Dispensations of the past."[18]

Examination of the Greatest Holy Leaf's letters written to individual believers and to Bahá'í communities throughout the world provides insight into the extent to which she clarified the believers' vision and enhanced their understanding of the implications of this historic document. She was instrumental in preserving the unity of the Bahá'í community and in orienting its members to Shoghi Effendi, the newly appointed Guardian.

These letters illustrate the sensitive manner in which she assisted the believers to gain a deeper understanding of the Covenant as set out in the Master's will and testament. She uses a number of striking images to underline the importance of having an appointed Center of the Covenant, a point of authority to which the believers must turn. In one of her letters she writes,

> This fact of there being only one Centre and of turning unto a single holy Being is, in the Kingdom of His Cause, as the shaft or spindle of a millstone, and all the other laws and ordinances must needs revolve around this one. In the temple of God's religion the Centre of the Cause can be likened to the heart, for upon it depends the life of the human body as one entity, as well as the relationships of its organs and their essential growth and vitality. In human society the Centre of the Cause can be compared to the sun, whose magnetic force controls the movements and orbits of the planets. The Centre of the Cause is also like the spine of a book, for by it the pages are all banded together into one book, and without the spine the papers would become loose and scattered. [19]

In another letter she observes,

> A clear Covenant makes our duty plain; an explicit and lucid Text explains the revealed Book; a specifically named Centre has been designated, toward whom all must turn, and the pronouncement of him who is the Guardian of the Cause and the interpreter of the Book has been made the decisive decree. . . .

The hope is that we may arise with a new spirit and be confirmed with bountiful blessings, and urge on our steeds in the field of service, of purity and sincerity, and of high endeavour. . . .[20]

Responding to questions about the Covenant raised by a believer in the East, the Greatest Holy Leaf provided the following elucidation:

It appears from your letter that you had written prior to the receipt of the Will and Testament of the Centre of the Covenant. You have certainly perused it by now. This Text is His decisive decree; it constitutes the very life of those endued with understanding. In it the Pen of Bounty has set forth in the most powerful, comprehensive, clear and detailed manner the obligations devolving on every stratum of the Bahá'í community. . . . He has specifically named the centre to whom all must turn, thus solidly fixing and establishing the foundations of the Covenant, and has clearly appointed the centre, to whom all the people of Bahá must direct themselves, the Chosen Branch, the Guardian of the Cause of God. This great bestowal is one of the special characteristics of this supreme Revelation, which of all Dispensations is the noblest and most excellent.[21]

In addition to educating the Bahá'ís concerning the general provisions of the Covenant, Bahíyyih Khánum specifically oriented them towards the appointed Guardian. In one of her letters she describes how 'Abdu'l-Bahá, as the unerring "Physician," knew in advance that the believers would experience his passing as a devastating blow. To lessen its impact, she attests,

. . . He prepared a highly potent remedy and compounded a unique and incomparable cure—a cure most exquisite, most glorious, most excellent, most powerful, most perfect, and most consummate. And through the movement of His Pen of eternal bounty He recorded in His weighty and inviolable Testament the name of Shoghi Effendi—the bough that has grown from the two offshoots of the celestial glory, the branch that has branched from the two hallowed and sacred Lote-Trees.* Then he winged His flight to the Concourse on High and to the luminous horizon. Now it devolves upon every well-assured and devoted friend, every firm and enkindled believer enraptured by His love, to drink this healing remedy at one draught, so that the agony of bereavement may be somewhat alleviated and the bitter anguish of separation dissipated.[22]

In another instance, she underlines the clear and explicit manner in which Shoghi Effendi's appointment is made, stating that "The Will and Testament of 'Abdu'l-Bahá is His decisive decree; it gathers the believers together; it preserves their unity; it ensures the protection of the Faith of God. It designates a specific Centre, irrefutably and in writing establishing Shoghi Effendi as Guardian of the Faith and Chosen Branch, so that his name is recorded in the Preserved Tablet, by the fingers of grace and bounty." On yet another occasion, when responding to news about the activities of a Covenant-breaker, the Greatest Holy Leaf reiterates the major points of the Covenant:

The essential point is this: praise be to God, the way of His holy Faith is laid straight, the Edifice of the Law of God is well-founded and strong. He to whom the people of Bahá must turn, the Centre on which the concourse of the faithful must fix their gaze, the Expounder of the Holy Writings, the Guardian of the Cause of God, the Chosen Branch, Shoghi Effendi, has been

---

* This refers to Shoghi Effendi's ancestry. He was a descendant of both the Báb and Bahá'u'lláh (see glossary).

clearly appointed in conformity with explicit, conclusive and unmistakable terms. The Religion of God, the laws and ordinances of God, the blessed teachings, the obligations that are binding on everyone—all stand clear and manifest even as the sun in its meridian glory. There is no hidden mystery, no secret that remains concealed. There is no room for interpretation or argument, no occasion for doubt or hesitation. The hour for teaching and service is come. It is the time for unity, harmony, solidarity and high endeavour.[23]

News of the believers' recognition of Shoghi Effendi was a source of great joy and happiness to the Greatest Holy Leaf. Writing in response to such information, she indicates, "The good news has come that the Will and Testament of 'Abdu'l-Bahá, may our lives be sacrificed for His meekness, has been read at the meetings of the friends, and we here are rejoiced to learn of their unity and their steadfastness and loyalty, and of their directing themselves toward the designated Centre, the named and specified Guardian of the Cause of God, the interpreter of the Book of God, the protector of His Faith, the keeper of His Law, Shoghi Effendi. This news brought extreme joy." Indeed, the Greatest Holy Leaf spells out the importance of the believers' acceptance of Shoghi Effendi and his designated functions. Responding to a letter, she writes, "The purport of your letter is highly indicative of your steadfastness in His Cause, of your unswerving constancy in the Covenant, of having set your face toward Shoghi Effendi, the authorized Point to whom all must turn, the Centre of the Cause, the Chosen Branch, the bough that has branched out from the twin heavenly Trees. Indeed, this is the essential thing, this is the meaning of true devotion, this is the unshakeable, the indubitable truth whereby the people of Bahá, the dwellers of the Crimson Ark, are distinguished."[24]

It is clear from her letters that the Greatest Holy Leaf set about rallying the Bahá'ís and focusing their attention on the newly appointed Guardian, the point of authority to whom all Bahá'ís must turn, and she thereby enabled the nascent community to move forward in unity to its next stage of development.

Bahíyyih Khánum's loving concern for Shoghi Effendi and her assiduous efforts to focus the Bahá'í community on this chosen successor of 'Abdu'l-Bahá were motivated not only by her deep affection and concern for her grandnephew but also were guided by the clear and explicit directive in 'Abdu'l-Bahá's will and testament that the believers must "take the greatest care of Shoghi Effendi . . . that no dust of despondency and sorrow may stain his radiant nature." To this end, she helped the believers understand the reason for Shoghi Effendi's absences from the Holy Land. She was a reliable source of accurate, factual and, no doubt, reassuring information about why the newly appointed Guardian had felt it necessary to leave the Holy Land. She also kept the community informed about when he was scheduled to return. For example, in one of her letters to a Spiritual Assembly she writes: "The Chosen Branch, the Guardian of the Cause of God, Shoghi Effendi, because of the intense grief and suffering and pain inflicted by this terrible event, has desired to spend a period alone, in a quiet spot, where he can devote his time to prayer and supplication, and communion with God. He, therefore, left us some time ago, but our hopes are high that in a very short time he will come home to the Holy Land. For the moment, then, this wronged and sad one has answered, however briefly, the letter from your distinguished Assembly." From the final sentence, it is interesting to observe, in passing, that the Greatest Holy Leaf was, according to the terms of her appointment by Shoghi Effendi, actively engaged in overseeing the administration of the Faith in the Guardian's absence.[25]

The Greatest Holy Leaf, in a poignant and dramatic letter written in 1924, frankly sets forth the critical impact of the Bahá'ís' actions on the Guardian's three protracted absences from the Holy Land. She recalls the condition of Shoghi Effendi immediately after 'Abdu'l-Bahá's passing in November 1921: "Broken in health, his heart brimful of sorrows, he returned to this blessed place. At that time the unfaithful, with extreme perversity and at a high point of rebellion, were openly and secretly spreading their calumnies, and this behaviour of theirs added still more to the Guardian's burden of grief. He left, therefore, and spent some time in seclusion, carrying on the affairs of the Faith, seeing to its interests and its institutions, communing with God, and imploring His help." During his absence, she explains, "there were such evidences of staunchness and loyalty and high resolve and unity and love and fervour among all the friends, men and women alike, both of East and West, and in the Holy Land—that on the one hand the Centre of Sedition [Mírzá Muḥammad-'Alí], and the arrogant and the malevolent, found themselves utterly defeated, their hopes of making a breach in the Faith bitterly disappointed, while on the other, the exemplary quality and sound condition of the believers . . . was a comfort to the Guardian's heart." As a result, Shoghi Effendi returned to the Holy Land in December 1922, his health restored and energized to carry out his sacred obligations.[26]

The Greatest Holy Leaf goes on to recount how, on his return to the Holy Land, the Guardian immersed himself in correspondence with the Bahá'ís and the Spiritual Assemblies. His letters described the believers' responsibilities, and the Bahá'ís received the letters with love and gratitude. Before long, however, it became evident that "among some of the believers a certain ill-feeling had arisen, and further, that some did not, as they should, respect and duly defer to their Spiritual Assembly." She graphically describes the impact of this information on the Guardian, commenting, "It is obvious what an effect this kind of news . . . had on the Guardian's heart, and what an unfavourable reaction it produced. The result was that for the second time his health failed, and then, at the importunity of this evanescent soul, and the urgent entreaties of the Holy Household and the repeated appeals of those in close association with him—he went away last summer."[27]

The Greatest Holy Leaf reports that the Guardian's several months' absence in 1923 proved beneficial to his health and enabled him to reengage actively with the Bahá'í community. The loyalty and activities of the believers consoled his heart and filled him with a renewed sense of confidence. Sadly, however, the pattern described by the Greatest Holy Leaf was to repeat itself, leading once more to his abrupt departure in the spring of 1924. She tells the believers what happened: "once again in some communities, he noted from certain letters an absence of spirituality and good-fellowship among some of the friends, and a lack of respect among some for their Assemblies. Once more, as a result of this, his heart was filled with sorrow and once again he decided on departure." She confides in the Bahá'ís that she and the other women of the holy family have done all in their power to cheer Shoghi Effendi's heart and have begged him to reconsider his decision—but to no avail.[28]

The next section of this amazing letter consists of a message that Shoghi Effendi instructed her to convey to all the Bahá'ís. It reads as follows:

> He told us: "My heart is sensitive. Just as I feel the ill-feeling that exists between individuals, and am injured by it, so too do I treasure the excellent qualities of the believers; indeed, I hold these dearer than words can tell. After that most dread ordeal, the one and only solace of my heart was the loyalty, the staunch-

ness, the love of the friends for the Blessed Beauty and for 'Abdu'l-Bahá. Nothing can ever detract from the value of such excellent qualities, and I am deeply grateful to all the friends, men and women alike, for this. And yet, this love of theirs, with all its fervour, can never, by itself, bring the Ark of the Faith to the longed-for shore. It can never prove the claims of the people of Bahá to the people of the world. To safeguard the religion of God and reinforce its power, the friends must make use of effective means: their love must be so great that they worship one another, and shut any mutual ill-feeling out of their hearts.

"If, for example, the non-Bahá'ís should ask the friends, 'What differentiates you from all the rest?', and if, to this, the friends answer, 'In the pathway of our love for the Centre of our Faith, we would sacrifice our lives and possessions,' those of the civilized world would never be content with such a reply. They would merely say: 'Your love, your sacrifice for a single individual cannot possibly serve as a remedy for the chronic ills which plague society today.' If the friends then answer: 'Our religion provides principles and moral teachings whose value the wisest of the day cannot deny,' this will be the response: 'Noble principles and teachings will produce an effect on human character, and heal the mortal sicknesses which afflict society, only at such time when those who claim to believe in and support them are themselves the first to act upon them, and to demonstrate and incorporate the value and the benefits of them in their own everyday transactions and lives.' Unless this comes about, there is nothing to distinguish the Bahá'ís from the rest."

He also told us: "The people of the world are carefully watching the Bahá'ís today, and minutely observing them. The believers must make every effort, and take the utmost care to ward off and remove any feelings of estrangement, and consider themselves duty-bound to comply with the decisions of their Spiritual Assemblies. To the same degree that ill-feeling among some of the believers has cast its shadow on my heart, to that same degree will my heart reflect their mutual agreement, understanding and loving affection, and their deference to the authority of their Spiritual Assemblies. And whenever I shall feel such lights reflected, I will at once return to the Holy Land and engage in the fulfilment of my sacred obligations. Convey this message of mine to all the friends."[29]

The Greatest Holy Leaf's letter concludes with the stark pronouncement, "It is now two weeks since he made this touching statement and left the Holy Land." Finally, she refers the believers to the passage in the Will and Testament of 'Abdu'l-Bahá about taking care of Shoghi Effendi, and she expresses the hope that they will make such constructive efforts that the beloved Guardian will be attracted back to the Holy Land.[30]

Ruḥíyyih Khánum, the Guardian's widow, provides a telling glimpse of the depth and tenderness of the relationship between the Greatest Holy Leaf and the young Guardian. She states that, following the passing of 'Abdu'l-Bahá, Shoghi Effendi became the very center of the Greatest Holy Leaf's life. Ruḥíyyih Khánum recalls that when she was visiting while on pilgrimage with her mother in 1923, there was a large meeting attended by the Bahá'í men in the central hall of 'Abdu'l-Bahá's house in Haifa. She describes what transpired on that occasion:

. . . my mother and Edith Sanderson were seated there beside the Guardian but I had joined the women in a room opening on to it. We sat in the dark so that we could leave the door open (in those days the eastern men and women, following the custom of the country, were entirely sequestered) and hear a little of what was going on. It seems that some oriental believer, suddenly overcome by emotion, had got up and flung himself at the feet of Shoghi Effendi; we in our room could not see what had happened but only hear a great hubbub going on outside. The Greatest Holy Leaf, so slender and frail, jumped to her feet with a loud cry, fearing that something had happened to the young Guardian. She was quieted when someone brought news that nothing serious had occurred, but her anguish had been so evident the scene imprinted itself on my mind forever.[31]

The Greatest Holy Leaf gave particular attention to educating the believers concerning the specific provisions of the Master's will and testament that pertain to firmness in the Covenant and the avoidance of contact with those who endeavor to destroy the unity of the Faith. For example, in her letter written to a Spiritual Assembly in the East, Bahíyyih Khánum describes in detail some of the activities of the Covenant-breakers—activities that 'Abdu'l-Bahá had merely alluded to in his will and testament. She thereby ensured that the Bahá'ís gained a fuller understanding of the dangers confronting the embryonic Faith not only at the time of Bahá'u'lláh's passing, but also with the passing of 'Abdu'l-Bahá, when the Covenant was again being subjected to the same kinds of threats and dangers from the disaffected and ambitious.[32]

Writing to the believers in the West, the Greatest Holy Leaf underlines the responsibilities of the Bahá'ís in relation to the Covenant. She counsels them thus:

> Dear friends! A great obligation of every Bahá'í is vigilance to protect and shield the stronghold of the Faith from the onslaught of the enemies. In these days their activity has waxed strong. They are constantly on the alert, and exert the utmost endeavour to cause such harm as would impede the onward march of the Cause.

Association with such people will cause discord and unrest among the friends and will be detrimental to the progress of the Cause. Therefore it is urgent that the friends exercise great wisdom and vigilance lest through the evil schemes of the enemies a breach be made in the Faith. The few people whom 'Abdu'l-Bahá pronounced as injurious to the Cause must be shunned by all the friends, as Shoghi Effendi himself tells us to do in his second letter to the American believers. [33]

Guiding the Ongoing Work of the Bahá'í Community

In addition to educating the believers concerning the explicit provisions of 'Abdu'l-Bahá's will and testament and the significance of the Bahá'í Covenant, Bahíyyih Khánum attended to the ongoing work of the Bahá'í community in the Holy Land and abroad.

The Greatest Holy Leaf supervised the completion of a number of tasks that had been initiated by 'Abdu'l-Bahá. For example, in the last year of his life the Master invited Curtis Kelsey, an American believer, to install the electricity generators and the lighting for the Bahá'í shrines in Haifa and Bahjí. This project was completed in 1922 under the supervision of the Greatest Holy Leaf while Shoghi Effendi was in Europe. Nathan Rutstein, Curtis Kelsey's biographer, describes what happened when the task was finished immediately before Curtis's departure from the Holy Land. It illustrates the sensitivity, practicality, and authority of the Greatest Holy Leaf:

> One day while packing for his trip home, Curtis was asked to come to the Master's house. When he arrived he was led to 'Abdu'l-Bahá's room where he found the Greatest Holy Leaf and three of the Master's daughters waiting for him. After greeting him warmly, they moved closer to him, actually encircling him. One of the daughters praised him for the work he had done. . . . when that same daughter insisted that he take money for his trip home,

Curtis said, "No, all my affairs are in order." He couldn't think of taking money from the Master's family. But the other daughters were adamant about the importance of his taking the money. He was equally adamant in refusing it. Finally, the Greatest Holy Leaf reached out and, taking hold of Curtis' hand, said, "Kelsey, you need this money to pay for your return home," and she placed the money in his hand.

"I will take it," Curtis said, "if you will let me return it after getting home."

"No," she responded firmly.

Curtis sensed that the Greatest Holy Leaf had issued a divine command reminiscent of the way 'Abdu'l-Bahá responded when firmness was called for. Curtis graciously accepted the money and thanked them for it. He left the room, wondering how they knew what his financial condition was, when he hadn't told a soul about it.[34]

The Greatest Holy Leaf's guiding hand is also evident in the completion of another project that began in the lifetime of the Master. Prior to his passing, 'Abdu'l-Bahá requested the American Bahá'ís to locate a Bahá'í teacher to serve as director of the Tarbíyat School for Girls—a Bahá'í school that had been established in 1909. The new director would replace Miss Lillian Kappes, who had died at her post in Tehran. Dr. Genevieve Coy arose to accept this assignment. In a letter dated 11 July 1922 addressed to the Spiritual Assembly of Tehran, the Greatest Holy Leaf states,

His Holiness 'Abdu'l-Bahá . . . after the ascension of Miss Kappes to the Abha Kingdom, gave instructions that one of the maidservants of God in America be selected and sent to Teheran to take her place. Therefore they have selected and sent this faithful, radiant and attracted maidservant of God, Miss Coy. For nearly one month she was in Haifa, associated with these longing and sorrowful maidservants of God, and she attained to visiting the holy Tombs and Thresholds. Now she is about to depart, under the protection and care of God and, please God, she will reach Teheran safely. [35]

She concludes by expressing her hopes that the Spiritual Assembly will extend to Miss Coy every assistance so that "she may be engaged with a gladdened and joyous soul and spirit in the education and training of the girls in the Tarbiat School." [36]

The willing support and acceptance of the guidance of the Greatest Holy Leaf is illustrated by an extract from a letter of the Spiritual Assembly of Tehran that was published in *Star of the West* in February 1923. The letter states,

Her holiness the Greatest Holy Leaf . . . in a holy tablet has especially introduced and recommended this revered lady [Miss Coy] to such a degree that all the friends are desirous and longing to serve her. We hope that the important services and steps which Miss Kappes took in the way of the promulgation of knowledge and the moral education of the Bahai girls of Teheran may be matured and completed in the time of this honored lady, and the girls' Tarbiat School may, according to the desire of the friends, reach the high point of honor and improvement so that well educated, learned and spiritual girls who will serve brilliantly the movement for freedom and the progress of the Bahai women of the East may be graduated therefrom. [37]*

---

* The provision of schooling for girls was of particular significance as it defied contemporary social convention. The Tarbíyat School faced considerable opposition from conservative Muslims, and eventually from the government. It was closed by order of the ministry of education in 1934.

The Greatest Holy Leaf continued to nurture and cherish the deep friendships some of the early believers in the West had established with her brother 'Abdu'l-Bahá, and she enlarged the embrace of these loving relationships to include the newly appointed Guardian, Shoghi Effendi. Addressing one such friend, she writes,

It is a very long time since we have had any news from you and we are quite longing to have one of your interesting and beautiful letters, that brings us always comfort because of your sincerity, your love for the Cause and your constant energy in the work for the Cause. You have ever been one of the Master's best friends, you are one of the oldest American believers, one of the firm and enthusiastic workers, and we are always happy to hear from you. The joy of our hearts is to hear that the friends are active and sincere in the spreading of the teachings.

We always long to hear about the friends, to know that in America they are arising with sincere energy to assist our beloved Guardian, to make his heart happy so that he may return to the Holy Land and again take up, with renewed vigour, the burdens that are too great when he feels that the friends are not uniting with him to carry out the instructions of the Beloved. We know that these instructions and teachings are the balm for the wounds and ills of the world, and if the friends are not firm, sincere and united in the principles as given by Bahá'u'lláh, explained and amplified by 'Abdu'l-Bahá, and do not teach them clearly and keep them pure and unadulterated, then how can the ills of mankind be alleviated? All other teachings have failed to eliminate the existing prejudices between peoples and religions and unite them upon the basis of pure truth, and now that we have this blessed remedy which is a divine solvent, let us not be blind or neglectful, but energetically and courageously stand forth as true heralds of this Divine Remedy.[38]

The Greatest Holy Leaf served as the tangible link between the past, present, and future of the Faith. She instilled a sense of continuity and a clear vision based on the familiar guidance provided in the writings of Bahá'u'lláh and 'Abdu'l-Bahá. She helped the Bahá'ís to understand the continuing relevance of this guidance to the needs of the present, and she directed their attention to the contents of Shoghi Effendi's letters.

In directing the administrative affairs of the Bahá'í community, the Greatest Holy Leaf drew on the guidance contained in the letters written by Shoghi Effendi in the first months of his ministry. The Guardian's letters set the course for the development of the Faith, highlighted the needs, established the priorities for action, and enhanced the believers' understanding concerning the transition to the Formative Age of the Cause.

A number of broad, seminal themes are found in the letters that Shoghi Effendi wrote in the early years of his Guardianship. He stresses, for example, the importance of understanding and adopting, without reservation, the provisions of the Will and Testament of 'Abdu'l-Bahá. He calls attention to the significance of the institution of the Spiritual Assembly and to the vital necessity of establishing Local and National Spiritual Assemblies throughout the world. He sets out the means for the election of this important institution, outlines its functions, and describes its relationship to the Universal House of Justice, the crowning institution of the Bahá'í Administrative Order, to be brought into being in the future. He also explains the unique Bahá'í election process, emphasizes the importance of consultation as the means by which Spiritual Assemblies arrive at decisions, and describes the spiritual, personal, and intellectual qualities to be manifested by those who are elected to Assembly membership.

In addition, Shoghi Effendi's early letters refer to the challenges confronting the Faith during the transition to the Formative Age.

He reminds the believers of 'Abdu'l-Bahá's statement concerning a period of testing and stresses the importance of the believers' firmness in the Covenant, of their unity, and of their exerting efforts to teach the Cause.[39]

Bahíyyih Khánum reiterated these same themes many times in the letters she wrote during the Guardian's absences from the Holy Land. She also followed up and brought to fruition a number of initiatives, some of which Shoghi Effendi had instigated. The clear unity of purpose and the close collaboration between the Guardian and the Greatest Holy Leaf is illustrated in the arrangements made for the visit of Jináb-i-Fáḍil-i-Mazindarání, a distinguished Persian Bahá'í teacher, to North America to stimulate the teaching work.

In September 1922 the National Spiritual Assembly of the Bahá'ís of the United States and Canada sent a cable to Bahíyyih Khánum conveying an invitation to Jináb-i-Fáḍil-i-Mazindarání and his family to visit America. In February 1923, this individual arrived in New York, bringing with him a letter from Shoghi Effendi addressed to the Bahá'ís in North America. The Guardian's letter states,

> Our dear friend, Jináb-i-Fáḍil-i Mazindarání, accompanied by his family, has gladly and gratefully responded to the kind invitation of the American friends to visit them once more and extend his helping hand to the many friends who are so faithfully labouring throughout that continent for the Cause of Bahá'u'lláh. . . .
>
> That all the friends may realize more fully the urgent and supreme necessity of Teaching the Cause in these days, that they may arise to inaugurate a more strenuous, systematized and extensive campaign of service—these are the high aims he has set before himself and which he intends, with the unfailing help and whole-hearted support of every believer in America, to achieve in the immediate future.

May his second visit to your shores mark, in its character and results, a new and memorable era in the history of the Cause in that great country! [40]

A second example of the manner in which the Greatest Holy Leaf ensured that an important project initiated by Shoghi Effendi reached fruition concerns the preparation of an article on the Bahá'í Faith. The article was to be presented at a "Conference of Living Religions within the British Empire," to be held in London in 1924 as part of the British Empire Exhibition. In January 1924 Shoghi Effendi had written to the American National Spiritual Assembly requesting that it prepare a paper for this event in collaboration with the British National Assembly. In June 1924 the Greatest Holy Leaf, in a letter written on her behalf to the British National Spiritual Assembly, mentions that she has sent a follow-up cable to the American Assembly inquiring about the status and progress of the paper and calling attention to the fact that it had to be submitted by July. Indeed, the article was completed, submitted on time, and presented at the conference. [41]

Fostering the Expansion of the Bahá'í Faith

Given the emphasis on the importance of teaching the Faith contained in the writings of Bahá'u'lláh and 'Abdu'l-Bahá and in the letters of Shoghi Effendi, it is only to be expected that the Greatest Holy Leaf in her letters gave considerable attention to fostering and encouraging teaching activities among the Bahá'ís. For example, writing in 1922, she refers to the words of 'Abdu'l-Bahá to inspire the believers to take action:

Your letter of 12th October 1922 is just received and refreshed in our memory the many beautiful days that you spent here when the Beloved Lord, 'Abdu'l-Bahá, was still on this earth. Those are days that many events of history could never efface from the hearts, nay rather the further we go in the scale of life the deeper become the impressions thereof within the meshes of our inner life.

I read your letter with full attention and in the course of the reading the words of the Master were ringing in my ear; words that have descended like showers on all souls and hearts that could understand. Now is the time when we should forget everything and concentrate our thoughts upon the advancement of the Cause of God and strive day and night that the principles and teachings of His Holiness Bahá'u'lláh and the words of the Master may find full expression in the hearts of the true friends.

When I think over the history of the Cause and the many difficulties that all its promoters have undergone I unhesitatingly am convinced that the sincere friends who have watched the events will not lose a moment but will with all their hearts and souls sacrifice everything of worth in order to realize that for which the Divine plan has been working.[42]

When one of the Bahá'ís reported meeting with a number of Chinese students and speaking with them about the Faith, the Greatest Holy Leaf wrote, "I was very glad to know of your meeting with the Chinese students, and I am sure your effect and influence shall be great upon them because their fresh and receptive minds are ready to grasp the importance of this Manifestation; and when you go to China, which you may if you think it wise, your influence and success, I hope, will be still more." She offers the following encouragement to the Bahá'í to persist in her efforts:

I pray God that He should confirm you in your teaching, and when you go to China, He should make you a pioneer in carrying the Message of this Dispensation to the farthermost countries of the world and to the most obscure.

The members of the Holy Family join me in extending to you their love and Bahá'í greetings, and may the spirit of 'Abdu'l-Bahá guide you and keep you.[43]

The Greatest Holy Leaf clearly understood the importance of sustained efforts in relation to the work of teaching the Faith, even when the results do not immediately materialize. In one of her letters she encouraged the Bahá'ís in the following words:

You have written that your number is small; but it is decidedly true that it is not numbers that count, it is, rather, the sincerity and devotion of the hearts. It is the heart that, subduing within itself all earthly cares, shines forth resplendent in the realm of love and selflessness, attracting to itself the souls of the weary and depressed, soothing their wounds with the balm of this Message. This new Revelation has in reality been the water of life unto the thirsty, a sea of knowledge unto the searcher, a message of condolence to the weary and a new spirit and life to the whole world. And now it remains that we, the humble servants of our Lord should be confirmed, through our own effort and through His bounty to diffuse this light everywhere and to carry this Glad Tidings to every cottage and princely home.[44]

In yet another letter she informs the friends of her intention to pray, personally, at the Shrine of 'Abdu'l-Bahá for the success of their teaching activities. Thus she writes, "I pray at the Holy Shrine of our beloved Lord, 'Abdu'l-Bahá, to favour you with the realization of the desire of your heart which contributes to the joy and happiness of the beloved Guardian of the Cause, that is, service towards the unity of the dear friends and the promulgation of the divine Teachings which alone can redeem this lifeless world."[45]

Above all, Bahíyyih Khánum stresses the supreme importance and the timeliness of teaching the Faith, helping the friends to understand the link between this vital activity and the achievement of personal happiness and contentment. "Now is the time," she asserts in one of her letters, "to arise and serve with all our powers, that we may grow happier day by day, and fill our hearts with warmth and joy."[46]

Fostering Awareness of Bahá'í Administrative Functioning

Bahíyyih Khánum took specific steps to steer the Bahá'í Faith from the Heroic to the Formative Age. She fostered awareness of the importance of establishing Spiritual Assemblies and encouraged and trained the believers to conduct their activities according to Bahá'í administrative procedures. Her vision and the guidance she provided were derived both from her clear understanding of the needs of the Faith at this stage in its development and from the guidance contained in the seminal letters of Shoghi Effendi. So crucial were these new directions that she immediately underlined their importance in the letters she wrote after the Guardian's departure from the Holy Land in 1922 and continued to do so during her tenure of "headship." Ruḥíyyih Khánum provides the following description of some of the actions the Greatest Holy Leaf took at this time: "On 8 April [1922] the Greatest Holy Leaf wrote a general letter to the friends. She first acknowledges the letters of allegiance they have sent and says Shoghi Effendi is counting upon their co-operation in spreading the Message; the Bahá'í world must from now on be linked through the Spiritual Assemblies and local questions must be referred to them."[47]

With regard to the encouragement of Bahá'í administrative functioning, it is instructive to examine the manner in which the Greatest Holy Leaf, herself, modeled appropriate administrative behavior. Her letters provide useful insight into how to manifest the "spirit of frank and loving consultation," which, the Guardian writes, is the "keynote of the Cause of God."[48]

Bahíyyih Khánum's letters are direct and personal, sensitive and responsive to the needs of the individual and the particular situation she was addressing. Thus we read the following: "It would be our wish to answer each letter individually, but the shock of our bereavement was so sudden, and the work to which we were compelled to attend, was so overwhelming, that time failed us. Now, we wish you to realize that your words of steadfast faith and love were our greatest solace throughout the days of our grief, for we felt that you would each and all faithfully and loyally strive to carry on the work for which the life of our Beloved Master was spent." Acknowledging the receipt of letters addressed to Shoghi Effendi and herself, the Greatest Holy Leaf expresses appreciation for the services of the believer. She writes, "Your numerous letters written to the beloved Guardian and myself have all arrived and brought with them the sweet perfume of your devotion, sincerity, strong faith and active and beautiful services you are inexhaustibly rendering to the Cause of God. You should be happy, dear Bahá'í sister[,] in being so wonderfully confirmed in your spiritual life. . . ." She then provides news of the Guardian and of his anticipated imminent return to the Holy Land and concludes with these words of encouragement: "The Ladies of the Holy Family and I are always remembering you dear friends of 'Abdu'l-Bahá and praying for your confirmation and happiness. I am thankful to all the dear friends who so faithfully and lovingly responded with their excellent deeds to my affectionate appeal for greater unity and love. May the Blessed

Beauty [Bahá'u'lláh]and 'Abdu'l-Bahá reward them richly and crown their sincere services with great results."[49]

A study of the letters of Bahíyyih Khánum reveals that her approach to the administration of the affairs of the Faith was practical, systematic, goal-directed, and forward-looking. She did not hesitate to introduce change when circumstances required it or the guidance of Shoghi Effendi mandated it. Her letters call attention to spiritual and administrative principles and provide necessary information. For example, in a letter addressed to the Spiritual Assemblies in the East, she writes, "A few days ago I sent out a general letter. A detailed, and recent, letter from the Guardian to all the people of Bahá was likewise sent out, and it is certain that you will be reading it; it is essential to circulate it among all the friends. What I mean is, that because of my great and spiritual love for you, the steadfast lovers of God and His Covenant, I have now set about writing this present letter as well." In this same letter she refers to statements concerning dissension in the Will and Testament of 'Abdu'l-Bahá and in other tablets, and she warns the believers about the dangers of contending with the provisions of the Covenant. To help the believers understand these provisions she announces, "Although up to now, because of the dictates of wisdom, the Will and Testament has not been in general circulation, and has been entrusted only to the Spiritual Assemblies of the various countries, at this time a photocopy has been made from the Master's original Text, which is in His own hand, and it will soon be sent out, to increase the spiritual joy of you who are essences of loyalty and trust, that every individual believer, every steadfast one in the Covenant who so desires, may read it and make a copy of it."[50]

Yet another letter illustrates the Greatest Holy Leaf's systematic approach by informing the believers about what transpired as a result of an appeal she had made to the Bahá'í community. This same passage also focuses attention on the importance of understanding the station of the National Spiritual Assembly and of supporting this nascent institution. She writes, "Since my last affectionate appeal to the beloved of God and 'Abdu'l-Bahá's spiritual children, the dear friends in every land have indeed shown a wonderful spirit which has inspired us all with joy and gratitude. For their confirmation and success we ardently pray at the Holy Shrines. I hope and pray that your National Spiritual Assembly will this year be favoured with divine support and unprecedented prosperity." [51]

The Greatest Holy Leaf not only supported the embryonic National Spiritual Assemblies but also actively encouraged the establishment of Local Spiritual Assemblies throughout the Bahá'í world and helped the Bahá'ís to understand the functions of these institutions. She thus assisted the believers to understand more deeply the guidance on this subject contained in the Guardian's letters.

To foster a greater understanding of the importance of Bahá'í administrative institutions, the Greatest Holy Leaf stressed the link between the activities of the believers and their administrative organs, and the spiritual transformation of the world at large. She states, "It is clear and evident that the body of mankind in this day stands in dire need of such members and organs as are capable, useful and active, so that their movements and activities, their bearing and behaviour, their tender feelings, lofty sentiments and noble intentions may at all times reflect heavenly virtues and perfections and become the expressions of divine attributes and saintly characteristics, thus breathing a new life and spirit into all the dwellers of the world and causing the inner ties and spiritual relationships to be fostered and fortified in all fields of human endeavour." [52]

Conveying her pleasure at the formation of a new Local Spiritual Assembly, the Greatest Holy Leaf writes, "We rejoiced greatly to learn of the unity among the friends, their staunchness, their

ardour, and the fact that they have established a Spiritual Assembly."
She then spells out what the believers must do to strengthen the foundations of this institution: "It is clear that the stronger grow the bonds of yearning love among the believers, and the fiercer its fire, the more will they find themselves embraced by the bounties of the Ancient of Days, and receiving the continuous confirmations of the Greatest Name.* Thus will the Assemblies of the friends become reflections of the gardens of the Concourse on High, mirroring forth the radiance of the Abhá Kingdom." In the same letter, she attests that the Central Figures of the Faith—the Báb, Bahá'u'lláh, and 'Abdu'l-Bahá—all rejoice when the teachings of the Cause are faithfully put into practice: "From Their supernal realms and Their immortal heights, He the exalted Báb, and He Who is the Beauty of the All-Glorious, and the wondrous presence of 'Abdu'l-Bahá, all These are gazing down upon Their faithful loved ones, beholding what they do under all conditions, their behaviour and conduct, and all their words and ways, waiting to cry 'Well done!' when They see the Teachings carried out, and 'Blessed art thou!' to whoso may excel in doing the bidding of his Lord."[53]

Beyond encouraging the formation of Spiritual Assemblies, Bahíyyih Khánum also gave guidance to help the Assemblies understand their responsibilities and how they should function. In the following extract from one of her letters she calls attention to the role of the Assembly in creating and maintaining unity among the believers and in promoting the teachings of the Faith. She writes,

Praise be to God that through the gracious assistance of the Abhá Kingdom those devoted friends have been enabled to achieve that which befits the glory of the Cause of God and the protec-

---

* A reference to the name of Bahá'u'lláh.

tion of the community of the followers of Bahá'u'lláh. This is none other than to foster unity and fellowship under all conditions, to strengthen the bonds of harmony and concord in all things, and to avoid political matters. It is particularly important to refrain from making unfavourable remarks or statements concerning the friends and the loved ones of God, inasmuch as any expression of grievance, of complaint or backbiting is incompatible with the requirements of unity and harmony and would dampen the spirit of love, fellowship and nobility. Therefore it is incumbent upon the members of the exalted Spiritual Assembly to exercise the utmost care with firm determination and not to allow the doors of complaint and grievance to be opened, or permit any of the friends to indulge in censure and backbiting. Whoever sets himself to do so, even though he be the very embodiment of the Holy Spirit, should realize that such behaviour would create disruption among the people of Bahá and would cause the standard of sedition to be raised.

In these days when the peoples of the world are thirsting for the teachings of the Abhá Beauty—teachings that provide the incomparable, life-giving waters of immortality—when we Bahá'ís have pledged ourselves to proffer these living waters to all mankind and are known to be prepared to endure every suffering and tribulation, how pitiful it would be if, despite all this, we were to neglect our binding obligations and responsibilities and to occupy ourselves with disagreeable discussions that provoke irritation and distress and to turn our attention to matters that lead to ill-feeling, to despondency and unhappiness and reduce the penetrating influence of the Word of God.[54]

A letter addressed to the Spiritual Assembly of Tehran not only illustrates the role the Greatest Holy Leaf played in receiving contributions to certain Bahá'í funds, but also clearly demonstrates her familiarity with current world events and her understanding of the potential benefits of international cooperation and of their impact on the emergence of a Bahá'í identity. The letter states,

> The cheque for the amount of two hundred pounds that you had sent as your contribution to the Temple Fund* has been received and duly forwarded to Chicago. Behold what a pervasive power this evidence of co-operation and support, this spirit of selfless consecration is bound to release in the realm of the heart and spirit. Consider to what extent the world of human virtues will be enriched and adorned by this munificent act, and how glorious the light that this manifestation of unity and solidarity is likely to shed upon all regions. Indeed, this mighty endeavour has been accomplished despite the adverse economic situation in Persia, where the evidences of hardship, privation and depression are clearly apparent. But since the object of this noble enterprise and praiseworthy effort is to enhance the glory of the Cause of God, therefore it will unfailingly attract divine blessings and bounty.[55]

From the foregoing, it is evident that the Greatest Holy Leaf was able to communicate the importance and practical necessity of forming Spiritual Assemblies. She helped the Bahá'ís to appreciate the functions of the Assemblies, the role these institutions were to play in the unfoldment of the Bahá'í Administrative Order, and the responsibility of the believers to cherish and support the evolving Bahá'í Assemblies.

---

* A fund set up to provide for the construction of the Bahá'í House of Worship near Chicago in Wilmette, Illinois.

The Haifa Spiritual Assembly

Formed in the first year of the Guardian's ministry, the early days of the operation of the Haifa Spiritual Assembly coincide with the period of the "headship" of Bahíyyih Khánum. First elected in December 1922, the Assembly was not only responsible for organizing meetings of the local Bahá'í community; it also assumed the important function of keeping in touch with Bahá'í Spiritual Assemblies throughout the world. In a letter published in *Star of the West* the Assembly describes its mandate in the following terms:

> . . . inspired by his [the Guardian's] unceasing efforts to bring greater cooperation and interrelation between the Bahá'í centers the world over, we, the members of the newly constituted Spiritual Assembly of Haifa, have the great pleasure of extending a warm hand to our brothers and sisters across the seas who are working hard in order to carry out the unique principles of this Divine Dispensation. The more we hear the good news of the progress of the Cause the more do we realize the fulfillment of the words of the Master when with a radiant smile he spoke of the vast field of service which lies before the sincere and loyal friends of God.[56]

The existence of the Haifa Spiritual Assembly at the heart of the Bahá'í World Center, operating in concert with the Greatest Holy Leaf, was undoubtedly a source of encouragement to the Bahá'ís in different parts of the world to form Local Spiritual Assemblies in their own areas and to extend the range of the functions undertaken by this institution—an institution that constitutes the very foundation on which Bahá'u'lláh's Administrative Order is destined to be built.

The Haifa Spiritual Assembly contributed significantly to the emergence of the consciousness of a global Bahá'í community by disseminating news about developments of the Bahá'í Faith in all parts of the world. To this end the Assembly prepared informative reports in the form of letters that were published in the periodical *Star of the West*. In addition, the Assembly wrote circular letters in Persian that were sent to the Assemblies in the Orient. These reports fostered greater awareness of the nature of Bahá'í activities in both the East and the West, and they helped to forge a sense of Bahá'í identity.

A perusal of the Haifa Assembly's letters in *Star of the West* illustrates how the dissemination of information served to knit together the widely scattered Bahá'í communities throughout the world. For example, in March 1923 the Assembly reports on some of the activities that had occurred in Haifa—the holding of the Nineteen Day Feast* and the establishment of a youth teaching group. In addition, the Assembly shares news of the formation of Spiritual Assemblies in various places in the Middle East and of the activities of the Bahá'ís in 'Ishqábád, Russia, and in Persia.[57]

In its letter of April 1923, the secretary of the Haifa Assembly shares the good news that Spiritual Assemblies had been formed in Egypt; in Hamadán, Persia; and in Acre, where one of the members elected to serve was an elderly believer who had accompanied Bahá'u'lláh on His exiles. The secretary quotes a letter from the newly constituted Assembly in Hamadán concerning the activities of the Bahá'í schools for girls and boys in that town and refers to reports from 'Ishqábád and from the Bahá'ís in Germany. This same

---

* A meeting held on the first day of every Bahá'í month, each consisting of nineteen days, is the heart of Bahá'í community life at the local level. It consists of devotional, consultative, and social elements.

issue of *Star of the West* mentions the travels of Mr. and Mrs. Hyde Dunn—two American Bahá'ís who traveled to Australia and New Zealand to teach the Faith—and records the following comments of Mr. Dunn concerning Shoghi Effendi and the activities of the Greatest Holy Leaf: "The wonderful bounty and gift to the Cause in dear Shoghi Effendi are amazing . . . to all of us. It is a most glorious day in which we live—a day that will not be followed by a night. Again, the Greatest Holy Leaf seems more to us than ever before. 'The leaves shall be the healing of the nations.'"[58]

The circular letters from the Haifa Spiritual Assembly to the believers in the Orient contained information about the progress of the Faith in the East and in the West. Choice items of news were translated and shared with the Eastern friends. For example, Martha Root's* services in China and Japan and a letter from Shoghi Effendi about these activities were translated and inserted in the monthly circular letter and mailed to different Assemblies and the friends in the Orient.[59]

A letter from the Haifa Spiritual Assembly written around two years after 'Abdu'l-Bahá's passing graphically underlines the growing interconnection between the widely scattered Bahá'í communities and the extent to which events that transpired in one locality impacted the Bahá'í world as a whole. The Assembly reports having received a letter from the Persian National Spiritual Assembly, which illustrates its desire to alert the believers to the economic hardships being experienced by their coreligionists in Germany, a country burdened by the conditions of the peace treaty concluded at the end of World War I. The National Assembly's letter mentions that

---

* An outstanding American Bahá'í teacher who traveled around the world and introduced the message of Bahá'u'lláh to many countries that had not previously heard of the Bahá'í Faith.

"A special circular letter regarding the economic conditions in Germany and the suffering of the friends there has been sent [by the National Spiritual Assembly] to all the different provinces in Persia with the hope that spiritual or material help may be forthcoming." The National Spiritual Assembly's letter goes on to say, "The news of the progress of the Cause in Australia has wonderfully encouraged the teaching in Persia, as it shows the heavenly influence of the Divine Teachings throughout the world." The Assembly comments, "The more we experience the more do we realize the significance of the words of His Holiness Bahá'u'lláh and the Master. These are treasures which, if rightly understood, will give the firm believer a key for the solution of any problem which may arise in social organization. It is through this power that many illiterate friends in Persia are able to overcome the arguments of any religious leader."[60]

Identification with the sufferings of fellow Bahá'ís and the desire to render assistance to alleviate their difficulties is further illustrated in the following report of the Haifa Assembly issued in late 1923:

> Our last Nineteen Day Feast had a charm of its own as it was the first one after the return of Shoghi Effendi to Haifa. As a sign of gratitude for this blessing the host proposed that more contributions be sent to our brothers and sisters in Germany. As a result of this proposal the sum of about forty Egyptian pounds was contributed and will be forwarded to the friends in Germany.
>
> In addition, when news of the earthquake in Japan was received from the Bahá'í pioneer, Agnes Alexander, contributions were made by the believers in Haifa and dispatched to Japan.[61]

The role of the Haifa Spiritual Assembly in arranging for the activities of the Bahá'ís in Haifa emphasized the importance of the institution of the Spiritual Assembly. Its actions in disseminating news of the progress of the Faith in the East and West helped to demonstrate that the Faith was, indeed, a world religion, and to strengthen a sense of Bahá'í identity. The work of the Haifa Assembly thus complemented and supported the initiatives the Greatest Holy Leaf undertook. It was her function to give overall direction to the administrative affairs of the Cause and to provide the necessary guidance to enable the believers to carry out the tasks assigned by the head of the Faith.

In later years, as Shoghi Effendi developed the scope of the administrative work at the World Center of the Faith, the functions of the Haifa Spiritual Assembly were absorbed by the Bahá'í World Center.

Protecting the Bahá'í Faith

The Greatest Holy Leaf made a significant contribution to the protection of the fledgling Bahá'í Faith, both from the attacks of those who were attempting to violate the Covenant concerning 'Abdu'l-Bahá's appointed successor, and from the persecutions by its enemies in Persia, the land of its birth.

As mentioned in chapter 3, on 22 January 1922, soon after the passing of 'Abdu'l-Bahá, His disaffected half-brother Mírzá Muḥammad-'Alí and his cohorts forcibly seized the keys to the Shrine of Bahá'u'lláh from the Bahá'í caretaker. They claimed that, according to the provisions of Islamic law, since they were the nearest surviving relatives of Bahá'u'lláh, custody of the shrine should pass to them. Shoghi Effendi immediately referred the matter to the governor of Acre, who took possession of the keys pending a full investigation by the British Mandatory Government to determine the question of rightful ownership.

Resolution of the situation required the unceasing efforts of Shoghi Effendi over a long period of time. In his absence, the Great-

est Holy Leaf actively monitored the situation and took the necessary steps to follow up the matter with the British authorities. In
this regard it is interesting to examine the following extract from a
letter written in May 1922 to the Bahá'ís in Iran. In it Bahíyyih
Khánum describes the current state of affairs, writing, "Now, after
the passage of four months, the Government has rendered its ver-
dict, to the effect that the question should be put to the Bahá'í
community, and that whatever decision the Bahá'ís arrive at will be
conclusive. If the Bahá'í community considers Mírzá Muhammad-
'Alí to be excommunicated, then he has no rights whatever to the
takeover."[62]

In light of these circumstances, the Greatest Holy Leaf called for
a systematic campaign of action on the part of the believers and the
Bahá'í Assemblies throughout the world. She therefore instructed
them to make representations to the British authorities and provided the following specific guidance:

Therefore, wherever Bahá'ís reside, they must, through the given
city's Spiritual Assembly, and bearing the signature of named individuals who are members of the elected body, inform the British
authorities in Jerusalem, either by cable or letter sent through His
Majesty's ambassadors or consuls, that the Bahá'í community, in
conformity with the explicit writings and the Will and Testament
of His Eminence 'Abdu'l-Bahá, Sir 'Abbás Effendi, texts well known
and available in His own hand—recognize His Eminence Shoghi
Effendi as the one to whom all Bahá'ís must turn, and as the Guardian of the Cause of God, and that they have no connection whatever, either material or spiritual, with Mírzá Muhammad-'Alí,
whom they consider to be excommunicated from the Bahá'í Faith,
according to the explicit writings of 'Abdu'l-Bahá.

It should be the request, therefore, of Bahá'ís of all countries, both men and women, in every important centre, wherever they may reside throughout the world, that the officials of His Britannic Majesty's Government in Palestine, its Headquarters being Jerusalem, issue a categorical order that the key of the Holy Tomb—which is the Point of Adoration and the sanctuary of all Bahá'ís in the world—be restored to His Eminence Shoghi Effendi, the Chosen Branch, and in this way to render the Bahá'í community, whether of the East or of the West, more appreciative than ever of British justice. [63]

To facilitate this action, she enclosed copies of a sample letter and cable and she instructed, "The message is to be signed by the representatives and known followers of the Bahá'í Faith in that city." [64]

When Shoghi Effendi returned to Haifa in December 1922, he continued to pursue a number of initiatives and contacts with various authorities. Finally, the case was decided. In February 1923, the British High Commissioner in Palestine decided in favor of the Bahá'ís and returned the key to the Guardian, just over one year after it had been forcibly taken from the legitimate Bahá'í custodian of the Shrine of Bahá'u'lláh.[65]

A further example of Bahíyyih Khánum's strategic approach to mobilizing the Bahá'í community for the protection of the Faith is illustrated by her letter to the Bahá'ís of the West in August 1922. Written at a time when there were widespread outbursts of persecution against the Bahá'í Faith in the land of its birth, the Greatest Holy Leaf vividly describes the scope and nature of some of these attacks:

Sad news has come to us out of Iran in recent days, and it has intensely grieved the entire Bahá'í world: they have, in most parts of that land, set bonfires of envy and malevolence, and hoisted the banner of aggression against this much-wronged community; they have left no means untried, no plot or strategy neglected, and have arisen with extreme hostility and spite to pull out by their very roots the trees of this garden of God. . . .

. . . They are taking the men and women believers captive, and making orphans of the children. They are plundering the believers' property, sacking their hearths and homes.[66]

Given the pressing danger of the situation and the lack of protection afforded the Persian Bahá'ís from the authorities, the Greatest Holy Leaf urgently called for the Bahá'í community in different parts of the world to take action: "During occurrences of this kind, it is incumbent upon the believers in other countries to immediately adopt prudent and reasonable measures, that through wise methods such fires may be put out."[67]

Bahíyyih Khánum set out a two-pronged approach for the Bahá'ís to follow—to make representations to the Persian ambassador in each country and to encourage the governments to raise the issue of the persecution of the Bahá'ís with their ambassadors in Tehran. Additionally, the Greatest Holy Leaf gave explicit instructions concerning how to proceed in each instance.

In relation to the former, she writes, "At this time it is urgently needful, and it is the request of this grieving servant, that the assembly of the believers in that area act at once, and take the case to the ambassador of the Iranian government." To help the Bahá'ís respond to this instruction, she provided detailed guidance concerning the points to be made in the representation to the Iranian ambassador:

Let them tell him, "The holy Cause of Bahá'u'lláh has so unified us who are His world-wide followers, and has brought us so close together, that we have become like a single body. If the foot of a Bahá'í, in the farthest Eastern land, is so much as scratched by a thorn, it is even as if we Bahá'ís here in the West had suffered the same. We have now received word from Írán that in S͟híráz, in Sulṭánábád, in Hamadán, in Kás͟hán, even in Ṭihrán, and in other places as well, the fanaticism of the ignorant and heedless has been fanned into flame, and that agitators are stirring up the populace—with the result that our brothers and sisters, who are but well-wishers of all humankind and are indeed the world's only hope for peace, and are obedient and helpful citizens of Iran and her government, find themselves under attack and pushed into the heart of the fire.

"We therefore request the representative of Iran to ask his government to safeguard our brothers in Iran from the aggressions of their enemies, and to deliver that flock of God's lovers from the claws of the wolf, and provide for their security and well-being. By bringing us word of this outcome, Írán will earn the deep and heartfelt gratitude of thousands of Bahá'ís who reside in these countries, and widespread appreciation will be voiced by us in our many gatherings, of her government's good offices on our behalf." [68]

As to the second part of her strategic intervention, the Greatest Holy Leaf issued the following guidance:

And further, if it be possible, you should make this same representation through your own ambassador in Ṭihrán, so that he may direct the attention of the Iranian authorities to these persecutions, and awaken that government to the possibility of divine retribution and to the shameful stigma occasioned by such actions directed against this innocent community by the heedless and ignorant amongst the mass of the people.

Let him make them aware that there are thousands of adherents of this Faith of the love of God around the world, who are gazing in astonishment and disbelief at the savage acts now being perpetrated against their brothers, and are eagerly waiting to hear that the government has come to the rescue of this unique, this law-abiding people, who are the well-wishers of mankind, from the attacks of the ravening wolves.[69]

A third area in which the Greatest Holy Leaf significantly contributed to the protection of the Faith was through the guidance she gave the believers regarding their response to the Covenant-breakers' activities, especially in Iran. Not only did she educate the believers about the necessity of safeguarding the Cause, but she also helped them to understand the motivation of those who attacked the Bahá'í Covenant, and she issued detailed instructions to help Bahá'ís and their Assemblies respond to specific situations. In a letter addressed to the Spiritual Assembly of Hamadán, Iran, she writes:

In this momentous matter there must be no laxity, no inattention, for a whisper might become an axe laid to the root of the Tree of the Faith—a word from an ambitious soul could be a spark tossed into the harvest of the people of Bahá. We take refuge with God! May He guard us ever, from the recklessness of the insistent self.

For the harbouring of an evil purpose is a disease which shuts out the individual from all the blessings of Heaven, and casts him deep into the pit of perdition, of utter ruin. The point to make is that anyone, high or low, rich or poor, learned or unlettered, although to all appearances he may be a jewel among men, and the fine flower of all that is best—if he gives utterance to some pronouncement or speaks some word from which can be detected the scent of self-worship, or a malicious and evil purpose, his aim is to disintegrate the Word of God and disperse the gathering of the people of Bahá. From such individuals it is a solemn obligation to turn away; it is an inescapable duty to pay no heed whatever to their claims.[70]

In another letter written to a believer in the East, Bahíyyih Khánum alludes to the activities of ‘Abdu’l-Ḥusayn Ávaríh, who had been a distinguished early believer but, after the passing of ‘Abdu’l-Bahá, attempted to undermine the authority of the Guardian. He refused to recognize the legitimacy of the Spiritual Assemblies and sought to gain the allegiance of the followers of the Faith in the East. Shoghi Effendi subsequently expelled him from the Faith.[71] Commenting on the destructive effect of Ávaríh’s behavior, the Greatest Holy Leaf states,

> Indeed, it is true to say that malice will cause one’s intelligence and understanding to fade, and the king of reason to become subservient to the satanic self and its promptings. Time and again has this matter been put to proof and the following blessed passage from the Will and Testament amply demonstrates this significant truth and serves to heighten the sense of alertness and vigilance. How wondrous is His Word: “No doubt every vainglorious one that purposeth dissension and discord will not openly declare his evil purposes, nay rather, even as impure gold, would he seize upon divers measures and various pretexts that he may separate the gathering of the people of Bahá.”[72]

Further, in a letter written in May 1924, the Greatest Holy Leaf directly addresses “the question of Ávaríh,” a former member of the Bahá’í Faith who became alienated from it when he found his ambition for personal power frustrated by the provisions of the

Covenant. She describes the attempts that had been made to guide him and restrain him in his destructive efforts to create disunity between the Spiritual Assemblies and the believers. Furthermore, she spells out in detail his efforts to disrupt the Bahá'í communities in Cairo, Beirut, and Baghdad by means of spreading false information about the provisions of the Covenant as a prelude to the eventual overthrow of the institutions expressly provided for in 'Abdu'l-Bahá's will and testament. Ávaríh's machinations, while disturbing at the time, have no lasting impact. She concludes her letter with an explanation as to why she decided it was necessary to provide an account of what actually took place, and she offers the following words of assurance to enable the believers to put the situation into perspective: "The point is that although such talk and such behaviour have no effect and no importance whatsoever, and do not merit our attention, still this disloyalty of his in these days of trial and sorrow is such that, unable to bear the situation any longer, this grieved and helpless one has felt obliged to set down a brief account of what actually took place."[73]

The Greatest Holy Leaf's contribution, in collaboration with the members of the holy family to whom Shoghi Effendi entrusted supervision of the Faith's affairs during his absences from the Holy Land, was indeed unique. Might not the tribute he penned at the time of her passing in 1932 provide an intimate glimpse into his loving appreciation for the services she rendered during this vital period of transition? His testimony reads,

Which of the blessings am I to recount, which in her unfailing solicitude she showered upon me, in the most critical and agitated hours of my life? To me, standing in so dire a need of the vitalizing grace of God, she was the living symbol of many an attribute I had learned to admire in 'Abdu'l-Bahá. She was to me a continual reminder of His inspiring personality, of His calm resignation, of His munificence and magnanimity. To me she was an incarnation of His winsome graciousness, of His all-encompassing tenderness and love.

It would take me too long to make even a brief allusion to those incidents of her life, each of which eloquently proclaims her as a daughter, worthy to inherit that priceless heritage bequeathed to her by Bahá'u'lláh. . . .[74]

When Shoghi Effendi returned to Haifa, refreshed and eager to assume the reins of the Cause, he addressed a letter dated 24 September 1924 to 'The beloved of the Lord and the handmaids of the Merciful throughout the Continent of America." In this letter he reflects on the effects of his prolonged absences and sets out his confident vision of the future development of the Faith. He writes,

> Looking back upon those sullen days of my retirement, bitter with feelings of anxiety and gloom, I can recall with appreciation and gratitude those unmistakable evidences of your affection and steadfast zeal which I have received from time to time, and which have served to relieve in no small measure the burden that weighed so heavily upon my heart.
>
> I can well imagine the degree of uneasiness, nay of affliction, that must have agitated the mind and soul of every loving and loyal servant of the Beloved during these long months of suspense and distressing silence. But I assure you such remarkable solicitude as you have shown for the protection of His Cause, such tenacity of faith and unceasing activity as you have displayed for its promotion, cannot but in the end be abundantly rewarded by 'Abdu'l-Bahá, who from His station above is the sure witness of all that you have endured and suffered for Him.
>
> And now as I look into the future, I hope to see the friends at all times, in every land, and of every shade of thought and char-

acter, voluntarily and joyously rallying round their local and in particular their national centers of activity, upholding and promoting their interests with complete unanimity and contentment, with perfect understanding, genuine enthusiasm, and sustained vigor. This indeed is the one joy and yearning of my life, for it is the fountainhead from which all future blessings will flow, the broad foundation upon which the security of the Divine Edifice must ultimately rest. May we not hope that now at last the dawn of a brighter day is breaking upon our beloved Cause? [75]

Chapter 6

The Glorious Companion
of Shoghi Effendi

The deep bond between the Guardian and his great-aunt, Bahíyyih Khánum, transcended mere family relationship. A letter written on his behalf contains the assertion that "No one has understood the tender, spiritual and celestial bond between the Guardian and her who was the Remnant of Bahá, nor can any mind conceive that plane of being, nor reckon its sublimity." Throughout her long life, Bahíyyih Khánum was a constant source of loving encouragement to Shoghi Effendi. He testifies that he was "reared by the hands of her loving kindness," that his "frail being" was "leavened with her love, refreshed by her companionship, [and] sustained by her eternal spirit."[1]

In this chapter we will examine the nature of the relationship between Shoghi Effendi and Bahíyyih Khánum. We will also explore some of the ways in which the Guardian associated the "Liege Lady of the people of Bahá" with the activities and significant developments in the Bahá'í Faith, and we will describe the services of Bahíyyih Khánum in the very evening of her life.[2]

The Bond between the Guardian and the Greatest Holy Leaf

In chapter 5 we considered the manner in which Bahíyyih Khánum willingly assumed the "headship" of the Bahá'í Faith when this responsibility was assigned to her by the Guardian. We examined her constant endeavors both to educate the Bahá'í community concerning the provisions of the Bahá'í Covenant and to rally support for the duly appointed Guardian and his initiatives to orient and move the community to the next stage in its development.[3]

In letters of eulogy written at the time of her death, Shoghi Effendi provides insight into her great sensitivity and the nature of the assistance she rendered to him after the passing of 'Abdu'l-Bahá. "After the ascension of 'Abdu'l-Bahá to the realm of the All-Glorious," he confides, she who was "that Light of the Concourse on High enfolded me, helpless as I was, in the embrace of her love, and with incomparable pity and tenderness, persuaded, guided, and urged me on to the requirements of servitude." His rhetorical question underlines the measure of his gratitude to the Greatest Holy Leaf: "How can my lonely pen . . . recount the blessings she showered upon me since my earliest childhood—how can such a pen repay the great debt of gratitude and love that I owe her whom I regarded as my chief sustainer, my most affectionate comforter, the joy and inspiration of my life?"[4]

Confronted with the challenging work of the Guardianship and the imperative need to establish the Bahá'í Faith throughout the world, Shoghi Effendi not only drew upon the encouragement and support of the Greatest Holy Leaf, but also derived great inspiration from her personal qualities, which reminded him of 'Abdu'l-Bahá. Indeed, the Guardian calls attention to the fact that Bahá'u'lláh singled out His beloved daughter to be "a true example" to all her kin to follow. Reflecting on his appreciation for the Greatest Holy Leaf, Shoghi Effendi writes, "To me . . . she was the living symbol of many an attribute I learned to admire in 'Abdu'l-Bahá. She was to me a continual reminder of His inspiring personality, of His calm resignation, of His munificence and magnanimity. To me she was an incarnation of His winsome graciousness, of His all-encompassing tenderness and love." The Guardian testifies to the depth of the inspiration and guidance he derived from consideration of her outstanding qualities. He writes, "When, in the morning and the evening, I call her beloved face to mind, and let her smiles, that nourished the spirit, pass again before my eyes, and I think over all her bounty to me, all her unnumbered kindnesses, and remember that astonishing meekness she showed in her sufferings—then the flames of yearning love are kindled yet again. . . . "[5]

From a perusal of his letters, it is evident that the Guardian was greatly influenced by Bahíyyih Khánum's deep commitment to the Bahá'í Cause and her attachment to its followers. He makes the following disclosure in a letter eulogizing her qualities: "I can . . . feel in its calm intensity, the immense love thou didst bear for the Cause of thine Almighty Father, the attachment that bound thee to the most lowly and insignificant among its followers, the warm affection thou didst cherish for me in thine heart."[6]

The Greatest Holy Leaf's spirit of selfless service had a profound impact on Shoghi Effendi. Memorializing his great-aunt, he writes, "The memory of the ineffable beauty of thy smile shall ever continue to cheer and hearten me in the thorny path I am destined to pursue. The remembrance of the touch of thine hand shall spur me on to follow steadfastly in thy way. The sweet magic of thy voice shall remind me, when the hour of adversity is at its darkest, to hold fast to the rope thou didst seize so firmly all the days of thy life." Shoghi Effendi stresses the inspiration he derived from the contemplation of the Greatest Holy Leaf's exemplary life and the sacrifices she willingly made for the Cause of God, and he expresses his intention to follow her example. He writes, "And at such times I strengthen my resolve to follow in thy footsteps, and to continue onward in the pathway of thy love; to take thee as my model, and to acquire the qualities, and to make manifest that which thou didst desire for the triumph of this exalted and exacting, this most resplendent, sacred, and wondrous Cause."[7]

The Close Companion of Shoghi Effendi

Shoghi Effendi clearly treasured the companionship of the Greatest Holy Leaf. He avers that Bahíyyih Khánum was his "close companion," the "consolation" of his heart, and "the one great solace of his life." The importance of this tender relationship to Shoghi Effendi is captured in the poignant description, contained in a letter written on his behalf, which states, "That gem of immortality, that precious and exalted being, was the one consolation, the one companion of the Guardian in his sorrow-filled life; and she, with her sweet encouragement, her gentle words, her never-ceasing, soothing care of him, her smiles that came like fair winds from heavenly gardens, could always gladden and refresh his spirit."[8]

The uniqueness and, indeed, the mysterious nature of the bond between Bahíyyih Khánum and Shoghi Effendi are emphasized in another letter written on behalf of Shoghi Effendi: "For the subtle and spiritual attachment that the Guardian felt for her, and the heavenly tenderness and affection between that lovely fruit of the divine Lote-Tree* and himself, was a bond so strong as to defy description, nor can the mind encompass that exalted state. That secret is a secret well-concealed, a treasured mystery unplumbed, and to a plane such as this, the minds of the believers can never find their way."[9]

While it is not possible to appreciate the exact nature of the relationship between Shoghi Effendi and the Greatest Holy Leaf, the accounts of eyewitnesses and pilgrims do provide brief glimpses into this intimate bond. According to Ruhíyyih Khánum, Shoghi Effendi's widow, the manifold responsibilities associated with being head of the Bahá'í Faith made it difficult for the Guardian to have a wide range of deep and personal relationships with other people.

---

* "Lote-Tree" refers to Bahá'u'lláh; see glossary for further information.

His closest relationships were with the members of his family and, in the early days of his ministry, with his helpers and secretaries. Ruḥíyyih Khánum attests that, "However faithful and tender Shoghi Effendi's relationships were throughout his life with those closest to him, his supreme relationship was with the Greatest Holy Leaf."[10]

Ruḥíyyih Khánum recounts that, until the time of the Greatest Holy Leaf's death, it was Shoghi Effendi's custom to dine alone with his great-aunt each day. The meal was served on a small table in her bedroom. Indeed, towards the end of her life, the Guardian used to spend the greatest part of his leisure time in her company.[11]

It was also the Guardian's practice to visit with the Greatest Holy Leaf in her room after meeting with the pilgrims. He would sit and talk to her and, no doubt, share news of the progress of the Faith with her. On one such occasion, Bahíyyih Khánum was in bed when she heard the Guardian approaching. It is reported that "As soon as she heard the footsteps of Shoghi Effendi and the opening of the door she was at the point of rising from bed to sit in the presence of the Guardian. Although the distance is not far from the door to the bed, Shoghi Effendi literally ran from the door to the bed and gently restrained her, saying *'Já'iz níst'* (it is not permissible). He did not want her to be disturbed." The tenderness of this exchange is most touching, as is the desire of the Greatest Holy Leaf to show respect to the station of the Guardian.[12]

The close communion between Shoghi Effendi and his great-aunt, and the central role she played in his life are illustrated by a number of personal vignettes shared by Ruḥíyyih Khánum. She writes, "Nothing could be more revealing of this intense love he had for her than the fact that on the day we were married it was to her room, where everything was preserved as it was in her days, standing beside her bed, that the Guardian went to have the simple Bahá'í marriage ceremony of hand in hand performed. . . ." Indeed, Ruḥíyyih Khánum confides that, "The day he told me that he had chosen me to be his wife he placed on my finger the simple gold ring engraved with the symbol of the Greatest Name which the Greatest Holy Leaf had given him years before as his Bahá'í ring."[13]

She further illustrates the deep bond that linked the Guardian and the Greatest Holy Leaf, recounting, after Bahíyyih Khánum's passing, "The armchair he had always sat in in her room he moved to the place where he often sat for a respite in his work and continued to use it until the end of his life; his bedroom was filled with photographs of her, at different stages of her life, and more than one picture showing her monument."[14]

The passing of the Greatest Holy Leaf deprived the Guardian of his closest companion and was thus the cause of intense grief to him. The extent of his personal loss is apparent in the following passage from a letter written on his behalf:

> It cannot be imagined to what a degree this terrible and calamitous event has saddened him, and, more than words can tell, clouded the radiance of his heart. For that holy being, that resplendent person, with all her heart and soul and endless love, had ever fostered and cherished him in the warm embrace of her celestial tenderness. She was his single, dear companion, she was his one and only consolation in the world, and that is why he is so burdened down with the passing of her high and stately presence, and why the departure of that comely spirit is so hard for him to bear.[15]

Shoghi Effendi's Collaborator

Throughout his ministry as Guardian Shoghi Effendi associated the Greatest Holy Leaf with many of the major undertakings he initiated for the development of the Bahá'í Faith. In the early years of his ministry, Shoghi Effendi included references to his great-aunt in cables and communications he sent. He referred, for example, to "the Greatest Holy Leaf and I," thereby illustrating the close connection that existed between them. Likewise, in a postscript in his own handwriting appended to a letter written on his behalf to Henry and Clara Hyde Dunn—the Bahá'ís who introduced the Bahá'í Faith to Australia during the lifetime of 'Abdu'l-Bahá—Shoghi Effendi wrote, "Your achievements the rising Bahá'í generation will extol and magnify. You occupy most certainly an abiding place in the Greatest Holy Leaf's heart and my own, & we shall both continue to supplicate for you & your dear co-workers the Master's imperishable blessings."[16]

In addition to references to his great-aunt in his correspondence, Shoghi Effendi chose to ally Bahíyyih Khánum with his endeavors to foster the ongoing development of the Faith and with a number of its major undertakings, including the frustrated visit of Queen Marie of Romania and her daughter to the Bahá'í holy places, and the construction of the House of Worship in Wilmette, Illinois.

The Ongoing Work of the Faith

The Guardian engaged Bahíyyih Khánum as his collaborator in the ongoing work of the Faith. In a letter dated 24 November 1924 addressed to the American National Spiritual Assembly, Shoghi Effendi called attention to the turbulent state of society and the vital role of the Bahá'ís in ameliorating the situation by sharing the healing message of Bahá'u'lláh and demonstrating the efficacy of His teachings in their daily lives. The Guardian issued the following plea on behalf of the Greatest Holy Leaf and himself:

> I entreat you, dear friends, to continue, nay, to redouble your efforts, to keep your vision clear, your hopes undimmed, your determination unshaken, so that the power of God within us may fill the world with all its glory.

In this fervent plea joins me the Greatest Holy Leaf. Though chagrined in the evening of her life at the sorrowful tales of repression in Persia, she still turns with the deepest longings of her heart to your land where freedom reigns, eager and expectant to behold, ere she is called away, the signs of the universal triumph of the Cause she loves so dearly. [17]

It is evident, therefore, that Bahíyyih Khánum closely followed the activities of the worldwide Bahá'í community. She was conscious of its needs and of the unique opportunities for development that existed in different countries, and she was acutely aware of the challenges it faced in the land of its birth.

A further example of the combined efforts of the Guardian and the Greatest Holy Leaf to foster the advancement of the Faith and its teachings is illustrated by their encouragement to the Bahá'ís of India to participate in the All-Asian Women's Conference in 1931. Shoghi Effendi addressed a cable to the conference through the secretary of the National Spiritual Assembly of India. So keen was the Greatest Holy Leaf's and his interest in this important event that he wrote to the Indian National Assembly inquiring whether "the message sent on behalf of the Greatest Holy Leaf and myself" had arrived in time to be conveyed to the participants at the conference. On hearing that the cable had been presented, he expressed the hope that the Bahá'ís attending the conference "will take an active share in its proceedings and will thereby be putting to active effect the teachings of Bahá'u'lláh." He calls attention to the fact that "Various and innumerable contacts will naturally be made and the effort should be to take advantage of this unique opportunity." [18]

Queen Marie of Romania

Bahíyyih Khánum shared Shoghi Effendi's appreciation of the services rendered to the Cause of Bahá'u'lláh by Miss Martha Root, its "star servant" and outstanding teacher. Writing in *God Passes By*, his

written history of the Bahá'í Faith, the Guardian refers to the introduction of the Bahá'í Faith to Queen Marie in 1926 and her subsequent identification with its teachings as "the most superb and by far
the most momentous" of all of Martha Root's remarkable services.[19]

Queen Marie, the grand-daughter of two monarchs who received
tablets from Bahá'u'lláh—namely, Queen Victoria and Czar Alex-
ander II—was, according to Shoghi Effendi, "an accomplished au-
thoress; possessed of a charming and radiant personality; highly
talented, clear-visioned, daring and ardent by nature; keenly devoted to all enterprises of a humanitarian character, she, alone among
her sister-queens, alone among all those of royal birth or station,
was moved to spontaneously acclaim the greatness of the Message
of Bahá'u'lláh, to proclaim His Fatherhood, as well as the Prophet-
hood of Muḥammad, to commend the Bahá'í teachings to all men
and women, and to extol their potency, sublimity and beauty."
Shoghi Effendi describes Queen Marie's unique contributions to
the Bahá'í Faith in the following terms:

> Through the fearless acknowledgment of her belief to her own
> kith and kin, and particularly to her youngest daughter; through
> three successive encomiums that constitute her greatest and abid-
> ing legacy to posterity; through three additional appreciations
> penned by her as her contribution to Bahá'í publications; through
> several letters written to friends and associates, as well as those
> addressed to her guide and spiritual mother; through various
> tokens expressive of faith and gratitude for the glad-tidings that
> had been brought to her through the orders for Bahá'í books
> placed by her and her youngest daughter; and lastly through her
> frustrated pilgrimage to the Holy Land for the express purpose
> of paying homage at the graves of the Founders of the Faith—
> through such acts as these this illustrious queen may well deserve
> to rank as the first of those royal supporters of the Cause of God
> who are to arise in the future, and each of whom, in the words of

Bahá'u'lláh Himself, is to be acclaimed as "the very eye of mankind, the luminous ornament on the brow of creation, the fountainhead of blessings unto the whole world."[20]

The many services Queen Marie rendered to the Bahá'í Cause and the story of Martha Root's remarkable relationship with the queen have both been described elsewhere.* The account here will focus on Queen Marie's "frustrated pilgrimage to the Holy Land" because of its impact on the Greatest Holy Leaf.[21]

It was the intention of the queen and her daughter Princess Ileana to visit the Bahá'í holy places in the course of their travels in the Near East. In anticipation of receiving the royal guests, preparations were made in Haifa to ensure the success of this historic visit. 'Abdu'l-Bahá's home was made ready, and the Guardian arranged for Bahá'u'lláh's tablet to Queen Marie's grandmother, Queen Victoria, to be copied in fine Persian calligraphy and illuminated in Iran. This was to be a gift to the queen.

In March 1930 Shoghi Effendi forwarded to the queen a formal invitation to visit the World Center of the Faith. The invitation reads:

HER MAJESTY, THE DOWAGER QUEEN MARIE OF ROMANIA, ABOARD MAYFLOWER, ASWAN

FAMILY OF 'ABDU'L-BAHÁ JOIN ME IN RENEWING THE EXPRESSION OF OUR LOVING AND HEARTFELT INVITATION TO YOUR GRACIOUS MAJESTY AND HER ROYAL HIGHNESS PRINCESS ILEANA TO VISIT HIS HOME IN HAIFA. YOUR MAJESTY'S ACCEPTANCE TO VISIT BAHÁ'U'LLÁH'S SHRINE AND PRISON-CITY OF 'AKKÁ WILL APART FROM ITS HISTORIC SIGNIFI-

---

* See *Martha Root, Herald of the Kingdom: A Compilation*, comp. Kay Zinky, ed. A. Baram (New Delhi: Bahá'í Publishing Trust, 1983); see also M. R. Garis, *Martha Root: Lioness at the Threshold* (Wilmette, IL: Bahá'í Publishing Trust, 1983); and Della L. Marcus, *Her Eternal Crown: Queen Marie of Romania and the Bahá'í Faith* (Oxford: George Ronald, 2000).

CANCE BE A SOURCE OF IMMEASURABLE STRENGTH, JOY AND HOPE TO THE SILENT SUFFERERS OF THE FAITH THROUGHOUT THE EAST. OUR FONDEST LOVE, PRAYERS AND BEST WISHES FOR YOUR MAJESTY'S HAPPINESS AND WELFARE.[22]

When he received no reply, Shoghi Effendi sent another cable. An answer finally came, signed by the Romanian minister in Cairo, stating, "HER MAJESTY REGRETS THAT NOT PASSING THROUGH PALESTINE SHE WILL NOT BE ABLE TO VISIT YOU."[23]

The cancellation of the visit of Queen Marie and her daughter to the Bahá'í holy places was a source of deep disappointment not only to the queen herself but to the holy family as well. Shoghi Effendi himself testifies to "the keen disappointment of the aged Greatest Holy Leaf who had eagerly expected" the queen's arrival. Rúḥíyyih Khánum provides the following poignant details of what transpired:

> I remember Shoghi Effendi a number of times describing to me how the Greatest Holy Leaf had waited, hour after hour, in the Master's home to receive the Queen and her daughter—for Her Majesty had actually sailed for Haifa, and this news encouraged Shoghi Effendi to believe she was going to carry out the pilgrimage she had planned; time passed and no news came, even after the boat had docked. Later the Guardian learned that the Queen and her party had been met at the boat, informed her visit was impolitic and not permissible, been put in a car and whisked out of Palestine to another Middle Eastern country.[24]

Construction of the House of Worship in Wilmette

The Greatest Holy Leaf maintained a lively interest in the progress of the Bahá'í community in the West, from the days of the Master until the very end of her life. Shoghi Effendi attests that "Her earthly life, as it drew to a close, was much brightened by the brilliant accomplishments of her devoted lovers in the American continent." He, further, calls attention to "the predominating share" the American Bahá'ís assumed "in alleviating the burden which that most exalted Leaf bore so heroically in the evening of her life."[25]

Bahíyyih Khánum was particularly interested in the progress of the construction of the Bahá'í House of Worship in Wilmette, Illinois, that "unique edifice," which is characterized by Shoghi Effendi as "the first fruit of a slowly maturing Administrative Order, the noblest structure reared in the first Bahá'í century, and the symbol and precursor of a future world civilization."[26]

This historic undertaking, "the crowning achievement of the Administrative Order of the Faith of Bahá'u'lláh in the first Bahá'í century," was initiated during 'Abdu'l-Bahá's lifetime. He himself laid its foundation stone in 1912. The concluding stages of its construction are associated with the memory of the Greatest Holy Leaf, the Purest Branch, and their mother. The story of the construction of the House of Worship has been told elsewhere.* Needless to say, the small, embryonic Bahá'í community encountered great challenges in undertaking such a large and complex construction project. They struggled to raise the funds, acquire the land, and make the necessary arrangements for the work to begin. The contracts for the construction of the basement were awarded in 1920 and 1921. Even after the project began, the progress tended to be intermittent, since there were long periods of time when the work was held in abeyance pending the raising of sufficient funds to embark on the next phase of the construction.[27]

In 1928 the American National Spiritual Assembly allocated funds for the improvement of the interior of the basement, known as

---

* See Bruce W. Whitmore, *The Dawning Place: The Building of a Temple, the Forging of the North American Bahá'í Community* (Wilmette, IL: Bahá'í Publishing Trust, 1984).

Foundation Hall, and decided to use this as a venue, for the first time, for the Bahá'í National Convention in that same year. The event was a thrilling experience for the delegates and other attendees, who were excited to be meeting in the basement of the future temple. The occasion also provided a tangible reminder of the ongoing interest the Greatest Holy Leaf had in the progress of this remarkable building. The following report describes the scene at the opening of the convention:

> After several tablets and prayers of Bahá'u'lláh were read and chanted, Corinne True [the Bahá'í assigned by 'Abdu'l-Bahá to ensure that the Temple was constructed] stepped forward. During Mrs. True's pilgrimage in 1928 'Abdu'l-Bahá's sister, Bahíyyih Khánum, had given her a large package of tea and a bottle of attar of rose to be used at the inauguration ceremony. Mrs. True conveyed the love of Bahíyyih Khánum to the assembled Bahá'ís and then personally served each a cup of the special tea. Parvene Baghdadi, the young daughter of Dr. Zia Baghdadi, anointed each delegate with the attar of rose, the rare fragrance of which soon filled the huge room.[28]

In 1929 Shoghi Effendi presented a rare and valuable Persian carpet to the American National Spiritual Assembly. The carpet was to be sold and the funds used to further the next stage of the Temple's construction. In the letter announcing his gift, the Guardian stressed the significance of the completion of this enterprise for the prestige of the Faith, and he called attention to some of the challenges that lay ahead. He describes the acceleration of the work on the House of Worship as Bahíyyih Khánum's "fondest desire" and the importance she accorded this project. He refers to "the hopes and fears of the Greatest Holy Leaf, now in the evening of her life, with deepening shadows caused by failing eye-sight and declining strength swiftly gathering about her," and to the fact that she was "yearning to hear as the one remaining solace in her swiftly ebbing life the news of the resumption of work on an Edifice, the glories of which she has, from the lips of 'Abdu'l-Bahá, Himself, learned to admire." 29

When the superstructure of the Temple was complete in 1931, the delegates assembled in the auditorium for the convention. During the course of the convention the following cable was received from Shoghi Effendi:

"THE GREATEST HOLY LEAF JOINS ME IN REQUESTING DELEGATES AS-SEMBLED UNDER MASHRIQU'L-ADHKÁR'S SACRED DOME CONVEY ALL AMERICAN BELIEVERS EXPRESSION OUR HEARTFELT CONGRATULATIONS, BOUNDLESS JOY, PROFOUND GRATITUDE PRACTICAL COMPLETION SU-PERSTRUCTURE GLORIOUS EDIFICE. FERVENTLY APPEAL ALL ASSOCIATED THIS HOLY ENTERPRISE, CONSUMMATE THEIR ACHIEVEMENT BY UP-HOLDING WHATEVER MANNER NATIONAL REPRESENTATIVES MAY DEEM NECESSARY FOR PROVISION EXTERIOR ORNAMENTATION. INESTIMABLE BLESSING SHALL CROWN AMERICA'S SUSTAINED, SELF-SACRIFICING EN-DEAVOR." 30

Conscious that these were the waning years of Bahíyyih Khánum's life, Shoghi Effendi urged the American believers to press forward with the completion of the dome of the Temple. "My voice," he writes,

is once more reinforced by the passionate, and perhaps, the last, entreaty, of the Greatest Holy Leaf, whose spirit, now hovering on the edge of the Great Beyond, longs to carry on its flight to the Abhá Kingdom, and into the presence of a Divine, an al-mighty Father, an assurance of the joyous consummation of an enterprise, the progress of which has so greatly brightened the closing days of her earthly life. That the American believers, those stout-hearted pioneers of the Faith of Bahá'u'lláh, will unanimously respond, with that same spontaneous generosity, that same measure of self-sacrifice, as have characterized their response to her appeals in the past, no one who is familiar with the vitality of their faith can possibly question. [31]

Likewise, when the National Assembly took the decision to begin work immediately on the external decoration of the Temple, the Guardian cabled on 10 June 1932: "ASSEMBLY'S MOMENTOUS DECISION FRAUGHT WITH INCALCULABLE CONSEQUENCES, WORLD-WIDE BENEFITS. GREATEST HOLY LEAF FILLED WITH DELIGHT. BOTH DEVOUTLY PRAYING [FOR] UNRELAXING DETERMINATION [TO] CONSUMMATE HEROIC ENTERPRISE. ABIDING GRATITUDE." [32]

It is evident that the Greatest Holy Leaf shared the Guardian's great concern for the progress of the erection of the Temple and his delight at the efforts of the believers to move the project forward. In this regard, it is interesting to read the following extract from a letter written on behalf of the Guardian soon after the passing of his great-aunt. Reference is made to an incident that occurred at the Bahá'í National Convention in 1932 and her reaction to it. Those in attendance at this convention responded in an impressive manner to a fund associated with the name of the Greatest Holy Leaf that had been initiated in order to complete the exterior ornamentation of the House of Worship. One of the Bahá'ís, Mrs. Parsons, spontaneously removed a valuable pearl necklace from her neck as a contribution toward meeting the fund's goal. The letter states, "The expressions of zealous enthusiasm and hope, of genuine self-abnegation and love that the American believers and especially our precious sister Mrs. Agnes Parsons demonstrated in their last Convention meeting have greatly brightened the closing days of her life. Shoghi Effendi trusts that her memory will increasingly serve to cheer and hearten the friends in their ever-widening activities."[33]

The following testimonial to the importance accorded by Bahíyyih Khánum to the completion of the House of Worship in Wilmette was addressed to the American National Spiritual Assembly soon after her passing. The Guardian writes of his beloved collaborator:

> The passing of the Greatest Holy Leaf has filled my heart with unutterable sorrow. My comfort is the thought that the measure of success achieved, under your wise and able leadership, by the collective efforts of the American believers has brightened considerably the last days of her precious life. Would to God that the continued endeavours of this little band of her devoted lovers who have brought so great a joy to her blessed heart, may bring further satisfaction to her soul, and realize, at the appointed time, her dearest wish and fondest hopes for the Cause in your land. To complete the Temple, to clothe its naked dome, and terminate its exterior elaborate ornamentation, is the best and most effective way in which the American believers, the recipients of her untold favours, can demonstrate their fidelity to her memory and their gratitude for the inestimable blessings she showered upon them.[34]

The Evening of Her Life

In addition to being involved with important initiatives spearheaded by Shoghi Effendi, examples of which have already been mentioned, the Greatest Holy Leaf continued to serve the Bahá'í community until the very end of her life. Despite failing eyesight and declining health, which, at times, confined her to bed, Bahíyyih <u>Kh</u>ánum wrote letters of encouragement to Bahá'ís, and she played an active role with the Bahá'í pilgrims until her passing in 1932.

Her Letters

Though the volume of Bahíyyih <u>Kh</u>ánum's letters to the Bahá'ís and their institutions decreased towards the end of her life, they clearly illustrate her keen understanding of the state of the Bahá'í communities around the world and of the efficacy of Bahá'u'lláh's teachings for the solution of the world's problems. In one such letter she writes, "It always cheers my heart to hear from the dear friends whose hearts are so full of love and devotion, and desire to serve this Blessed Cause which has been proclaimed by Bahá'u'lláh to all the world, so that all national, racial, and religious prejudices will be abolished, and the world of humanity recognized as one home, and all men as brothers." She goes on to assure the recipient of her prayers, so that the individual's service to the Cause will be blessed. She offers the following encouragement: "One soul who becomes entirely selfless and devoted and filled to overflowing with the spirit of love and service will do much for the progress of the Cause in whatever locality he is. Be assured, if you arise to serve, the Beloved Master says *Nothing shall be impossible to you if you have faith. As ye have faith so shall your powers and blessings be.*" She concludes, "I convey to you the warm love and Bahá'í greetings of Shoghi Effendi, and all the family, and again assure you of our earnest prayers that you will be enabled to render much service to the Kingdom."[35]

A further example of the Greatest Holy Leaf's encouragement to the Bahá'ís is contained in an extract from a letter written in 1929, in which she expresses pleasure at meeting or hearing from the "dear friends in America." She explains that her pleasure derives from the fact that "the Beloved Master spoke so much to us about His visit to your land, and we feel confident that the teachings of the Blessed Perfection which He heralded forth have not fallen on barren soil and the day is not far distant when a rich harvest will be garnered therefrom." [36]

A letter written in 1929 to the Local Spiritual Assembly of Tehran illustrates the Greatest Holy Leaf's continuing commitment to the nurturance of Spiritual Assemblies. She rejoices in "the brilliant achievements won and the distinguished services rendered" by the members of the Assembly and assures them that her heart is, therefore, "filled with utmost joy and assurance." She then responds to a request from the Spiritual Assembly for information about the Houses of Bahá'u'lláh in Tehran, stating, "You have asked me about my own knowledge and recollections concerning the holy Houses in Tehran. Unfortunately, due to my tender age at that time, those blessed places and quarters have faded from my memory." [37]

Involvement with the Pilgrims

Bahíyyih Khánum was actively involved with the Bahá'í pilgrims until the closing days of her life. Those who had the privilege of meeting her were profoundly moved by the experience. Shoghi Effendi in his letters provides some insight into the impact Bahíyyih Khánum had on the pilgrims. He states, for example, "What a source of inspiration she was to the pilgrims who came from the four corners of the world to seek spirituality and attain a new birth by visiting the Holy Shrines. They should surely remember those blessed moments they spent in her room or in her presence elsewhere, and remembering her suffering, take courage in confronting the problems of their life." He concludes, "May God help us all to follow her example and like her be a blessing to others." [38]

Commenting on the good fortune of those who had the opportunity to meet his great-aunt, the Guardian, in another letter writ-

ten on his behalf, writes, "She was always such a source of courage
and hope to those pilgrims that came from all parts of the world
and had the pleasure of meeting her, that they left her presence
with added hope and greater determination to serve the Cause and
sacrifice their all in its path. This was especially true of them after
the passing away of the Master when they felt that she was the only
worthy remnant of Bahá'u'lláh's immediate kin."[39]

It is interesting to examine the reports of pilgrims and others who
were fortunate to spend time with Bahíyyih Khánum during the last
years of her life. Such reports provide glimpses into the nature of her
activities and the qualities she manifested. They bespeak a fruitful
time, despite the accumulation of physical disabilities.

Keith Ransom-Kehler, an American Bahá'í who visited the Holy
Land in 1926, left the following description of her impressions of
her meeting with the Greatest Holy Leaf and the other female members of the household of 'Abdu'l-Bahá:

Bahíyyih Khánum, the sister of 'Abdu'l-Bahá, has, from the age
of five, lived through experiences and calamities the like of which
no Occidental woman could faintly imagine. Exquisite, fragrant,
imperturbable, assured, she walks among the fluctuating conditions of the world like a star through its appointed course in the
heavens. After one has been stirred by the presence of women
like the sister and the wife of 'Abdu'l-Bahá, our curious little
evidences of "firmness" are practically meaningless. That self-con-
gratulatory state of the Occidental when he has performed some
little service for his cause is unknown in Haifa. . . . Day and night
the daughters of 'Abdu'l-Bahá, without stint and without rest,
are building up through their deeds of continual kindness those
solid barricades against the forces of ignorance, prejudice and
malevolence; those outposts of service, love and peace that mark
the boundaries of another world. We see in these . . . women a

faith that never wavers, a gift that never varies, a love that never tires—celestial caryatides, it might be, bearing on their heads the structure of the new civilization.[40]

Dr. Gertrude Richardson Brigham, an American Bahá'í who made her pilgrimage to the Holy Land in 1927, recalls that the afternoon she spent with the ladies of the holy household was, for her, the "greatest experience." She describes being greeted by 'Abdu'l-Bahá's widow and her meeting with the Greatest Holy Leaf thus: "Bahíyyih Khánum, the distinguished sister of 'Abdu'l-Bahá, came also, and they were both very sweet to me, and seemed pleased at my coming now when there were no other visitors. Bahíyyih Khánum looks frail, but both were in their usual health they said, and keenly interested in everything going on among the Bahá'ís."[41]

The vitality of the Greatest Holy Leaf and her sister-in-law, though advanced in years, left an abiding impression on Dr. Brigham, who recalled that "they were anxious to hear of the American Bahá'ís, and asked about several friends whom I knew only by name. They said that the news of the progress of Bahá'í work is their greatest joy, and that it is for that they live."[42]

Concerned that she might be staying too long and perhaps tiring the ladies, Dr. Brigham more than once suggested going, but they insisted that her visit was only too short. She recounts that during the course of the afternoon they talked of many matters and the women encouraged her to study carefully the Bahá'í teachings and to become actively involved in service to the Bahá'í Faith. One final bounty awaited Dr. Brigham. Just before Dr. Brigham's departure, the Greatest Holy Leaf, the custodian of the holy relics, conducted her into an adjacent room to view the portraits of the Báb, Bahá'u'lláh, and 'Abdu'l-Bahá. This was a special privilege reserved for Bahá'í pilgrims and a unique opportunity since these images have, as a matter of policy, not been reproduced and circulated within the Bahá'í community.[43]

In her capacity as custodian of the sacred relics and of the portraits of the Báb and Bahá'u'lláh, the Greatest Holy Leaf performed an important service not only to the visiting pilgrims but also to the generations of Bahá'ís who will follow in the course of the Bahá'í Dispensation. It is evident that she understood the significance of these items for posterity. She took great care of them—indeed, the portraits were kept in her room—and she demonstrated an attitude of deep reverence for what they represented. In this regard, the account of a believer who, as a child, lived in the house of 'Abdu'l-Bahá, provides the following sweet picture: "How many times I have gone into that room in great reverence and knelt down, as we used to before the portraits of Bahá'u'lláh and the Báb, and watched while the Greatest Holy Leaf sat there reverently unveiling the portraits and then closing them up again after the viewing was over."[44]

Bahíyyih Khánum had a love of beauty and enjoyed hearing Persian chanting. In his reminiscences, Abu'l-Qásim Faizí, who was subsequently appointed to a high rank by the Guardian, describes how, during his student days at the American University in Beirut, he was privileged to spend vacations in Haifa. On one such occasion, a small group of students was invited to perform for the Greatest Holy Leaf. They were ushered into the presence of the Greatest Holy Leaf and Munírih Khánum, the widow of 'Abdu'l-Bahá, and several other women of the household. He writes, "'We students were given seats facing this beautiful audience. Khánum sat still, her lily-white hands resting gently on her lap. She was a queen who inspired love and reverence and at her throne of grandeur we offered our grateful hearts. Her glance was full of love but she did not speak to us. The Master's wife, Munírih Khánum, spoke on her behalf. She greeted us when we arrived and thanked us warmly in

<u>Kh</u>ánum's name at the end of our programme of prayers, songs and Bahá'í poems.'"[45]

On yet another occasion when the students were invited to sing for Bahíyyih <u>Kh</u>ánum, Mr. Faizí recounts, "'This time she said she would like to hear one of the songs that labourers sing in Irán as they go home in the evening on their way back from work. She asked if there was anyone among us who knew these songs. We were surprised that <u>Kh</u>ánum should still remember such songs which she must have heard on the streets of Ṭihrán during her early childhood. Perhaps the sight of a group of young Persians or the music of the tár (. . . a Persian stringed instrument) had taken her memories back to those days.'"[46]

In her closing days the Greatest Holy Leaf continued to provide an inspiring example to the pilgrims. Though frail and burdened with age, she demonstrated a way of being that encouraged and inspired the Bahá'ís. Marjorie Morton, an early American Bahá'í, provides the following pen picture of Bahíyyih <u>Kh</u>ánum at this time:

We of the West knew her only in the latter days of her life. But we could not find it in our hearts to wish that we had known her in her youth or earlier womanhood rather than in the time of her fulfilment. She had none of the habits of mind which we have come to associate with age. We see old age musing, looking over its shoulder; sighing over memories flattened between pages turned with the years—distinct, perhaps, and sharp in outline, but dried of the fullness and colour of living emotions. She had no need to turn back the leaves, to recapture any shreds of vanished hours. The essential filaments of the past were woven with the threads of the present into today's pattern. Her now embodied all her yesterdays.[47]

Keith Ransom-Kehler, a distinguished American Bahá'í who was the last among the Western pilgrims to meet Bahíyyih Khánum, provides our final glimpse of the Greatest Holy Leaf. Mrs. Ransom-Kehler spent time in the Holy Land prior to her departure for Iran, where she was to undertake a special mission on behalf of the Faith. Her visit to the Greatest Holy Leaf took place just a month before her death. The following is recorded in her diary:

> From the Greatest Holy Leaf streamed an effulgence of beauty and heavenly love that I have never witnessed from any human being. To come into her presence was to hush and exalt the soul. She was like a bird at dawn, the coming of spring, a city on a far horizon; everything that wakes our wonder and reveals the depths and not the tumults of the heart.
>
> On two occasions she removed my Bahá'í ring and after holding it for some time replaced it reversed. Twice she blew on the palm of my hand, a sweet, cool, delicious breath and then exultantly exclaimed: "It is all right now."
>
> Her mind was never quite clear except on the occasion of my parting.
>
> She would reach out her delicate hand and, pressing my cheek close against her own, would make some lover-like exclamation. I was dissolved by her sweetness.
>
> For the most part she would chant in a low delicious voice some glorious Tablet or poem, smoothing my hand or holding me under the chin as she sang. [48]

Mrs. Ransom-Kehler explains that on the eve of her departure she was invited to take tea with the ladies of the household. Her diary records,

<u>Kh</u>ánum was very feeble, her visit to the Shrine of Bahá'u'lláh on the ascension night had been very hard for her. Every Sunday she insisted on going to the meeting on Mt Carmel: she had to be lifted in and out of the car. . . .

Her thoughtfulness, her loving kindness, her self-mastery, her complete dedication to the things of the spirit never ceased to the last hour that I saw her, just a month and a day before her ascension.

As I was making my farewells Ḍíyá [her niece] assisted her to her feet in spite of my protests. She folded me oh, so tenderly in her precious arms and said: "When you are come to Persia, I want you to give my love to every Bahá'í in all that land, to the men the same as to the women. And when you reach the holy city of Ṭihrán enter it in my name, and teach there in my name."[49]

From the foregoing discussion, it is evident that one of the major features of the closing years of the Greatest Holy Leaf's life was the deep bond uniting her with the Guardian. The close companionship they enjoyed was not only on a personal level. They shared a vision of the future unfoldment of the Bahá'í Faith and a mutual concern for its development and for the successful completion of timely programs and projects. Though her physical faculties were somewhat diminished, in her old age, as in the earlier phases of her life, the progress of the Bahá'í Faith was the dominating focus of Bahíyyih <u>Kh</u>ánum's existence. Service to the Cause of her beloved father was the joy of her being and the desire of her heart. Through her encouragement and her example, she succeeded in motivating the Bahá'ís to participate in the great arena of service.

The Hill of God Is Stirred

In the final phase of her life, Bahíyyih Khánum was increasingly burdened by the "discomforts, trials and illnesses" so often associated with advanced age. Shoghi Effendi attests that, despite being "weak and most of the time confined to her room," she was nevertheless "a source of constant joy and inspiration to those that met her." Indeed, he affirms that "All the sufferings that she had endured during her life and that had left their traces upon her feeble form, had not in the least affected her spirit of joy and hopefulness. She liked to see the people happy, and exerted all her efforts to make it easy for them to realize it." Marjorie Morton, an American Bahá'í, provides the following pen portrait of the Greatest Holy Leaf at the very end of her life. Mrs. Morton writes, "And when she came to die her failing faculties threw into sharper and intenser relief the nature of her heart and spirit. It was as if she first let slip away the mechanical devices of the mind and the transient sense perceptions while holding fast to the end the essential elements of her being, unclouded by extremity of bodily weakness and pain. Still her smile spoke strength, serenity, tenderness and the love that is both recognition and bestowal. And so she left for remembrance a last clear record of the pattern of her life."[1]

In this chapter we will examine the passing of the Greatest Holy Leaf, its immediate impact on the Bahá'í community, and the connection of her resting-place with the rise of the institutions of the Bahá'í Faith at its World Center.

The Passing of the Greatest Holy Leaf

Bahíyyih Khánum passed away in Haifa "at one hour after midnight, on the eve of Friday, July 15," 1932. She was in the eighty-sixth year of her life. In spite of her advanced age and the delicate state of her health, the Guardian paradoxically described her death as being "tragic in its suddenness." Characterizing the reaction of the Bahá'ís to the news of her ascension, he states, "Inevitable though this calamitous event appeared to us all, however acute our apprehensions of its steady approach, the consciousness of its final consummation at this terrible hour leaves us . . . prostrated and disconsolate."[2]

The news of Bahíyyih Khánum's death reached Shoghi Effendi when he was in Switzerland. He clearly lamented his absence. In a letter written at the time of her passing, he expresses his feelings of deprivation and regret. "Alas," he writes, "that I was prevented from being with her at the close of her earthly days, at that moment when she ascended to her Lord, her Master, and when her delicate body was placed in the tomb. Not mine that honour, that high privilege, for I was far away, deprived, bereft, excluded."[3]

On receiving news of Bahíyyih Khánum's ascension, Shoghi Effendi immediately informed the Bahá'ís in the East and the West. His cable of 15 July 1932 to the American National Spiritual Assembly describes the historical significance of her death and his personal reaction to it, specifies the location of her tomb on Mount Carmel, and calls for the initiation of a nine-month period of mourning. The cable reads,

GREATEST HOLY LEAF'S IMMORTAL SPIRIT WINGED ITS FLIGHT GREAT BEYOND. COUNTLESS LOVERS HER SAINTLY LIFE IN EAST AND WEST SEIZED WITH PANGS OF ANGUISH, PLUNGED IN UNUTTERABLE SORROW. HUMANITY SHALL ERE LONG RECOGNIZE ITS IRREPARABLE LOSS. OUR BELOVED FAITH, WELL-NIGH CRUSHED BY DEVASTATING BLOW OF 'ABDU'L-BAHÁ'S UNEXPECTED ASCENSION, NOW LAMENTS PASSING LAST REMNANT OF BAHÁ'U'LLÁH, ITS MOST EXALTED MEMBER. HOLY FAMILY CRUELLY DIVESTED ITS MOST PRECIOUS, MOST GREAT ADORNING. I,

FOR MY PART, BEWAIL SUDDEN REMOVAL MY SOLE EARTHLY SUSTAINER THE JOY AND SOLACE OF MY LIFE. HER SACRED REMAINS WILL REPOSE VICINITY HOLY SHRINES. SO GRIEVOUS A BEREAVEMENT NECESSITATES SUSPENSION FOR NINE MONTHS THROUGHOUT BAHÁ'Í WORLD EVERY MANNER RELIGIOUS FESTIVITY.[4]

In addition, the Guardian called upon the National Assembly to take a number of specific actions in relation to the Bahá'í community: "INFORM LOCAL ASSEMBLIES AND GROUPS HOLD BEFITTING MANNER MEMORIAL GATHERINGS, EXTOL A LIFE SO LADEN SACRED EXPERIENCES, SO RICH IMPERISHABLE MEMORIES. ADVISE HOLDING ADDITIONAL COMMEMORATION SERVICE OF STRICTLY DEVOTIONAL CHARACTER AUDITORIUM MA<u>SH</u>RIQU'L-A<u>DH</u>KÁR."[5]

Two days later on 17 July 1932, Shoghi Effendi penned a deeply touching tribute to his beloved great-aunt. This letter provides an intimate glimpse into the thoughts and feelings that were surging in his sorrowing heart. In it he eulogizes the life, station, and deeds of the Greatest Holy Leaf, and he highlights her unique contributions to the Faith. The letter, which was penned in the Guardian's own handwriting, was subsequently printed in a facsimile edition and distributed to the Bahá'ís in the West. It is also published in a book of selected letters of the Guardian entitled *Bahá'í Administration: Selected Messages 1922–1932.*[6]

The passing of Bahíyyih <u>Kh</u>ánum, "the last survivor of a glorious and heroic age," brings to a final close "the first and most moving chapter of Bahá'í history, marking the conclusion of the Primitive, the Apostolic Age of the Faith of Bahá'u'lláh." She was the living link between the Bahá'ís and the great historic period that incorporated the ministries of the three Central Figures of the Faith. A life that spanned all but two years of the entire Heroic Age of the Bahá'í Faith had come to an end. In one of his letters the Guardian testifies to the length of her services to the Faith, observing, "For more than eighty years this Exalted Leaf bore with a fortitude that bewildered every one who had the privilege of knowing her, sufferings and tribulations that few of our present-day believers did experience. And yet, what a joy and what a saintlike attitude she manifested all through her life. Her angelic face was so calm, so serene in the very midst of sufferings and pains. Not that she lacked tenderness of heart and sympathy. But she could overcome her feelings and this because she had put all her trust in God."[7]

The Funeral

Though he was not present at the funeral of his great-aunt, Shoghi Effendi selected the site where she was to be buried. He specified that her sacred remains were to repose on Mount Carmel in the vicinity of the holy shrines of the Báb and 'Abdu'l-Bahá.[8]

'Alí Nakhjavání, a Bahá'í who until early adulthood (and subsequently later in life) resided in Haifa, provides the following account of the events that transpired in the town at the time of Bahíyyih Khánum's funeral:

> When the Greatest Holy Leaf passed away in her eighty-sixth year, on 15 July 1932, an announcement was printed in Haifa and distributed to everyone concerned, Bahá'ís and others in Haifa, 'Akká and Jerusalem. At the top is set out stanza 33 of the *Hidden Words* of Bahá'u'lláh, from the Arabic: "O Son of Spirit! With the joyful tidings of light I hail thee; rejoice! To the court of holiness I summon thee; abide therein that thou mayest live in peace for evermore. Bahá'u'lláh."
>
> Then it states: "The family of the late Sir 'Abdu'l-Bahá 'Abbas

announces with profound sorrow the death of Bahíyyih <u>Kh</u>ánum, sister of the late Sir 'Abdu'l-Bahá 'Abbas, who passed away peacefully at 1 a.m. on the morning of July 15. The funeral procession from her home in the Persian Colony is at 4:30 p.m. Saturday, July 15th."

The passing of the Greatest Holy Leaf was the most significant event in Haifa since the passing of 'Abdu'l-Bahá. Many people gathered for the funeral; indeed, there were a hundred cars following the procession. . . . Apart from many dignitaries, the Mayor of Haifa was present and the representative of the northern district. There were people present not only from Haifa, but 'Akká, Abú-Sinán, Nablus, Jaffa and Jerusalem, and of course the Bahá'ís were present. The prayer for the dead was read in the Master's house in the main hall. Some of the friends served as pallbearers. The coffin was raised shoulder high on the shoulders of the friends and carried from the Master's house up to the Shrine. The coffin was brought in not through the main gate but through the small gate next to the school, almost immediately above the cluster of cypress trees where Bahá'u'lláh sat, and then down the path to the Shrine.[9]

Na<u>kh</u>javání goes on to say that, as he recalls, the coffin was not taken into the shrine but was placed outside, and prayers were read. He continues, "Then her coffin was raised again and carried along the same route to her resting-place. The site was chosen by Shoghi Effendi and he himself had instructed his father in Haifa exactly where the site should be and how the burial should take place. Shoghi Effendi also instructed the Bahá'ís to visit her resting-place every day for nine days. Every afternoon for nine days we gathered at her resting-place for prayers."[10]

Na<u>kh</u>javání also provides the following information about the impact of the passing of Bahíyyih <u>Kh</u>ánum on the local citizens. He recalls,

There were among the local Arabs those who had written eulogies (*Marthíyyih*) about the Greatest Holy Leaf and they wanted to read them. There was no time on the day of the funeral so this was set aside because evening came on and everybody had to go home. Very soon requests were made for a meeting in the Master's house for these poets and various officials to come and, as is the custom, offer condolences to the family, recite poems written in honour of the Greatest Holy Leaf and speak words of praise in her memory. This was immediately reported to Shoghi Effendi who said no. Instead, he said that on the fortieth day after her passing a luncheon should be held for the poor and all else who might come.[11]

The historic memorial luncheon was held on 25 August 1932. It took place in the garden of 'Abdu'l-Bahá's house in Haifa. Nakhjaváni captures the activity and excitement of the occasion: "Some of us were cooking, others were cleaning, others were laying tables and others were serving. Your humble servant was among those who were serving. A long table was laid seating 100 people. We had ten or eleven turnovers; over 1,000 people came. This is how it went on until 3 or 4 o'clock in the afternoon. A tent had been erected in the garden where those who were waiting to be seated could shelter from the hot summer sun." In addition to this gathering, Nakhjaváni reports that "Shoghi Effendi also gave the sum of £100—a considerable amount in those days—to the municipality of Haifa asking that it be distributed to the needy in the name of the Greatest Holy Leaf. An announcement was made in the papers and the municipality set up a special committee to screen applications for assistance and distribute the money to those genuinely in need."[12]

Though Shoghi Effendi was deprived of the privilege of attending the funeral of the Greatest Holy Leaf, his widow, Ruḥíyyih Khánum, states that immediately upon hearing the news, "his first act was to plan for her grave a suitable memorial which he hastened to Italy to order." Describing this monument, she writes, "No one could possibly call this exquisitely proportioned monument, built of shining white Carrara marble, anything but what it appears—a love temple, the embodiment of Shoghi Effendi's love."[13]

Nine-Month Period of Mourning

In his cables announcing the passing of Bahíyyih Khánum, Shoghi Effendi called for the suspension of "every manner [of] religious festivity" for a period of nine months, from 15 July 1932 until 15 April 1933. The significance of this period is further clarified in a letter dated 15 July 1932 to the Bahá'ís of the East, in which the Guardian writes,

> O faithful friends! It is right and fitting that out of honour to her most high station, in the gatherings of the followers of Bahá'u'lláh, whether of the East or the West, all Bahá'í festivals and celebrations should be completely suspended for a period of nine months, and that in every city and village, memorial meetings should be held, with all solemnity, spirituality, lowliness and consecration—where, in the choicest of language, may be described at length the shining attributes of that most resplendent Leaf, that archetype of the people of Bahá. If it be possible for the individual believers to postpone their personal celebrations for a period of one year, let them unhesitatingly do so thus to express their sorrow at this agonizing misfortune.[14]

In subsequent letters written on his behalf, Shoghi Effendi provided additional information to assist the believers to understand his intention concerning the suspension of certain types of activities. We read, for example, "Concerning the suspension of festivities for a period of nine months it should be made clear that what is meant by this is that all gatherings, whether outdoor or indoor, which are not of a strictly devotional character should be abolished all through the period of our mourning. However, meetings and services that are wholly spiritual as well as those that are necessary for the carrying on of the administration should continue to be held as usual." In another letter, the Guardian's secretary writes, "The Nineteen Day Feast being of a quasi-administrative character should continue to be held, but should be conducted with the utmost simplicity and should be devoid of any features associated with feasts and entertainment. The celebration of Naw-Rúz, the anniversary of the birth of Bahá'u'lláh and of the Báb should be altogether cancelled as a token of our deep mourning for so distinguished and precious a member of Bahá'u'lláh's family." One final example serves to emphasize not only the purpose of the period but the manner in which the Bahá'ís were to use their time: "These nine months during which the Guardian has asked the friends to discard feast days, are meant to be months of mourning for the passing away of the Greatest Holy Leaf. The friends should also use it as a period of redoubled energy in serving the Cause in expression of our deep love for her as well as for the Cause she so much suffered for."[15]

Circulation of Tablets

To help the Bahá'ís gain a deeper appreciation for the Greatest Holy Leaf and her unique station as "the outstanding heroine of the Bahá'í Dispensation," Shoghi Effendi forwarded to the believers in the East and the West, through their institutions, copies of tablets revealed by Bahá'u'lláh and 'Abdu'l-Bahá in her honor. "These passages," the Guardian attests, "disclose, to the extent that our finite minds can comprehend, the nature of that mystic bond which, on the one hand, united her with the Spirit of her almighty Father, and on the other, linked her so closely with her glorious Brother, the perfect Exemplar of that Spirit." He further states that her memory "will long live enshrined in these immortal words—a memory the ennobling influence of which will remain an inspiration and a solace amid the wreckage of a sadly shaken world."[16]

It was Shoghi Effendi's intention that these writings concerning the Greatest Holy Leaf would be used in the gatherings held in her memory. Writing to the Persian Central Assembly, the Guardian states that these verses "should be repeatedly recited, most movingly with devotion and lowliness, and great attention and care, so as to perpetuate her blessed memory, and extol her station, and out of love also for her incomparable beauty."[17]

Response of the Bahá'ís to the Mourning Period

Fragmentary details concerning the response of the Bahá'í community throughout the world to the passing of the Greatest Holy Leaf can be gleaned from the survey of current Bahá'í activities contained in *The Bahá'í World,** volume 5, and other published sources.

In *The Bahá'í World* it is reported that the worldwide Bahá'í community responded with profound grief to Bahíyyih Khánum's passing. The embryonic National Spiritual Assemblies communicated the news to the members of their local communities, and the National Assemblies themselves exchanged messages of condolence with each other. Spiritual Assemblies held special memorial gatherings, and for nine months, Bahá'ís throughout the world suspended

---

* A Bahá'í periodical, published from 1925 to the present day, that surveys news of the current developments of the Bahá'í Faith.

all religious festivities. United in grief and inspired by the example of the Greatest Holy Leaf's life, the members of the Bahá'í Faith arose to new heights of service to the Cause.[18]

As the most experienced administrative bodies, the National Spiritual Assembly of the United States and Canada and the National Spiritual Assembly of Persia were given special responsibilities during this period. For example, the American National Assembly arranged for the facsimile reproduction of Shoghi Effendi's moving, handwritten tribute to his great-aunt, a service for which he expressed his deep gratitude. Shoghi Effendi also requested the Assembly to take "whatever measures are required" for the "prompt and wide circulation" among the believers in the Western world of the passages he translated from the writings of Bahá'u'lláh and 'Abdu'l-Bahá concerning the Greatest Holy Leaf.[19]

The publication and circulation of these materials enhanced the believers' understanding of Bahíyyih Khánum's unique station in the Bahá'í Faith and her remarkable contribution to its advancement, as can be seen from the following report:

> When on July 15th, 1932, the world was shaken by the news of the passing to the Great Beyond of the Greatest Holy Leaf there was need indeed to have recourse to every promise and divine assurance that from the Realm of the Limitless her radiant spirit would guide and support the grief-stricken and sorrowing hearts of those who longed to fly to the comfort and solace of the Guardian whose unutterable woe seemed inassaugeable. Only in such moments as these is humanity drawn more closely together in the common sense of loss and the effect upon the believers of the Western world was deep and lasting. A sense of irreparable loss through the breaking of the physical ties which bound to the believers the last "Remnant of Bahá'u'lláh entrusted to our frail and unworthy hands by our departed Master."[20]

In addition to holding special memorial gatherings, the American believers responded to the last appeal of the Greatest Holy Leaf to expedite the construction of the House of Worship in Wilmette— a project the Guardian described as being near to her heart.

The Persian National Spiritual Assembly was assigned the task of circulating the passages from the Bahá'í writings about the Greatest Holy Leaf "immediately and with great care, to the countries of the East, through their Local Spiritual Assemblies." The Guardian characterized this task as "a great bounty especially set apart for the trustees of His devoted loved ones in that noble homeland."[21]

Throughout Persia, memorial gatherings were held in honor of the Greatest Holy Leaf. Indeed, in Tehran, 21 July 1932 was designated as a special day on which all the Bahá'ís were to refrain from going to work. At Naw-Rúz, a traditional Persian period of celebration, no Bahá'í festivities were held. The scope and flavor of special activities undertaken by the Persian Bahá'ís during the months of mourning is suggested by the following report:

> In Ṭihrán for nine consecutive days memorial services were given, and following that these services continued every nineteen days for nine months; on these occasions incidents from the life of the Greatest Holy Leaf were told, and Tablets revealed for her chanted; during the mourning period ten memorial suppers were offered, and over seven hundred fed. To many gatherings Keith Ransom-Kehler, delegate to Persia from the National Spiritual Assembly of America, spoke unforgettably in the memory of the Greatest Holy Leaf; outstanding occasions were at the home of Mírzá 'Abdu'l-Ḥusayn Káẓimuf, where she addressed one hundred and twenty women guests at a memorial luncheon, and again at the Ḥaẓíratu'l-Quds, when she described her meetings with the Greatest Holy Leaf and gave the messages that this most exalted of women had sent through her to Persia, messages

which had the pathos of a final leave-taking. The Persian Bahá'ís have felt very keenly the passing of the Greatest Holy Leaf, and for her sake they are working with redoubled effort to bring about that Bahá'í World Order whose founding she had witnessed, whose establishment was so dear to her heart.[22]

Keith Ransom-Kehler, as mentioned in chapter 6, was the last among Western pilgrims to meet the Greatest Holy Leaf. She arrived in Tehran at the end of June 1932. In addition to undertaking a special mission on behalf of the American National Spiritual Assembly, the purpose of her sojourn in Persia was to strengthen the bonds of unity and understanding between the East and West and to visit the historic sites associated with the Bahá'í Faith. Her unique contribution to the memorial gathering held in honor of the Greatest Holy Leaf is further described by two of the Persian Bahá'ís. They report that "Mrs. Ransom-Kehler had brought with her greetings and messages of love from the household in Haifa. In a beautiful talk she gave these messages to the friends gathered in the garden to welcome her. A message from Bahiyyih Khanum was especially emphasized. It proved to be her last message to the Persian friends. 'When saying good-bye to the Greatest Holy Leaf,' Mrs. Ransom-Kehler said, 'she told me to give to the men as well as to the women the same message of love equally. She said also, "When you enter the holy city of Tihrán, enter it in my name and when you speak, speak in my name."'" The report continues, "Mrs. Ransom-Kehler was able to give a public talk at the first of nine memorial services held on nine successive days in various quarters of the town in honour of the Greatest Holy Leaf. In referring to the message given to her by the Greatest Holy Leaf Mrs. Ransom-Kehler said that she now realized that it was indeed a parting message and signalized the fact that her material life was fast approaching an end."[23]

Another account provides a vivid word picture of a gathering addressed by Keith Ransom-Kehler:

A great number of the friends, young and old, children and adults, were seated on two symmetrically built flights of steps leading to a spacious elevated veranda covering the front part of a typical Persian house of old style belonging to one of the friends. The steps, the veranda and the rooms in the background were simply packed with friends. Eager faces were seen from all points gazing at the sister from the Occident with such pure feelings of Bahá'í love and gladness of heart that Mrs. Ransom-Kehler could scarcely control the tears as she said, "Only the unlimited power of Bahá'u'lláh is able to attract such a love and unity and bring about this soul-to-soul communion between the East and the West."[24]

The holding of memorial gatherings and the commemoration of the life of the Greatest Holy Leaf were not confined to North America and Persia, but formed part of the activities of the worldwide Bahá'í community. For example, in Australia, fitting commemorative evenings were held to mark the passing of Bahíyyih Khánum. It was reported that "The hearts were deeply moved by the realization of what a source of comfort and strength she was to all in the Holy Household and to the Guardian in particular." Likewise, the Bahá'ís in New Zealand reported that "Following the sad news of the passing of the Greatest Holy Leaf, a memorial meeting was held at which were read excerpts from the Writings in reference to her wonderful life of sacrifice and loving service, and the tribute written by Shoghi Effendi. Those present who had had the privilege of meeting her when visiting Haifa spoke of the loving welcome she gave them, and of how even being in her presence and the touch of her hand had such an influence that it would be an ever blessed memory."[25]

The Bahá'ís' Grief

The Guardian graphically captures the intense sorrow experienced by the individual believers at the time of the passing of the Greatest Holy Leaf. In one of his letters he writes,

The community of Bahá, whether in the East of the world or the West, are lamenting like orphans left destitute; fevered, tormented, unquiet, they are voicing their grief. Out of the depths of their sorrowing hearts, there rises to the Abhá Horizon this continual piercing cry: "Where art thou gone, O torch of tender love? Where art thou gone, O source of grace and mercy? Where art thou gone, O symbol of bounty and generosity? Where art thou gone, O day-spring of detachment in this world of being? Where art thou gone, O trust left by Bahá among His people, O remnant left by Him among His servants, O sweet scent of His garment, shed across all created things!"[26]

It is clear from the letters of the Guardian that many of the Bahá'ís who had been privileged to meet Bahíyyih Khánum experienced a sense of deep personal loss at her passing. To some her death was experienced as the passing of a dear and personal friend. Shoghi Effendi attests that "The loss of the Greatest Holy Leaf will be bitterly felt by all those friends who had the pleasure and privilege to meet her." In a letter written on his behalf the Guardian offered the following consolation to one of the bereaved friends: "You should be very happy to have had the privilege of meeting her upon this physical plane of existence, for the world has seen only very few such souls who have suffered so much for the sake of God and yet kept their cheer and uttered words of hope and encouragement to those who were around them." Indeed, some of the friends expressed regret at not having had the opportunity to meet the Greatest Holy Leaf during her earthly life. They were counseled by Shoghi Effendi not "to feel depressed about it," and encouraged by his assurance that "this beloved soul" would, "from the Heaven of her Almighty Father," guide the believers to serve the Cause which had been so dear to her.[27]

As the believers' understanding of the significance of the passing of the Greatest Holy Leaf deepened and as they became aware of

the extent of the Guardian's loss, many of the Bahá'ís were moved
to address letters of condolence to him. Shoghi Effendi acknowledged in person all of these messages of sympathy from Bahá'ís
and friends in the East and West. He derived solace and encouragement from these letters of condolence, as indicated by the following extracts from two of his letters:

> Your highly impressive and touching message brought much re-
> lief to my weary soul. I thank you from the depths of my heart.
> I greatly value the sentiments expressed on behalf of a local com-
> munity, the members of which have, by their services, their de-
> votion and loyalty, contributed, to so great an extent, to the joy
> and satisfaction of the hearts of both 'Abdu'l-Bahá and the Great-
> est Holy Leaf. . . .[28]

> I greatly value the expression of your loving sympathy and am
> greatly relieved by the sentiments your message conveyed. I will
> pray that you may be assisted, individually and collectively, to
> follow her inspiring example, to bring happiness to her soul, and
> to proclaim far and wide the purity of her life, the immensity of
> her love, and the supreme nobility of her character.[29]

The letters of Shoghi Effendi not only educated the believers
concerning the station of the Greatest Holy Leaf, but they also served
as important vehicles for the expression of deep emotions of loss
and longing. Furthermore, they served to inspire and mobilize the
Bahá'ís and to focus their attention on activities that would promote the development of the Faith. We read, for example, "The
Guardian sends messages of consolation to you and all the friends
in this bereavement, and he says that in this calamitous time all
must bow down their heads and be acquiescent, arise in faithful
service to His Cause, and model themselves upon that most ex-

alted, sacred and resplendent presence [the Greatest Holy Leaf]." In yet another letter, the Guardian's secretary writes that Shoghi Effendi is "eagerly awaiting to see the friends as ever burning with the desire to serve a Cause for the sake of which our departed Holy Leaf gave up her entire existence."[30]

The passing of the Greatest Holy Leaf marks the conclusion of the Heroic Age of the Faith, the age associated with the ministries of Bahá'u'lláh and 'Abdu'l-Bahá. She was the last living link between the believers and that early, turbulent chapter of the Bahá'í Cause. Her unique contribution to the Faith extended from her early childhood to her final years. She was instrumental in helping the Bahá'í community to move forward into its Formative Age, a period associated with the establishment and development of the Bahá'í administrative institutions at the World Center of the Bahá'í Faith and throughout the world.

The Resting-Place of the Greatest Holy Leaf and the Rise of the Institutions at the World Center of the Faith

Shoghi Effendi calls attention to the spiritual potency of the resting-place of the Greatest Holy Leaf, and he establishes a linkage between her grave and the rise of the institutions of the Faith.

The Significance of Bahíyyih Khánum's Resting-Place

The Guardian personally specified that her grave should be in the vicinity of the Shrine of the Báb on Mount Carmel. He likewise emphasized the spiritual significance of visiting her grave.

"Blessed, a thousand times blessed, is he who loves thee," he writes in relation to the Greatest Holy Leaf, "and partakes of thy splendours, and sings the praises of thy qualities, and extols thy worth, and follows in thy footsteps; who testifies to the wrongs thou didst suffer, and visits thy resting-place, and circles around thine exalted tomb, by day and by night."[31]

As mentioned earlier, Shoghi Effendi designed the monument marking the resting-place of his great-aunt. His design symbolically links the structure of her monument with the threefold structure of the Bahá'í Administrative Order. In a letter written on his behalf, we find the following description: "The steps of her holy resting-place represent Local Spiritual Assemblies. . . . The columns, that is the pillars, are like the National Spiritual Assemblies, while the dome, which is raised following the placing of the columns, symbolizes the Universal House of Justice which, in accordance with the Master's Will and Testament must be elected by the secondary Houses of Justice, that is, the National Spiritual Assemblies of East and West." The symbolism of the monument of the Greatest Holy Leaf thus embodies the vision of the establishment of the Bahá'í Administrative Order throughout the world and foreshadows the election of the Universal House of Justice, the supreme governing and legislative body of the Bahá'í Faith, at its World Center on Mount Carmel.[32]

In previous chapters reference has been made to the construction of the Shrine of the Báb on Mount Carmel, in accordance with the Plan of Bahá'u'lláh, and the designation of Mount Carmel in Bahá'u'lláh's Tablet of Carmel as the site of the world administrative center of the future Bahá'í commonwealth. Indeed, the Bahá'í writings envisage that the cities of Haifa and Acre will be linked as "a single grand metropolis" that will "enshrine the spiritual as well as the administrative seats of the future Bahá'í Commonwealth."[33]

The burial of the Greatest Holy Leaf on Mount Carmel in 1932 constitutes "a further testimony to the majestic unfoldment and progressive consolidation of the stupendous undertaking launched by Bahá'u'lláh on that holy mountain." The significance of the location of her resting-place to the unfoldment of the Bahá'í Administrative Order was reinforced a few years later when, in accordance with the "cherished wish [of the] Greatest Holy Leaf," Shoghi Effendi transferred the remains of her younger brother, also known as the Purest Branch; their mother, the saintly Navváb; and the wife of 'Abdu'l-Bahá to a permanent site on Mount Carmel. This spot, Shoghi Effendi attests, is designed to constitute the focal center of the administrative institutions at the Bahá'í World Center. Writing in one of his letters, the Guardian states,

> Their resting-places are in one area, on an elevation close by the Spot round which do circle the Concourse on High, and facing the Qiblih* of the people of Bahá—'Akká, the resplendent city, and the sanctified, the luminous, the Most Holy Shrine. . . .
>
> For joy, the Hill of God is stirred at so high an honour, and for this most great bestowal the mountain of the Lord is in rapture and ecstasy.[34]

Commenting on the spiritual significance of "the conjunction of the resting-place of the Greatest Holy Leaf with those of her brother and mother," Shoghi Effendi forecasts that this action

> . . . incalculably reinforces the spiritual potencies of that consecrated Spot which, under the wings of the Báb's overshadowing Sepulcher, and in the vicinity of the future Mashriqu'l-Adhkár which will be reared on its flank, is destined to evolve into the

---

* Literally "that which faces one; prayer direction; point of adoration": the focus to which the faithful turn in prayer. The Qiblih for Muslims is the Kaaba in Mecca; for Bahá'ís it is the Shrine of Bahá'u'lláh at Bahjí

focal center of those world-shaking, world-embracing, world-directing administrative institutions, ordained by Bahá'u'lláh and anticipated by 'Abdu'l-Bahá, and which are to function in consonance with the principles that govern the twin institutions of the Guardianship and the Universal House of Justice. Then, and then only, will this momentous prophecy which illuminates the concluding passages of the Tablet of Carmel be fulfilled: "Erelong will God sail His Ark upon thee (Carmel), and will manifest the people of Bahá who have been mentioned in the Book of Names."[35]

In *God Passes By,* Shoghi Effendi's history of the first one hundred years of the Bahá'í Faith, he describes the significance of the resting-place of the Greatest Holy Leaf and its centrality to the emergence of the Bahá'í World Center:

> The conjunction of these three resting-places, under the shadow of the Báb's own Tomb, embosomed in the heart of Carmel, facing the snow-white city across the bay of 'Akká, the Qiblih of the Bahá'í world, set in a garden of exquisite beauty, reinforces, if we would correctly estimate its significance, the spiritual potencies of a spot, designated by Bahá'u'lláh Himself the seat of God's throne. It marks, too, a further milestone in the road leading eventually to the establishment of that permanent world Administrative Center of the future Bahá'í Commonwealth, destined never to be separated from, and to function in the proximity of, the Spiritual Center of that Faith, in a land already revered and held sacred alike by the adherents of three of the world's outstanding religious systems.[36]

Underlining the nature of the spiritual impact the institutions that are destined to evolve on Mount Carmel will have on the forces of history, Shoghi Effendi writes:

To attempt to visualize, even in its barest outline, the glory that must envelop these institutions, to essay even a tentative and partial description of their character or the manner of their operation, or to trace however inadequately the course of events leading to their rise and eventual establishment is far beyond my own capacity and power. Suffice it to say that at this troubled stage in world history the association of these three incomparably precious souls who, next to the three Central Figures of our Faith, tower in rank above the vast multitude of the heroes, Letters, martyrs, hands, teachers and administrators of the Cause of Bahá'u'lláh, in such a potentially powerful spiritual and administrative Center, is in itself an event which will release forces that are bound to hasten the emergence in a land which, geographically, spiritually and administratively, constitutes the heart of the entire planet, of some of the brightest gems of that World Order now shaping in the womb of this travailing age.[37]

The Emergence of the Bahá'í World Center

The impetus for the development of the Bahá'í World Center derives from Bahá'u'lláh's instructions in the Tablet of Carmel. This seminal document constitutes the charter for the evolution of the World Center of the Faith. It envisages the establishment of its supreme institution, the Universal House of Justice, and the emergence of other agencies of the Bahá'í Administrative Order.

Inspired by the words of Bahá'u'lláh in the Tablet of Carmel, Shoghi Effendi set in train the establishment of the administrative center on Mount Carmel. During the course of his lifetime, he completed the superstructure for the Shrine of the Báb and initiated a process of construction destined to culminate in the erection of the administrative seats of the institutions at the Bahá'í World Center. The first of the monumental buildings to be erected was the International Bahá'í Archives. In a letter addressed to the Bahá'ís of the world in 1954, the Guardian foreshadowed that "The raising of this Edifice will in turn herald the construction, in the course of successive epochs of the Formative Age of the Faith, of several other structures." "These Edifices," he states, "will, in the shape of a far-flung arc, and following a harmonizing style of architecture, surround the resting-places of the Greatest Holy Leaf, ranking as foremost among the members of her sex in the Bahá'í Dispensation, of her Brother, offered up as a ransom by Bahá'u'lláh for the quickening of the world and its unification, and of their Mother, proclaimed by Him to be His chosen 'consort in all the worlds of God.'"[38]

The construction of the International Bahá'í Archives Building was completed in 1957 during the lifetime of Shoghi Effendi. The interior finishing and furnishing took place during the six-year period of the custodianship of the Hands of the Cause in the Holy Land.* Pilgrims who have the opportunity to visit the International Bahá'í Archives will, doubtless, be struck by the unique contribution of the Greatest Holy Leaf to its rich collection of artifacts and relics associated with the Founders of the Faith. It was Bahíyyih Khánum who had been the custodian of the portraits of Bahá'u'lláh and the Báb, and these portraits now have a place of honor in the archives building. Likewise, it was the Greatest Holy Leaf who preserved the blood of Bahá'u'lláh—blood that was drawn as part of a routine health procedure common in the East. It was she who arranged the locks of her father's hair, collected one hair at a time from His brush and comb. In addition, there is a cabinet devoted to items associated with Bahíyyih Khánum herself. Such items include examples of her handwriting, her Bahá'í ring and personal seal, a lock of her hair, and some of her clothing—head scarves,

---

* After the passing of Shoghi Effendi in 1957, the twenty-seven eminent Bahá'ís known as Hands of the Cause of God—whom Shoghi Effendi had appointed as the "Chief Stewards" of the Faith to stimulate its propagation and ensure its protection—assumed leadership of the religion until the Universal House of Justice was formed in 1963. During the six-year temporary custodianship of the Hands of the Cause from 1957 to 1963, they elected nine of their number to serve as "Custodians" of the Faith in Haifa.

dresses, a pair of well-worn slippers, and a small handbag. Ruḥíyyih Khánum, who arranged the collection of materials in the Archives, characterized the items associated with the Greatest Holy Leaf as "all the touching little things that remain of one infinitely loved and which convey a sense of nearness to a personality worthy of emulation and all our devotion."[39]

In 1972 the Universal House of Justice, which was first elected in 1963, took steps to implement the vision of Shoghi Effendi concerning the construction of the edifices along an avenue taking the form of an arc on Mount Carmel, the focal center of which is oriented towards the resting-place of the Greatest Holy Leaf, her brother, and their mother. The first step in the process was to be the erection of the Seat of the Universal House of Justice. Mr. Ḥusayn Amánat was the architect appointed to design the new building. In preparing the plans, he reportedly designed the dome of the building to be reminiscent of the dome of the monument erected at the resting-place of the Greatest Holy Leaf. He is said to have done so "because of the well-known statement of Shoghi Effendi in which he likened the administrative order of the Faith of Bahá'u'lláh to the monument of the Greatest Holy Leaf, the dome representing the Universal House of Justice."[40]

The structure of the Seat of the Universal House of Justice was completed in 1982. Though not fully prepared for occupancy, the building was inaugurated on 17 July 1982. The ceremonial inaugural event was a seminar held on the occasion of the commemoration of the fiftieth anniversary of the passing of the Greatest Holy Leaf—thereby establishing a special link between Bahíyyih Khánum and the Universal House of Justice.

The formal occupation of the Seat of the Universal House of Justice, which took place in February 1983, was described by the House of Justice as an "AUSPICIOUS EVENT," which signalized "ANOTHER PHASE IN [the] PROCESS [of the] FULFILLMENT [of the] SAILING

OF GOD'S ARK ON [the] MOUNTAIN OF THE LORD AS ANTICIPATED IN [the] TABLET [of] CARMEL."[41]

Soon after the Universal House of Justice occupied its permanent seat on Mount Carmel, the edifice was used as the venue for the initial session of the Fifth International Bahá'í Convention. On Friday 29 April 1983, the quinquennial election of the House of Justice took place in the reception concourse of its seat. It was reported that the hall was "filled to capacity" with 590 delegates from 119 National Spiritual Assemblies. The occasion was graced by the presence of eight Hands of the Cause, the members of the Universal House of Justice, and fifty-seven Continental Counselors, in addition to the four Counselor members of the International Teaching Center.[42]

The Arc and the Terraces on Mount Carmel

'Abdu'l-Bahá's visionary plans for the development of Mount Carmel included the construction of nineteen monumental terraces reaching from the former German Templer Colony* at the foot of the mountain to its summit. In 1986 the Universal House of Justice announced its decision to construct the terraces of the Shrine of the Báb and the remaining buildings Shoghi Effendi had envisioned on the arc on Mount Carmel. It is interesting to note that the Greatest Holy Leaf took an active interest in the early stages of the unfoldment of 'Abdu'l-Bahá's grand design for the beautification of this sacred site.

In one of her letters, the Greatest Holy Leaf recounts that, after the completion of the basic structure of the Shrine of the Báb, it was 'Abdu'l-Bahá's wish and intention "to open a path that would lead directly from the Shrine to the German Avenue." There were, how-

---

* A group of German Christians known as the Temple Society *(Tempelgesellschaft)*, or Templers, had settled at the foot of Mount Carmel in the late 1860s and early 1870s to await the second coming of Jesus Christ.

ever, many obstacles preventing the execution of this project. For example, for many years 'Abdu'l-Bahá was unable to purchase the necessary land. Ultimately, in the time of the British mandate, the land was acquired. The municipal engineer prepared a design for the path leading up to the shrine and issued the order for the path to be opened. Bahíyyih Khánum reports, "This design received the blessed attention of 'Abdu'l-Bahá Who graciously approved it and expressed His satisfaction and appreciation to the Municipal Engineer. Later on, with the aid of divine confirmations, enough land was purchased from the remaining tracts through which the path passed."[43]

Not only was the Greatest Holy Leaf intensely interested in this project, but she also made a financial contribution to assist in its completion. Ruhíyyih Khánum, recounting a story the Guardian once told her about the Greatest Holy Leaf, states that when he "had insisted that she [Bahíyyih Khánum] receive as an inheritance from 'Abdu'l-Bahá a small sum of money, she had offered a large part of it to defray the expense of building the next terrace in front of the Shrine of the Báb in fulfilment of her Brother's cherished plan."[44]

Shoghi Effendi completed in preliminary form the nine terraces from the foot of the mountain leading up to the Báb's shrine. At a later date, the Universal House of Justice appointed the architect Mr. Faríburz Ṣahbá to complete the design of the terraces above and below the shrine and to supervise the construction of the remaining buildings on the arc.

The plan of the Universal House of Justice called for the construction of the administrative seats of the International Teaching Center and the Center for the Study of the Texts, and an extension to the International Bahá'í Archives Building. The construction of the International Bahá'í Library would be deferred to a later time. These edifices, designed by Ḥusayn Amánat, the architect of the Seat of the Universal House of Justice, have as their focal center the resting-places of the Greatest Holy Leaf, her brother, and their mother.

This vast construction project was completed in 2001 with the International Teaching Center's occupation of its permanent seat in January 2001 and the public inauguration of the terraces of the Shrine of the Báb in May of that same year. In a message addressed to the Bahá'ís gathered at the events marking the completion of the construction projects on Mount Carmel, the Universal House of Justice provides the following assessment of the significance of the occasion:

> The majestic buildings that now stand along the Arc traced for them by Shoghi Effendi on the slope of the Mountain of God, together with the magnificent flight of garden terraces that embrace the Shrine of the Báb, are an outward expression of the immense power animating the Cause we serve. They offer timeless witness to the fact that the followers of Bahá'u'lláh have successfully laid the foundations of a worldwide community transcending all differences that divide the human race, and have brought into existence the principal institutions of a unique and unassailable Administrative Order that shapes this community's life. In the transformation that has taken place on Mount Carmel, the Bahá'í Cause emerges as a visible and compelling reality on the global stage, as the focal centre of forces that will, in God's good time, bring about the reconstruction of society, and as a mystic source of spiritual renewal for all who turn to it.[45]

Might not the achievements the Universal House of Justice mentions represent the first fruits in the process referred to by Shoghi Effendi in 1939, a process that is intimately linked to the Greatest Holy Leaf, when he wrote: "The transfer of the sacred remains of the brother and mother of our Lord and Master 'Abdu'l-Bahá to Mount Carmel and their final interment within the hallowed precincts of the Shrine of the Báb, and in the immediate neighborhood of the resting place of the Greatest Holy Leaf, constitute, apart from their historic associations and the tender sentiments they arouse, events of such capital institutional significance as only future happenings, steadily and mysteriously unfolding at the World Center of our Faith, can adequately demonstrate."[46]

Hence it is evident that during her life Bahíyyih Khánum exerted, and after her passing has continued to exert, an influence on the unfoldment of the Bahá'í Cause. The spiritual potencies associated with her resting-place interact in a mystical way with the slowly maturing institutions at the World Center of the Bahá'í Faith.

Chapter 8

Archetype of the People of Bahá

In the previous chapters we have examined the contribution of Bahíyyih Khánum to the unfolding history of the Bahá'í Faith. In this final chapter we will explore the significance of her enduring legacy as the "archetype of the people of Bahá."[1] The term "people of Bahá" is a reference to the men and women who have identified themselves with the spiritual values and teachings of the Bahá'í Faith.

Role Model for Both Sexes

Most religions have identified an archetypal female figure that epitomizes the female ideal of the religion and serves to inspire and motivate women. However, Bahíyyih Khánum's designation as an "archetype" does not conform to any of the existing archetypal patterns that are traditionally identified. The Greatest Holy Leaf is neither simply a mother-earth type nor the typical mythical hero and martyr, nor is she exclusively a role model for women. Rather, her designation as the "archetype of the people of Bahá" removes that potential restriction. Her qualities and the example of her life are, therefore, not only relevant to women but also to men. This represents a departure from other religions, in which the female archetypal figure is regarded as embodying only the female ideal of the religion, an ideal that typically has been confined to such feminine qualities as purity and motherhood.[2]

Since Bahíyyih Khánum's qualities have, by definition, relevance to both women and men, both sexes can derive inspiration from the example of her life and can model their behavior on her qualities. An examination of the qualities she manifested will pave the way for a reconsideration of the characteristics that are traditionally associated with masculinity and femininity, and for a reformulation of the concept of heroism that is pertinent to contemporary times.

While reexamining the qualities associated with masculinity and femininity, it is noteworthy to observe that the Guardian equates some of the attributes manifested by the Greatest Holy Leaf with the qualities exemplified in the lives of the Manifestations of God. For example, in a passage addressing Bahíyyih Khánum, Shoghi Effendi observes, "during all thy days, from thine earliest years until the close of thy life, thou didst personify the attributes of thy Father, the Matchless, the Mighty. Thou wert the fruit of His Tree, thou wert the lamp of His love, thou wert the symbol of His serenity, and of His meekness, the pathway of His guidance, the channel of His blessings, the sweet scent of His robe, the refuge of His loved ones and His handmaidens, the mantle of His generosity and grace."[3]

While "serenity" and "meekness" are considered stereotypically feminine attributes, Shoghi Effendi shifts the balance. He generalizes their application to women and men by characterizing these two qualities as being among the attributes exemplified by Bahá-'u'lláh. Further, in the following extract from a letter the Guardian wrote at the time of Bahíyyih Khánum's passing, he compares her qualities not only to those of Bahá'u'lláh but also to those of the Báb and 'Abdu'l-Bahá. Shoghi Effendi specifically links the "resignation and serenity" expressed by the Greatest Holy Leaf with "the calm and heroic fortitude of the Báb." He notes that her "natural fondness of flowers and children" was also "so characteristic of Bahá'u'lláh," and that she shared with 'Abdu'l-Bahá "a generosity, a love, at once disinterested and undiscriminating." In this same passage, Shoghi Effendi provides the following list of some of the "outstanding attributes" that proclaim her as "a daughter, worthy to inherit that priceless heritage bequeathed to her by Bahá'u'lláh" and that set her apart from many of the heroes of the past:

A purity of life that reflected itself in even the minutest details of her daily occupations and activities; a tenderness of heart that obliterated every distinction of creed, class and colour; a resignation and serenity that evoked to the mind the calm and heroic fortitude of the Báb; a natural fondness of flowers and children that was so characteristic of Bahá'u'lláh; an unaffected simplicity of manners; an extreme sociability which made her accessible to all; a generosity, a love, at once disinterested and undiscriminating, that reflected so clearly the attributes of 'Abdu'l-Bahá's character; a sweetness of temper; a cheerfulness that no amount of sorrow could becloud; a quiet and unassuming disposition that served to enhance a thousandfold the prestige of her exalted rank; a forgiving nature that instantly disarmed the most unyielding enemy—these rank among the outstanding attributes of a saintly life which history will acknowledge as having been endowed with a celestial potency that few of the heroes of the past possessed.[4]

It is clear from a study of descriptions of her qualities that Bahíyyih Khánum was a strong, sensitive, and complex figure. She does not easily fit into any preconceived category, nor is she otherworldly. She manifested a consummate blend of detachment and engagement. She was sustained by her deep understanding of the teachings of the Bahá'í Faith, together with her keen awareness of the significance of the challenges she faced, and her unshakable confidence in the ultimate grace and mercy of God. She had a clear vision that guided her in determining courses of strategic action, reinforced her courage in times of challenge, and enabled her to bounce back during periods of severe testing. Through her qualities and actions, the Greatest Holy Leaf provides, to women and men alike, a consummate model of an individual who demonstrates resilience in the face of seemingly overwhelming odds.

This final chapter focuses on a number of Bahíyyih Khánum's outstanding characteristics as exemplified by her resilient response to hardship and suffering, her acceptance of responsibility, her leadership style, and her approach to change. Our aim is to identify links between the ideals and values she embodied and the pressing issues of concern to contemporary society, and thus to explore the implications of her example for those seeking to align themselves with the direction of social evolution.

Resilience in a World of Hardship

It is evident that the world is in a state of crisis—spiritually, economically, socially—and that this crisis is, in many instances, compounded by a lack of effective governance. The level of human suffering and hardship, of unrelieved stress and uncertainty, is daily increasing as the threats of war, terrorism, poverty, and oppression appear to loom ever closer. Survival and personal well-being depend not only on understanding the meaning of suffering, but on identifying constructive role models who are able, despite apparently overwhelming odds, to recover from misfortune and adjust to change.

Under such circumstances, it is natural for those seeking guidance and direction to turn to religion. One might well expect that, as the traditional repository of values and meaning, religion would be the source of insight for those endeavoring to understand the reason for their suffering and to determine how best to direct the course of their lives in times of hardship and uncertainty.

However, the religions of the world today are, in most instances, unable to meet this challenge in a way that is satisfying to the modern mind. One response ascribes suffering to the sinful nature of humanity, due to the original sin of an ancestor who has become a mythical figure from antiquity. Another tries to provide comfort by focusing entirely on the pleasures of the world beyond death, thus discouraging any attempts to ameliorate conditions in this world. Yet another seeks to circumvent the issue by asserting that all such suffering is in the mind and can be avoided by the appropriate mental discipline. In some parts of the globe the prevailing religious response is to encourage disengagement from the world as the panacea for relief from hardship. This approach advocates a remedy involving isolation, aloofness from social intercourse, and the extinction of all emotion.

From a Bahá'í perspective, suffering is considered to be an integral and inescapable part of life, but not an end in itself. 'Abdu'l-Bahá affirms, "When thou lookest about thee with a perceptive eye, thou wilt note that on this dusty earth all humankind are suffering." Indeed, He underscores the connection between suffering and personal and spiritual growth, stating,

The mind and spirit of man advance when he is tried by suffering. The more the ground is ploughed the better the seed will grow, the better the harvest will be. Just as the plough furrows the earth deeply, purifying it of weeds and thistles, so suffering and tribulation free man from the petty affairs of this worldly life until he arrives at a state of complete detachment. His attitude in this world will be that of divine happiness. Man is, so to speak, unripe: the heat of the fire of suffering will mature him. Look back to the times past and you will find that the greatest men have suffered most.[5]

It is important to note that the "state of complete detachment" to which 'Abdu'l-Bahá refers in no way implies a condition of masochistic or passive acceptance of one's lot in life. On the contrary, the Bahá'í Faith is not to be associated with any form of asceticism, or with a puritanical outlook. Shoghi Effendi affirms that the Bahá'í teachings do not seek "to deny anyone the legitimate right and privilege to derive the fullest advantage and benefit from the manifold joys, beauties, and pleasures with which the world has been so plentifully enriched by an All-Loving Creator."[6]

Bahá'u'lláh mandates an active stance for individuals confronted with tests and difficulties. He attests that "tribulation" leads individuals to search for spiritual meaning, and He encourages them to engage in constructive behavior. He offers the following counsel:

> Say: Tribulation is a horizon unto My Revelation. The day star of grace shineth above it, and sheddeth a light which neither the clouds of men's idle fancy nor the vain imaginations of the aggressor can obscure.
>
> Follow thou the footsteps of thy Lord, . . . undeterred by either the clamor of the heedless ones or the sword of the enemy. . . . Spread abroad the sweet savors of thy Lord, and hesitate not, though it be for less than a moment, in the service of His Cause. The day is approaching when the victory of thy Lord, the Ever-Forgiving, the Most Bountiful, will be proclaimed.[7]

The pervasiveness of hardship and suffering to the human condition and the stresses associated with contemporary life have intensified the need to gain an understanding of a wider range of new and creative ways of responding to hardship. This need is setting the agenda for social scientists and others who are keen to know why, for example, some people suffer real hardships and do not falter. There is a renewed interest in studying the subject of resilience—why some people have the capacity to face, overcome, and even be strengthened by the adversities of life, and to embrace change. In particular, these studies have attempted to identify the characteristics of resilient people with a view to finding ways of helping individuals and organizations to cope with life's exigencies.

The Dynamics of Resilience

Studies show that resilient people—those who are able to cope with adversity and bounce back from stressful experiences quickly and efficiently—have three distinguishing characteristics: an acceptance of reality, a strongly held belief that life is meaningful, and an ability to find creative solutions to seemingly insoluble problems.

In relation to the first characteristic, the acceptance of reality, it is interesting to note that while it is often thought that resilience stems from an optimistic nature, current research cautions against the danger of unrealistic optimism, which not only can lead to self-deception, avoidance, passivity, and inaction, but also can actually hinder the kind of down-to-earth assessment of the situation necessary both for survival and for planning constructive action. In contrast, realistic optimism not only helps the individual to understand the constraints inherent in the situation but also to anticipate and prepare for future challenges. It motivates the individual to marshal his or her resources and to engage actively in the task at hand, and it contributes to a sense of mastery and control over one's destiny.[8]

A second characteristic of resilient people is their conviction that life is meaningful, a belief that is very often buttressed by deeply rooted spiritual values. Such strong values infuse an environment with meaning because they offer ways to interpret and shape events. Rather than seeing themselves as victims, resilient people have the ability to find meaning in extreme suffering.

Viktor Frankl, an Auschwitz survivor and the originator of logotherapy, a psychotherapeutic approach that seeks to help individuals find an aim and purpose in their existence and to accept responsibility for life's decisions, stressed the fact that individuals may also find meaning in life even when confronted with a hopeless situation and when facing a fate they are unable to change. According to Frankl, the meaning of life arises from the responses that a person makes to life, to the situations and tasks with which life confronts him or her. While individuals cannot always control the conditions with which they are confronted, they can, to some extent, control their responses to them.[9]

Researchers affirm that finding meaning in one's environment is an important aspect of resilience and that it is the "dynamic of meaning making" that enables resilient people to build bridges from present-day hardships to a fuller, better future. Those bridges provide a clarity of vision and a way of interpreting experiences in a new light that helps to make the present manageable and removes the sense that the present is overwhelming and meaningless.[10]

A third characteristic associated with resilience is the ability to make do with whatever is at hand, to improvise the solution to a problem, to imagine possibilities for action, even in the face of an obvious lack of resources. Psychologists have related positive emotions to optimal functioning, suggesting, for example, that positive emotions not only increase creativity and broaden the range of possible solutions but also help to create positive expectations and a sense of trust and hope in the world.[11]

While some people are born resilient, recent studies indicate that resilience can be learned. One way to acquire the skills associated with resilience is to examine the lives of resilient people with a view to drawing inspiration and practical lessons about how to cope in times of stress and hardship. To this end, we offer the example of Bahíyyih K͟hánum, the "archetype of the people of Bahá."[12]

The Greatest Holy Leaf,
the Archetype of Resilience

The Greatest Holy Leaf was, in the words of Shoghi Effendi, "one of the greatest sufferers the world has yet seen," who bore her tribulations with a fortitude that was derived from her confidence "in the grace of God." The Guardian compared the nature of the tribulations borne by Bahíyyih Khánum to the trials borne by the Central Figures of the Bahá'í Faith.* He writes that upon her ascension into heaven, the "heavenly Crier" raised up his voice and cried out, "'O Most Exalted Leaf! Thou art she who did endure with patience in God's way from thine earliest childhood and throughout all thy life, and did bear in His pathway what none other hath borne, save only God in His own Self, the Supreme Ruler over all created things, and before Him, His noble Herald, and after Him, His holy Branch, the One, the Inaccessible, the Most High.'" He testifies to the severity of her sufferings: "The sufferings she bore in the pathway of God were the cruellest ones, the afflictions that assailed her were the severest of all. Fortitude was the rich dress she wore, serenity and tranquil strength were her splendid robe, virtue and detachment, purity and chastity, were all her jewels, and tenderness, care and love for humankind, her beauty's bright adornings."[13]

Not only were the Greatest Holy Leaf's sufferings intense but they also extended throughout her life. The Guardian affirms that

> she spent all the days of her precious life as an exile and a captive, and her every priceless hour was passed under tests and afflictions and ordeals that she endured at the hands of merciless foes. From early childhood she had her share of the sufferings of

---

* Refers to Bahá'u'lláh, the Báb, and 'Abdu'l-Bahá.

Bahá'u'lláh, subjected even as He was to hardships and calamities, and she was as well the partner in sorrows and tribulations of 'Abdu'l-Bahá.

For her there was never a night of peaceful sleep, for her no day when she found rest, and always, like a moth, would her comely person circle about the bright candle of the Faith. The words of her mouth were ever to glorify the Abhá Beauty, her only thought and her high purpose were to proclaim the Cause of God and to protect His Law, while the dearest wish of her glowing heart was to waft far and wide the sweet breathings of the Lord. [14]

The Guardian then calls attention to the significance of her actions. He writes, "Her heavenly ways were a model for the people of Bahá, and those who dwell in the pavilions of devotion and the denizens of the Abhá Paradise found in her celestial attributes their prototype and their guide." [15]

While there is a tendency in the West to equate suffering and martyrdom with defeat and failure, psychiatrist Abdu'l-Missagh Ghadirian suggests that they might alternatively be characterized as "the victory of the soul." He calls attention to the fact that a person's faith in God is a dynamic force rather than a static state of mind. He states, "As one's faith grows, so will one's ability to endure trials and tribulations that test one's sincerity and love of the divine reality." [16]

The Greatest Holy Leaf's response to trials and suffering is worthy of close examination. Her acceptance of pain and suffering should not be confused with either masochism or fanaticism. She did not seek personal gratification from pain and torment, nor was she driven by blind religious fervor or prejudice. From childhood she comprehended the nature of the dangers confronting the members of the infant Bahá'í community. Understanding the purpose of the events that engulfed her life enabled the Greatest Holy Leaf to choose her course of action. She exemplified a realistic optimism, chose to tread the path of a new spiritual truth, and accepted the adversities this entailed.

It is evident that the tribulations Bahíyyih Khánum experienced caused her great suffering and evoked deep feelings within her. She was, however, not simply ruled by her emotions, but was able to transcend them. The Guardian affirms that "For more than eighty years this Exalted Leaf bore with a fortitude that bewildered every one who had the privilege of knowing her, sufferings and tribulations that few of our present-day believers did experience. And yet, what a joy and what a saintlike attitude she manifested all through her life. Her angelic face was so calm, so serene in the very midst of sufferings and pains. Not that she lacked tenderness of heart and sympathy."[17]

The Greatest Holy Leaf's serenity and fortitude derived both from her keen sense, based on the sacred writings of the Bahá'í Faith, that life is meaningful, with meaning to be found even in suffering, and from her deep trust and confidence in the ultimate and unfailing grace and mercy of God. By persevering in her religious belief in the face of persecution, she was able to manifest spiritual values. Indeed, the Guardian attests that "No calamity, however intense, could obscure the brightness of her saintly face, and no agitation, no matter how severe, could disturb the composure of her gracious and dignified behaviour." Bahíyyih Khánum's confidence in the power of divine assistance and in the knowledge that God's will must ultimately prevail endowed her with true patience and the strength to endure. To the very end of her days, her clarity of vision imparted meaning to life and was the foundation of her realistic and confident hope in the future. This same vision was imparted to others through her example and galvanized the Bahá'í community after the passing of 'Abdu'l-Bahá."[18]

From an examination of her life, it is evident that Bahíyyih Khánum was neither paralyzed by events nor unmindful or unaware of what was transpiring. Rather than adopt a passive, helpless stance in relation to ordeals and tribulations, she actively sought out creative solutions to problems, taking advantage of whatever possibilities might be available. Nor did she engage in mindless, frenetic activity. Rather, her actions were designed to meet specific needs and situations.

As a child, Bahíyyih Khánum bore, with a spirit of acquiescence, uncounted ordeals including poverty, loneliness, and exile. At the same time, she took steps to lessen the trials and sufferings of others. In Baghdad, while yet in her teens, she was called upon by Bahá'u'lláh to undertake delicate missions, a challenge to which she responded with alacrity and joy, despite the very real dangers involved. During the stressful years in Adrianople, when the Bahá'í community was riven by disunity and division, she played a vital role in resolving the misunderstandings of some about the station of Bahá'u'lláh. In later life, after the passing of her father and again following that of 'Abdu'l-Bahá, she took the necessary actions to protect the Covenant and to stabilize the community. Shoghi Effendi notes that, despite her physical weakness and social isolation, the Greatest Holy Leaf "confronted the attacks of the hostile, and she suffered afflictions any one of which could well have shattered a mountain of iron. And yet the sweet and comely face of that spirit-like dove of holiness, was wreathed till her very last hour in life-giving smiles, nor did that patience and endurance, that greatness, that majesty and dignity, ever desert her delicate and fragile person."[19]

When dealing with difficulties Bahíyyih Khánum manifested both patience and loving-kindness. In contrast to the prevailing attitudes of present-day society, her response to "the attacks of the hostile" was neither adversarial nor vengeful. Her sole aim was to assist others, including those who attacked the Bahá'í Faith, to gain a deeper understanding and appreciation of the significance of Bahá'u'lláh's revelation. To this end, Shoghi Effendi observes, "She . . . had no other aim nor goal but these: to proclaim the Cause of God and exalt His Word; to praise and glorify the Blessed Beauty's [Bahá'u'lláh's] name; to bear 'Abdu'l-Bahá in mind and serve Him ever; to pity the sorely-troubled and give them endless, loving care; to cherish and comfort them, and bring them joy."[20]

The Greatest Holy Leaf is a model of resilience in the face of a lifetime of suffering and tribulation. Shoghi Effendi attests that, while these sufferings "left their traces upon her feeble form," they did not in the least affect "her spirit of joy and hopefulness," nor did they undermine her faith in the future. "Notwithstanding all this," he writes, "she never grumbled nor lost her faith in the future. She kept cheerful and tried to give cheer to others. She was a real source of inspiration to every person that met her." He underlines the significance and contemporary relevance of the example of her personal qualities to humankind, noting that

> She liked to see the people happy, and exerted all her efforts to make it easy for them to realize it.
>
> How badly we need such souls in the world at present when it seems so full of sorrows and discouragements! Every one is suffering and no person to give them courage and brighten their hearts.[21]

Fostering Resilience in Others

In addition to serving as a constructive role model of resilient behavior, the Greatest Holy Leaf took active steps to empower others by increasing their skills both to respond in a competent manner to the stresses of life and to adapt to change. Her personal interactions with pilgrims, as well as the letters she wrote, provide examples of her approach to promoting resilience in the members of the Bahá'í community.

Her contact with pilgrims as well as her correspondence were marked by an acute sensitivity to each person she addressed. Her response was tender, patient, loving, and tailored to each individual.

She expressed toward all an understanding of the difficulties with which they were confronted, empathized with them in their sorrows and trials, and acknowledged that she, too, had experienced grief, loss, and apprehension. Her recognition and validation of the reality of their stresses and strains was a source of encouragement to them and helped those in distress to feel more hopeful that they could do something to alleviate their situation.

Beyond encouragement, she also assisted the believers to find meaning in suffering. The Greatest Holy Leaf called their attention to the sufferings of Bahá'u'lláh and 'Abdu'l-Bahá and explained the transcendental reason they chose to submit to such trials—for the promotion of the Bahá'í Faith and, ultimately, for the peace and happiness of human society. She also stressed the fact that the believers have a choice in how they respond to life's vicissitudes. In this regard, she called attention to the example of 'Abdu'l-Bahá and his chosen role of self-sacrificing servitude.

Bahíyyih Khánum helped to forge a sense of identity among the Bahá'ís and to impart a guiding vision. To this end, she explained the dynamic of crisis and victory that drives the unfoldment of the Bahá'í Faith and helped the Bahá'ís to understand the significance of their current difficulties within this visionary context. Armed with this vision, the believers were empowered to assess the needs and opportunities of the situation, to mobilize their resources—however meager—and to devise constructive and confident actions appropriate to the moment and to the stage of development of the Faith. To increase confident action in the longer term, specifically in situations where the Bahá'í community lacked the requisite skills, the Greatest Holy Leaf often detailed a particular course of action to be followed. Her guidance educated the believers, increased their competence, and expanded their repertoire of coping skills.

While many lessons can be learned by examining the Greatest Holy Leaf as a role model for personal resilience in the face of adversity, her strategies for promoting resilience in others are also worthy of consideration. The empowerment of individuals to cope constructively with the spiritual, social, and economic crises of the contemporary world continues to be a critical, ongoing necessity.

Accepting Administrative Responsibility

Willingness to involve oneself in activities designed to benefit the entire society is one of the pressing needs in the world today. A sense of community has been lost, replaced by a single-minded pre-occupation with narrowly defined personal interests. Many people feel themselves to be alone, alienated from the society around them, surrounded by others who have no concern for their welfare and who should, in turn, not be the object of their attention.

There are a variety of causes for this disengagement of the individual from the wider society. It may be a response to the adversities one has experienced and to the weight of the manifold problems with which one is confronted. It may arise from despair at the growing turmoil and social disruption in the world, allied with a sense of helplessness about what one person can do to improve the situation. It may also be a consequence of a well-founded disenchantment with the hypocrisy of organizations that claim to promote beneficial change and disillusion at their ineffectiveness.

Under such circumstances, one might well be inclined to seek from religion that set of values and the motivation required to provide active and sustained participation in measures to improve the functioning of society. However, religious orthodoxy today is oriented to producing believers who will unquestioningly leave such matters to others and whose mind-set is one of passive obedience. Religious activists who discard such a mind-set tend to engage principally in protesting the established order and seeking immediate and radical change.

The Bahá'í Faith stands unique, for it contains as an integral element of its teachings an Administrative Order that constitutes far more than a mere system for organizing its community. This Administrative Order is a means of training its participants in attitudes and behaviors that constitute a pattern for the future functioning of society at large, so that they can create a nucleus for the governance of humanity in accord with the principles of freedom, justice, and unity. It calls for active involvement of all of its members, bringing to bear their talents and abilities, irrespective of their personal circumstances or the limitations to which they are subjected.

The Greatest Holy Leaf serves as an archetype for these participants. Undeterred by the circumstances in which she found herself, she provides an admirable model of administrative involvement worthy of emulation by all who follow in her footsteps and serve in an evolving Administrative Order, an Order that has grown vastly from the early beginnings to which Bahíyyih Khánum made so distinctive a contribution.

To examine this matter, we must first review some of the salient features of the Bahá'í Administrative Order. Within this context it will be possible to examine more fully the example Bahíyyih Khánum provides.

The Spiritual Foundation of the Social Order

From the Bahá'í perspective, the foundation of the social order should be fundamentally spiritual. Such a focus places the sacred at the heart of individual and community life. Emphasis on the spiritual has implications not only for the Bahá'í Faith's assumptions about social order and the nature of social institutions, but also influences its vision of social evolution and gives direction to the goals, strategies, and methods devised to bring about social change.

In this regard, Shoghi Effendi calls attention to the inseparability of the spiritual, social, and administrative dimensions of the Bahá'í Faith and its progressive unfoldment. He warns, "To dissociate the administrative principles of the Cause from the purely spiritual and humanitarian teachings would be tantamount to a mutilation of the body of the Cause." From this perspective alone, the Bahá'í Faith stands distinct among the world's religious systems.[22]

It is important to note that the Bahá'í administrative system derives its authority and its governing principles from Bahá'u'lláh Himself. Shoghi Effendi states, "this Administrative Order is fundamentally different from anything that any Prophet has previously established, inasmuch as Bahá'u'lláh has Himself revealed its principles, established its institutions, appointed the person to interpret His Word and conferred the necessary authority on the body designed to supplement and apply His legislative ordinances. Therein lies the secret of its strength, its fundamental distinction, and the guarantee against disintegration and schism."[23]

Shoghi Effendi analyzes the Bahá'í administrative system from the perspective of religious history and theories of social organization, distinguishing it from existing political and ecclesiastical institutions and underlining some of its unique features. He attests, "this vast Administrative Order is . . . both in theory and practice, not only unique in the entire history of political institutions, but can find no parallel in the annals of any of the world's recognized religious systems." He provides the following elaboration:

No form of democratic government; no system of autocracy or of dictatorship, whether monarchical or republican; no intermediary scheme of a purely aristocratic order; nor even any of the recognized types of theocracy, whether it be the Hebrew Commonwealth, or the various Christian ecclesiastical organizations, or the Imamate or the Caliphate in Islám—none of these can be identified or be said to conform with the Administrative Order which the master-hand of its perfect Architect has fashioned.

This new-born Administrative Order incorporates within its structure certain elements which are to be found in each of the three recognized forms of secular government, without being in any sense a mere replica of any one of them, and without intro-ducing within its machinery any of the objectionable features which they inherently possess. It blends and harmonizes, as no government fashioned by mortal hands has as yet accomplished, the salutary truths which each of these systems undoubtedly con-tains without vitiating the integrity of those God-given verities on which it is ultimately founded.[24]

From the foregoing it is clear that personal spiritual development, while an important goal for the individual Bahá'í, is, by itself, in-sufficient. For spiritual development is inextricably linked to the evolution of a Bahá'í system of social organization, which operates according to spiritual, humanitarian, and administrative principles derived from the teachings of the Bahá'í Faith. Thus there is a posi-tive and constructive interaction between the development of the individual and that of the social order. The Bahá'í Administrative Order serves as the means of promoting spiritual values in the world at large, and it offers an alternative model of governance, based on the implementation of these values, to those seeking effective solu-tions to the deficiencies of present-day administrative institutions.

It is beyond the scope of this book to attempt a detailed presentation of the various components of the Bahá'í system, their functioning and interaction. However, three aspects are of particular interest in review-ing the role of Bahíyyih Khánum, and they are discussed here.

A Lay Religion

A unique feature of the Bahá'í Faith is that it is a lay religion. The Faith is distinguished by its lack of a clerical class; no figures comparable to the rabbis, priests, ministers, or mullahs of other religions are responsible for administering to the needs of the Bahá'í community.

The structure of many religious communities that originated in past ages tends to be hierarchical, with the clergy being accorded a position superior to that of the laity. By virtue of this elevated position, the members of the clergy exercise authority over the mass of the faithful and enjoy certain rights and privileges not shared by their fellow believers. Historically, the clergy have, in the absence of explicit written provisions set out by the Founder of the religion, arrogated to themselves the exclusive right to provide authoritative interpretations of the scriptures. They assumed the right to determine matters of doctrine and ecclesiastical organization and to instruct the believers concerning all things spiritual and practical. In addition, the function of the clergy is typically to dispense blessings, administer sacraments such as those of baptism and penance, and generally mediate the individual believer's relationship to God.

In contrast, the function assigned to the laity is to obey and show reverence to the clerics. The role of the mass of the faithful, therefore, tends to be essentially passive—to receive the clergy's ministrations and to respond to their initiatives. Members of the congregation of believers are seen to fulfill their spiritual responsibility largely by accepting the clergy's services and guidance.

In the Bahá'í community, the absence of a clerical class means that the hierarchical distinction between clergy and layman is removed. The spiritual fate of each individual is not conditioned on the actions or statements of any other soul. The Bahá'í writings call for each believer to take personal responsibility to investigate spiritual truth, to deepen his or her understanding of the Bahá'í teachings, to endeavor to lead a life that manifests Bahá'í values and spiritual principles, to inform others about the message of Bahá'u'lláh, to be an active participant in Bahá'í community life and its administration, and to promote the welfare of the wider society. The active servant of humanity has replaced the passive congregation!

Shoghi Effendi draws attention to a number of unique and innovative provisions governing the organization of the Bahá'í community, referring, for example, to "The abolition of professional priesthood with its accompanying sacraments of baptism, of communion and of confession of sins, the laws requiring the election by universal suffrage of all local, national, and international Houses of Justice, the total absence of episcopal authority with its attendant privileges, corruptions and bureaucratic tendencies." He indicates that such provisions constitute "evidences of the non-autocratic character of the Bahá'í Administrative Order and of its inclination to democratic methods in the administration of its affairs."[25]

Although the Bahá'í Faith has no professional priesthood and no ordained clerical class, it does assign responsibility for administrative actions to certain individuals. The affairs of the community are administered by a system of democratically elected Spiritual Assemblies, assisted by individuals who are appointed to provide a counseling and educational function. The believers who serve in these capacities, however, do not have episcopal authority over the other members of the community, nor do they constitute an inherently superior and privileged class.

The Nature of Leadership

The Universal House of Justice is the international governing body of the Bahá'í Faith. Under its guidance, democratically elected National and Local Spiritual Assemblies exercise legislative, executive, and judicial authority over the Bahá'í community, thus providing the community's administrative leadership. In the conduct of the community's affairs, the Bahá'í institutions and the individual members of the community make use of Bahá'í consultation, a form of collective decision-making that seeks to arrive at the best solution or to uncover the truth of a matter through an approach that accords equal status to all participants. Although one individual presides at a meeting of consultation, this person does not have any special prerogatives. He or she chairs the gathering, facilitates the flow of the discussion, and encourages full participation in the decision-making process.

The Bahá'í writings set out a number of prerequisites for consultation that might also be considered, from a Bahá'í perspective, as essential to leadership behavior. Together they define a kind of leadership that differs markedly from charismatic and individualistic approaches now prevalent. 'Abdu'l-Bahá specifies that "The prime requisites for them that take counsel together are purity of motive, radiance of spirit, detachment from all else save God, attraction to His Divine Fragrances, humility and lowliness amongst His loved ones, patience and long-suffering in difficulties and servitude to His exalted Threshold. Should they be graciously aided to acquire these attributes, victory from the unseen Kingdom of Bahá shall be vouchsafed to them."[26]

'Abdu'l-Bahá also indicates that all members have the right and responsibility to express their views with absolute freedom, and they are encouraged to put forward their ideas with devotion, care, and moderation. Once a decision is made, all work to support it. Further, in addressing the chair of a Spiritual Assembly, 'Abdu'l-Bahá calls upon her to "Strive . . . with heart and soul, in prayerful humility and self-effacement, to uphold the Law of God and spread His sweet savours abroad." He encourages her to "Endeavour . . . to become the true president of the assemblies of spiritual souls, and a companion to the angels in the realm of the All-Merciful."[27]

The Bahá'í Faith should not be misconstrued as seeking to inhibit the legitimate exercise of individual initiative. On the contrary, it is clear to any who study carefully the Bahá'í teachings that many aspects of these teachings contribute to stimulating creative thought, including the principle of independent investigation of truth, the encouragement to eradicate prejudice and superstition, and the emphasis on training the mind. While Bahá'ís are called upon to follow Bahá'u'lláh's teachings, they are free—indeed encouraged—to strive to understand these teachings and to express that understanding in words and action.

Participation of Women

The Bahá'í Faith actively encourages the participation of all of its members—both women and men—in every aspect of Bahá'í community life. This stands in sharp contrast to other religious Dispensations in which women have been systematically disbarred from access to positions of administrative authority or decision-making in the organization of the religious community. In the religions arising in Western Asia, for example, rabbis, priests, and mullahs were all male. Although in some instances female religious orders were established to perform an educational or healing function, their female leaders were assigned authority only over other women.

In contemporary times, the movement for equality has found limited expression in some modification of this segregation. Within certain liberal denominations of Judaism and Christianity, women are to be found exercising ecclesiastical functions over congregations that include men and women, and in Islam a small number of female scholars have recently emerged.

The Bahá'í Administrative Order is distinguished by the involvement of women in positions of responsibility at local, national, and international levels. Bahá'í women have been called upon to serve as Hands of the Cause of God* and as Counselor† members of the In-

---

* Eminent Bahá'ís appointed to stimulate the propagation and ensure the protection of the Bahá'í Faith.

† Members of a Bahá'í institution concerned with the expansion and development of the Bahá'í Faith.

ternational Teaching Center—a senior institution at the World Center of the Faith—discharging vital responsibilities worldwide in stimulating the expansion of the Bahá'í community, preserving its integrity, and fostering its spiritual life. In addition, women are elected to membership of Spiritual Assemblies, and they participate at the grassroots level of Bahá'í community life through consultations at a wide variety of spiritual, educational, and social gatherings.

From its inception, the Bahá'í Faith has valued the contribution of women in the affairs of the Faith, and active measures have been taken to promote women's involvement, even in countries where the traditional culture has inhibited their active participation in all aspects of community life. It is from this context and against this background that the significance of the Greatest Holy Leaf's role in the administrative functioning of the Bahá'í community needs to be examined.

The Role of the Greatest Holy Leaf in the Administration of the Faith

It is evident, from a study of the events of her life and from the letters she addressed to the Bahá'í community, that the Greatest Holy Leaf willingly, and with touching humility, assumed the heavy administrative responsibilities assigned to her during the absences of 'Abdu'l-Bahá and the Guardian from the World Center of the Faith. She did not allow herself to be held back either by cultural constraints concerning the role of women or by increasing age. She was motivated by her vision of the significance and importance of Bahá'u'lláh's teachings regarding social evolution. She clearly understood the provisions of the Bahá'í Covenant and the importance of the Administrative Order to which it gave rise. In her personal life, she also embodied and modeled the values of this Order, thereby setting an example to individual believers and the members of the Bahá'í institutions alike.

Bahíyyih Khánum's deep understanding of the significance of the Covenant of Bahá'u'lláh is evident in her wholehearted support of its appointed Center, 'Abdu'l-Bahá, and after his passing, of its designated Guardian, Shoghi Effendi. Following the death of Bahá'u'lláh, they were the compass points towards which she oriented her life and established her priorities for service. Through her example and loving encouragement, the Greatest Holy Leaf likewise helped the believers give their allegiance first to the Master and then to the Guardian, thereby preserving the unity of the Faith and steadying its course during these two challenging periods of transition in leadership. The Greatest Holy Leaf's commitment to the Covenant was such that not only did she personally arise to serve and protect it, but the letters she wrote, especially during her tenure in guiding the affairs of the Faith, served as a vital means to educate the believers, to assist them to grasp the importance of the Covenant and understand both its unique features and the functions of its embryonic institutions.

Bahíyyih Khánum's letters demonstrate her profound comprehension of the Covenant of Bahá'u'lláh and 'Abdu'l-Bahá. They also illustrate the clarity with which she described the features of the Covenant as well as the nature of the requirements it placed on the believers to uphold and obey its provisions. She calls attention, for example, to the clear and explicit manner in which Shoghi Effendi's appointment as Guardian was made, and the implications of this appointment for the unity of the community, noting that "The Will and Testament of 'Abdu'l-Bahá is His decisive decree; it gathers the believers together; it preserves their unity; it ensures the protection of the Faith of God. It designates a specific Centre, irrefutably and in writing establishing Shoghi Effendi as Guardian of the Faith and Chosen Branch, so that his name is recorded in the Preserved Tablet, by the fingers of grace and bounty. How grateful should we be that such a bounty was bestowed, and such a favour granted." In another letter she underlines the authority of the Guardian, ordained in the written text, and elaborates on the responsibility of the believers in relation to the Covenant, stating that "A clear Covenant makes our duty plain; an explicit and lucid Text explains the revealed Book; a specifically named Centre has been designated, toward whom all must turn, and the pronouncement of him who is the Guardian of the Cause and the interpreter of the Book has been made the decisive decree. All this is out of the grace and favour of our Beloved, the All-Glorious, and the loving-kindness of Him from the splendours of Whose servitude earth and heaven were illumined."[28]

Bahíyyih Khánum took specific steps to foster the believers' awareness of the importance of establishing National and Local Spiritual Assemblies, while she encouraged and helped train them to conduct their activities according to Bahá'í administrative principles. Her vision and the guidance she provided were drawn both from her own understanding of the needs of the Faith at the particular stage in its evolution and from the seminal letters of the Guardian, which detailed the theory and guiding principles underlying the operation of these embryonic institutions.

From a perusal of her letters it can be seen that, in reiterating the guidance contained in Shoghi Effendi's letters, she was able to communicate to the believers the importance and practical necessity of forming Spiritual Assemblies. She helped the Bahá'ís to appreciate the functions of these Assemblies, the role the institutions of the Faith were to play in the unfoldment of the Bahá'í Administrative Order, and the responsibility of the believers to cherish, serve, and support these evolving institutions. In one visionary letter addressed to the members of a Spiritual Assembly, she stresses the link between the activities of the believers and their administrative bodies, and the spiritual transformation of the world at large. Thus she writes,

It is clear and evident that the body of mankind in this day stands in dire need of such members and organs as are capable, useful and active, so that their movements and activities, their bearing and behaviour, their tender feelings, lofty sentiments and noble intentions may at all times reflect heavenly virtues and perfections and become the expressions of divine attributes and saintly characteristics, thus breathing a new life and spirit into all the dwellers of the world and causing the inner ties and spiritual relationships to be fostered and fortified in all fields of human endeavour.[29]

The Greatest Holy Leaf clearly understood the priority need of the moment in the overall process of the spiritualization of humanity—the establishment of the institutions of the Bahá'í Administrative Order. Beyond that, she grasped the supreme importance of the example these institutions could offer to those searching for alternative models of governance and social organization.

Qualities of Administrative Service

Though the Greatest Holy Leaf did not serve as a member of any elected Bahá'í administrative institution, she respected and upheld the authority of the embryonic Local and National Spiritual Assemblies. She actively supported and promoted the development of these institutions and rejoiced in their achievements. In her correspondence with these bodies, she fostered the maturity of Assembly functioning by calling attention to two elements vital to the consultative process and to decision-making—first, recognition of the importance of the guidance contained in the sacred writings of the Faith and in the letters of Shoghi Effendi, and second, the use of this guidance in assessing the current needs and in establishing priorities of action for the ongoing progress of the Bahá'í community.

Bahíyyih Khánum embodied and modeled the values of the Bahá'í Administrative Order. She manifested such qualities as "unquestioned loyalty, . . . selfless devotion, . . . a well-trained mind, . . . recognized ability and mature experience," attributes identified by Shoghi Effendi as the distinguishing characteristics of the members of Spiritual Assemblies. In addition, her letters illustrated the application of the spiritual and intellectual qualities that 'Abdu'l-Bahá called for in the practice of consultation. It is interesting to note that, in relation to this process, 'Abdu'l-Bahá counseled the believers to "proceed with the utmost devotion, courtesy, dignity, care and moderation to express their views." "They must," he stated, "in every matter search out the truth and not insist upon their own opinion, for stubbornness and persistence in one's views will lead ultimately to discord and wrangling and the truth will remain hidden." He stressed that the "members must with all freedom express their own thoughts, and it is in no wise permissible for one to belittle the thought of another." Rather, the individual "must with moderation set forth the truth, and should differences of opinion arise a majority of voices must prevail, and all must obey and submit to the majority." Finally, 'Abdu'l-Bahá emphasized the importance of supporting the decision of the Assembly, asserting that "whatsoever thing is arranged in harmony and with love and purity of motive, its result is light, and should the least trace of estrangement prevail the result shall be darkness upon darkness."[30]

The style and content of the Greatest Holy Leaf's letters provide a useful example of how to achieve the delicate balance of "devotion, courtesy, dignity, care and moderation" in the full and free expression of views called for by the Master. Indeed, the sensitive, moderate, articulate, yet forthright manner in which the Greatest Holy Leaf communicated with the believers and their institutions is instructive and worthy of careful study.[31]

While the Greatest Holy Leaf was always courteous, she did not flinch from calling attention to deficiencies or from taking firm action, should the need arise. Her willingness to sever relationships with the members of Bahá'u'lláh's family who betrayed their spiritual principles by their violation of the Covenant at the time of her father's death, her refusal to receive her treacherous half-brother Mírzá Muḥammad-'Alí in the house of 'Abdu'l-Bahá during the days immediately following the passing of the Master, and her courageous and steadfast strategy of resistance against the machinations of those who rose to attack the Faith at a later time provide telling examples of Bahíyyih K͟hánum's determination to take a firm and principled stand in order to uphold the provisions of the Covenant, to protect the Bahá'í Faith, and to preserve the unity of its community.

The Greatest Holy Leaf's approach to service was based on spiritual and administrative principles, and it was practical, systematic, evolutionary, goal-directed, strategic, and forward-looking. Her actions reflect a keen sense of responsibility. During her childhood and adolescence she grasped with gratitude the opportunity to undertake delicate missions assigned by her father, Bahá'u'lláh, remaining ever willing to extend the range of her services and to take on tasks that were onerous and challenging. Supreme among these activities was her role later in life of giving leadership to the Faith during the travels of 'Abdu'l-Bahá and the absences of Shoghi Effendi during the early years of his Guardianship. In this capacity she made an invaluable contribution to preserving the unity of the Bahá'í community and to ensuring that the Administrative Order was established along sound lines.

The Greatest Holy Leaf gave systematic attention to the on-going work of the Faith. She made a conscious effort to be well informed about the conditions of the worldwide Bahá'í community and to be aware of world events. Her letters provided a reliable source of information about developments in the Faith and conveyed guidance based on the instructions of 'Abdu'l-Bahá and the Guardian. During the period of time when she supervised the direction of the Faith, she monitored the completion of projects undertaken during 'Abdu'l-Bahá's ministry and followed up new initiatives the Guardian set in motion, including the all-important task of appealing to the government to regain custody of the keys to the Shrine of Bahá'u'lláh that had been seized by the enemies of the Faith.

Cognizant of the important contribution of the individual Bahá'í to the unfoldment of the Faith and to social evolution, the Greatest Holy Leaf gave particular attention to stimulating individual initiative. From her letters it can be seen how she constantly encouraged the Bahá'ís. She provided inspiration through her poignant descriptions of the sacrificial exploits of their spiritual forebears. She called attention to the challenges confronting the Bahá'í community and to the opportunities for service that these difficulties provided. Through her expressions of pleasure when the believers took hesitant steps in a new direction or embarked on a new activity, she endorsed measures that would increase their level of competence and reinforce their courage and perseverance.

Apart from the multifaceted responsibilities placed on her shoulders in the absence of 'Abdu'l-Bahá and the Guardian, the Greatest Holy Leaf had a number of ongoing administrative functions. One such example is the role she performed in relation to visiting Bahá'í pilgrims. From the time of Bahá'u'lláh, and more particularly during the ministry of 'Abdu'l-Bahá and the early years of the Guardianship, Bahíyyih Khánum was actively involved with the pilgrims who traveled to the Holy Land to attain the presence of the head of the Faith and, later on, to visit the holy shrines. As the "last survivor" of the Heroic Age, the Greatest Holy Leaf greatly inspired the pilgrims with her reminiscences about the early days of the Faith.

The pilgrims were also deeply touched by her firm faith, serenity, and confident vision. Further, in her capacity as the trusted custodian of the sacred relics and historical items associated with the birth of the new revelation, the Greatest Holy Leaf displayed these precious archival treasures to the visiting pilgrims. Finally, the Greatest Holy Leaf was responsible for attending to the pilgrims' physical needs. She was involved in overall coordination of the pilgrims' housing and in arranging for the preparation of their food.[32]

Bahíyyih Khánum's actions illustrate the potential impact of a life committed to individual and social transformation and to the creation of administrative institutions that embody spiritual and civic values. Her loyal and patient support of these embryonic Bahá'í institutions, her confidence in their evolution, and her willingness to assume administrative responsibility serve as a model to counteract the prevailing climate of distrust and disengagement characterizing the present-day relationships between those who govern and those who are governed.

Responsibilities of Rank

An enduring aspect of human society has been its classification of the population with regard to rank, from the village level with its chiefs and elders to complex urban entities with rulers, ecclesiastics, educators, traders, and craftsmen, all assigned their particular position in a rank-ordered society.

During the present time of change in which thoughtful people are raising questions about the form that society should best take in the future, it is natural that the need for rank be scrutinized and its features, both positive and negative, assessed. We therefore consider this issue here, because the conduct of the Greatest Holy Leaf, who is assigned a high rank in the Bahá'í Dispensation, provides useful insight into the role to be played by people of rank in the Bahá'í social system.

The Dilemma of Rank

Criticism is often quite justifiably directed at the role exercised by people of rank in society. In many instances, rank is associated with a class of people who are accorded unwarranted privileges and allowed to exercise power over others for their personal advantage. In extreme cases they are allowed to use this power to violate the law without fear of restraint or punishment. Rank often leads to arrogance and a manifest sense of superiority towards others.

In the contemporary world, the issue of rank and privilege continues to be a source of contention and disunity. Social scientists maintain that conflicts are likely to occur when there are perceived divergent interests between two or more parties. They describe three general types of conflict: conflicts of interest (e.g., a dispute over territory or a scarce resource), conflicts over values (e.g., a conflict over religion, ideology, or ethnicity), and conflicts over relationships (e.g., conflicts between a minority and a majority, between a ruling class and a ruled class).[33]

A number of theorists have studied the impact of asymmetrical relationships on the promotion of conflict and social division. Asymmetrical relationships are characterized by a large power differential between the parties. In such settings, the system of relationships between the various elements of society is hierarchically structured. The findings suggest that those people at the bottom, by reason of their involuntary membership in certain ethnic, class, or other groups, are generally unable to obtain fair access to the social, economic, political, legal, educational, and other resources typically enjoyed and presided over by those at the top of the hierarchy. These dominant and more powerful parties tend to devalue the less powerful parties, deprive them of recognition, and exclude them from participation in the decision-making process. The dominant partners also tend to use force, coercion, and violence to achieve the desired ends and as a strategy for conflict resolution.[34]

Hence in societies with highly crystallized class systems, the presence of individuals and groups who derive their high social status from family background, from wealth, education, or professional position may well be regarded as a source of conflict and may militate against recognition of the oneness of the human family and constitute a barrier to social evolution. Indeed, the attitudes of superiority manifested by the members of powerful elites often give rise to adversarial relationships with people of lower status. Likewise, to preserve their prerogatives and high position they use their considerable influence to support the status quo.

However, it is clear that there are manifest benefits to a society from the existence of ranks within it. The organization of society requires differentiation of functions, with some assignments carrying with them a degree of authority, either legal or moral. If rank is associated with outstanding achievement, it can foster aspiration among people of talent and capacity whose striving to develop their abilities brings with it the reward of a high rank in society. Their rank gives greater weight to statements they make within their fields of competence. In this way, those of recognized accomplishment are able to exert a beneficial influence on the progress of the society. Beyond that, it may well be argued that it is only fitting that individuals should show a proper measure of respect for those who have excelled in a skill of value to society or who occupy a position in which they can perform functions that will aid in the upliftment of the general population.

The dilemma of rank is therefore a matter of devising a form by which it can play a positive role in social cohesion and progress while avoiding the negative aspects that are detrimental to justice and unity. This leads us to a detailed consideration of the Bahá'í concept of rank.

The Bahá'í Concept of Rank

The Bahá'í writings do not convey a detailed description of the form of society anticipated for the future. Nevertheless, certain salient features evident from a perusal of these texts will, no doubt, receive elaboration as society develops.

The Universal House of Justice has clarified that "the proper functioning of human society requires the preservation of ranks and classes within its membership." Further detail is provided in a number of places in Bahá'í literature, principally in *The Secret of Divine Civilization,* where 'Abdu'l-Bahá sets out the principal ranks in society, assigning a high position to wise and skillful statesmen, people of learning, and those engaged in the endeavor to improve society and to increase the comfort of the citizens.[35]

Bahá'u'lláh underlines the significance of rank and of its role in society. According to Bahá'u'lláh, the key to social cohesion and progress is "the unity of rank and station." He indicates that the fundamental dynamic principle driving such unity is the realization that individuals "should regard themselves as being on the same level as the others and in the same station." This realization in turn is motivated by one's awareness that a person's nobility resides in his or her being "a repository of the sign of God." To emphasize the importance of this underlying spiritual perspective on social relationships, Bahá'u'lláh calls attention to the destructive influence of those who regard themselves as superior in knowledge, learning, or virtue, and those who exalt themselves or seek preference, since these behaviors undermine the basis of society. Such an approach addresses, at the fundamental level of spiritual values, the negative impact of asymmetrical relationships with their inherent attitudes of superiority and authoritarian domination.[36]

In conjunction with the legitimacy assigned to the existence of ranks in a Bahá'í society is the recognition that rank is here given a unique form that resolves the dilemma described in the preceding section. The social advantages of rank are maintained, and the potential for injustice and oppression is removed.

Functionality is intimately associated with the Bahá'í concept of rank. It may be assigned in recognition of outstanding accomplishment in activities of benefit to society, or it may be an aspect of Bahá'í administrative responsibilities that an individual is called upon to assume through election or appointment.

In a passage concerning "the protection and preservation of the station of God's servants" Bahá'u'lláh affirms that His followers "should not deny any soul the reward due to him," and that they "should treat craftsmen with deference." In another place He praises people of learning "who dedicate themselves to the guidance of others and are freed and well guarded from the promptings of a base and covetous nature"; they are lauded as "stars of the heaven of true knowledge," and He states, "it is essential to treat them with deference." Implicit in this call for deference is that such individuals are, because of their accomplishments and character, distinguished from the generality of society and thus accorded a social rank.[37]

Rank exists in the Bahá'í Administrative Order. The Hands of the Cause of God are, in many passages, described as being of "exalted rank." The Universal House of Justice, following the appointment of Continental Counselors, clarified that "the Boards of Counselors outrank the National Institutions of the Faith." Here again, the element of functionality is paramount, with the House of Justice affirming that each Board of Continental Counselors "has the necessary rank to enable it to ensure that it is kept properly informed and that the Spiritual Assemblies give due consideration to its advice and recommendations. However, the essence of the relationships between Bahá'í institutions is loving consultation and a common desire to serve the Cause of God rather than a matter of rank or station."[38]

Particular attention should be directed to the rank assigned to the members of the family of Bahá'u'lláh since the abuse of rank has historically been due, very often, to actions of those without merit who are given privilege or deference for no reason other than family relationship. Bahá'u'lláh calls upon His followers to show respect to the members of His family. Referring to His male descendants, the *Aghsán*,* He states, "It is enjoined upon everyone to manifest love towards the Aghsán," and "It is incumbent upon everyone to show courtesy to, and have regard for the Aghsán, that thereby the Cause of God may be glorified and His Word exalted." However, this designation carries with it the restriction that "God hath not granted them any right to the property of others" and the functional responsibility placed on His family members in these words: "We exhort you to fear God, to perform praiseworthy deeds and to do that which is meet and seemly and serveth to exalt your station." Shoghi Effendi in a letter written on his behalf provides the following elaboration of this theme: "The higher the station of those who have the privilege of being related by ties of blood to the Centre of the Cause the greater indeed must be their responsibility to serve, and thus prove in deeds their worthiness to occupy such an exalted and responsible position."[39]

Bahá'í history shows that rank arising from family relationship can be lost through failure to exercise the duties associated with it. The members of Bahá'u'lláh's family who violated His Covenant "were precipitated, without exception, from the enviable positions they

---

* Literally "Branches," the sons and other male descendants of Bahá'u'lláh.

occupied." Shoghi Effendi, in praising the Greatest Holy Leaf and her mother and her martyred brother, describes them as "these three incomparably precious souls who, next to the Central Figures of our Faith, tower in rank above the vast multitude of the heroes, Letters, martyrs, hands, teachers and administrators of the Cause of Bahá'u'lláh." Such a description carries with it a further confirmation that rank conferred through relationship to Bahá'u'lláh carries high responsibilities, which were met by these three distinguished family members to the exclusion of those who failed in their duties.[40]

More generally, those assigned rank in the Bahá'í Administrative Order are warned in the strongest terms about the dangers of abusing their position. The Universal House of Justice refers to a letter written on behalf of the Guardian: "He pointed out how, in the past, it was certain individuals who 'accounted themselves as superior in knowledge and elevated in position' who caused division, and that it was those 'who pretended to be the most distinguished of all' who 'always proved themselves to be the source of contention.'" The House of Justice has stated that "those who occupy ranks should never exploit their position or regard themselves as being superior to others." Bahá'u'lláh Himself affirms, in a passage quoted by the House of Justice in that message, that "'Indeed, man is noble, inasmuch as each one is a repository of the sign of God. Nevertheless, to regard oneself as superior in knowledge, learning or virtue, or to exalt oneself or seek preference, is a grievous transgression. Great is the blessedness of those who are adorned with the ornament of this unity and have been graciously confirmed by God.'"[41]

The Universal House of Justice comments, "Courtesy, reverence, dignity, respect for the rank and achievements of others are virtues which contribute to the harmony and well-being of every community, but pride and self-aggrandizement are among the most deadly of sins."[42]

The following statement of the Universal House of Justice offers an admonition to those occupying a rank in society and a reassurance to those who do not: "The true spiritual station of any soul is known only to God. It is quite a different thing from the ranks and stations that men and women occupy in the various sectors of society."[43]

An innovative feature of the Bahá'í Faith is the important distinction made between rank and spiritual station. In a tablet of Bahá'u'lláh we read the following:

> Know thou moreover that in the Day of His Manifestation all things besides God shall be brought forth and placed equally, irrespective of their rank being high or low. . . . When the Word of God is revealed unto all created things whoso then giveth ear and heedeth the Call is, indeed, reckoned among the most distinguished souls, though he be a carrier of ashes. And he who turneth away is accounted as the lowliest of His servants, though he be a ruler amongst men and the possessor of all the books that are in the heavens and on earth.[44]

While personal accomplishment is encouraged and the expertise and contributions of people of rank are respected and appreciated, the ultimate aim in life, for a Bahá'í, is to attain spiritual excellence. Bahá'u'lláh affirms that "Man's merit lieth in service and virtue and not in the pageantry of wealth and riches." Likewise, 'Abdu'l-Bahá indicates that "man's highest distinction is to be lowly before and obedient to his God" and that "his greatest glory, his most exalted rank and honor, depend on his close observance of the Divine commands and prohibitions." He further observes, "the happiness and greatness, the rank and station, the pleasure and peace, of an individual have never consisted in his personal wealth, but rather in his excellent character, his high resolve, the breadth of his learning, and his ability to solve difficult problems."[45]

The Bahá'í writings call attention to a number of qualities that are associated with spiritual distinction—to which all believers aspire, irrespective of rank. Bahá'u'lláh states, for example, "Whoso is endued with courtesy hath indeed attained a sublime station," and 'Abdu'l-Bahá indicates that "man's supreme honor and real happiness lie in self-respect, in high resolves and noble purposes, in integrity and moral quality, in immaculacy of mind."[46]

'Abdu'l-Bahá emphasizes the importance of service to humanity in one's spiritual life, noting that "the honor and distinction of the individual" reside in being "a source of social good." Elaborating on this theme he states, "The highest righteousness of all is for blessed souls to take hold of the hands of the helpless and deliver them out of their ignorance and abasement and poverty, and with pure motives, and only for the sake of God, to arise and energetically devote themselves to the service of the masses, forgetting their own worldly advantage and working only to serve the general good." Furthermore, 'Abdu'l-Bahá allies "true religious faith" with the implementation of the high goals set out above, noting that the individual "who puts his faith in God and believes in the words of God . . . will for the sake of God abandon his own peace and profit and will freely consecrate his heart and soul to the common good."[47]

Search for Novel Approaches to Leadership

Given the emphasis in the Bahá'í teachings on principled behavior and a service orientation, and recognizing the important role people of rank and capacity play in fostering social cohesion and enhancing the process of social transformation, it is interesting to note that recent research in the fields of conflict resolution and management have endeavored to identify novel approaches to peacemaking and to leadership that differ from those that prevail in present-day society. In relation to the former, attention has been focused, for example, on means of reducing conflict in society. It has been found that, among other things, establishing symmetric relations that are based on a sense of equality between contending parties, and the substitution of a participatory approach for a power-oriented approach to problem-solving constitute important means of resolving conflict. A Committee for the Psychological Study of Peace has expanded the concept of conflict resolution to encompass the idea of a "culture of peace," described in the following terms:

> Conceptually, a culture of peace should be viewed not as a conflict-free utopia but as a culture in which individuals, groups, and nations have productive, cooperative relations with one another and manage their inevitable conflicts constructively. It is a culture in which there are caring and just relations among individuals, groups and nations based on full realization of their positive interdependence with one another and with their environment. Thus a culture of peace entails much more than the absence of war—it entails social justice, norms of equity and multicultural sensitivity, and social relations conducive to nonviolence, sustainable development, and human well-being.[48]

Such findings correlate with the Bahá'í perspective on rank and provide useful insights into the dynamics that give rise to social cohesion and progress.

In the field of management, a recent study investigated the management styles of individuals who are successful in transforming a good organization into an excellent one. The findings, described as "counterintuitive," noted that "People generally assume that transforming companies from good to great requires larger-than-life leaders—big personalities." However, contrary to conventional wisdom and to "much of management theory to date," the study found that "an individual who blends extreme personal humility with intense professional will" possesses the combination of qualities needed to catalyze sustained change in an organization.[49]

There are a number of significant implications of a leadership style characterized by humility and will. According to the study referred to above, humility is manifested in the form of "a compelling modesty." The individual, for example, is never boastful and shuns public adulation; he or she acts with "quiet, calm determination," motivates others by reference to "inspired standards" rather than by "inspiring charisma," and is ambitious for the organization rather than self-promoting. Besides extreme humility, such individuals display a strong professional will, as exemplified by their determination to uphold high standards and to inspire others in the organization to do likewise. They also take strategic action to ensure the long-term success of the organization and empower others to participate in this process.[50]

In light of the foregoing discussion concerning the Bahá'í concept of rank and of the ways in which it differs from contemporary understandings of rank, we offer the example of Bahíyyih Khánum, the highest-ranking woman in the Bahá'í Dispensation, as a means of gaining additional insights into the responsibilities associated with rank.

The Rank and Station of the Greatest Holy Leaf

Bahá'u'lláh conferred upon His daughter, Bahíyyih Khánum, an exalted and privileged station. Addressing her in the following words, He states, "Verily, We have elevated thee to the rank of one of the most distinguished among thy sex, and granted thee, in My court, a station such as none other woman hath surpassed. Thus have We preferred thee and raised thee above the rest, as a sign of grace from Him Who is the Lord of the throne on high and earth below."[51]

Though the Greatest Holy Leaf's rank derived from her family background, family membership was not sufficient in and of itself. It is evident that her elevation to such a high station was, in large part, dependent on her actions and the qualities she manifested. In describing the sacrificial services Bahíyyih Khánum rendered in the time of Bahá'u'lláh and in the early days of 'Abdu'l-Bahá's ministry, the Guardian affirms that

> Whether in the management of the affairs of His Household in which she excelled, or in the social relationships which she so assiduously cultivated in order to shield both Bahá'u'lláh and 'Abdu'l-Bahá, whether in the unfailing attention she paid to the everyday needs of her Father, or in the traits of generosity, of affability and kindness, which she manifested, the Greatest Holy Leaf had by that time abundantly demonstrated her worthiness to rank as one of the noblest figures intimately associated with the life-long work of Bahá'u'lláh.[52]

It is also apparent that the Bahá'í community became progressively aware of her rank as the range of her functions increased. Shoghi Effendi attests that when the enemies of the Faith created difficulties during the time of Bahá'u'lláh's incarceration in the prison-city of Acre, the Greatest Holy Leaf's "value and high rank" became known throughout the community. Understanding of the rank of the Greatest Holy Leaf increased when her functions become somewhat public— when, for example, she served as 'Abdu'l-Bahá's "competent deputy" and "vicegerent" during his travels in the West—and again during the early years of the Guardianship when, during Shoghi Effendi's absences from the World Center, she had the major responsibility of overseeing the affairs of the Faith. The Guardian's decision, announced in the following letter, to call for an extended period of mourning following the passing of the Greatest Holy Leaf further reinforced the believers' appreciation of her rank. The letter states,

> O faithful friends! It is right and fitting that out of honour to her most high station, in the gatherings of the followers of Bahá'u'lláh, whether of the East or the West, all Bahá'í festivals and celebrations should be completely suspended for a period of nine months, and that in every city and village, memorial meetings should be held, with all solemnity, spirituality, lowliness and consecration—where, in the choicest of language, may be described at length the shining attributes of that most resplendent Leaf, that archetype of the people of Bahá. [53]

Finally, her integral role in the unfoldment of the Bahá'í Administrative Order is underlined by the location of her grave, which serves as a focal point for the edifices housing the major institutions of the Bahá'í Faith on Mount Carmel.

Functions Associated with Her Rank

As already mentioned, authoritative leadership of the Bahá'í community is vested in democratically elected institutions operating at the local, national, and international levels of society, rather than in individuals, thereby avoiding some of the abuses traditionally associated with rank and privilege. Within the Bahá'í Administrative Order, consequently, people of rank, including the Greatest Holy Leaf, do not have the right to direct or exercise authority over the Bahá'í community.

Bahíyyih Khánum did not seek power or position for herself, though she willingly fulfilled the administrative tasks to which she was assigned. Rather, the Greatest Holy Leaf ensured that the believers turned for guidance to 'Abdu'l-Bahá and, later, to Shoghi Effendi, and she directed the attention of the members of the community to the authoritative guidance contained in the teachings of the Faith.

In her capacity as acting head of the Bahá'í Faith, the Greatest Holy Leaf oversaw the day-to-day activities of the worldwide Bahá'í community. She was the designated point of contact for the believers and their institutions, the source of reliable information, and the one to turn to when problems arose. She collaborated with the Spiritual Assemblies, offering them advice and encouraging them to plan courses of action consonant with the guidance contained in the writings of the Faith. She fostered the development of these embryonic institutions, giving them space to exercise initiative in line with local conditions.

The Greatest Holy Leaf was also a force for unity in the Bahá'í community as evidenced by her actions to protect the community against the attacks of the Covenant-breakers, her patient education of the community, her expressions of loving concern, and her forging of relationships with government officials. She took wise steps to promote acceptance of the leadership of the Spiritual Assemblies by members of a community who were more used to a charismatic style of individual leadership, and to forge a greater cohesion and a sense of identity in the worldwide community.

In carrying out her functions, the Greatest Holy Leaf derived her inspiration and direction from the seminal writings of the Faith, and she drew upon the example of both her father, Bahá'u'lláh, and her brother, 'Abdu'l-Bahá. She motivated the believers by directing them to the standard set out in the Bahá'í teachings, and she exerted a moral influence by calling upon the friends to put into practice the guidance contained in the sacred writings. It is evident that she gained the respect of the believers not only because of her designated rank, but also because of her unique qualities, the exemplary way in which she carried out her assigned functions, and the enormous contribution she made to the development of the Bahá'í community.

The Nature of Her Relationships

Examining the Greatest Holy Leaf's relationships with others helps to shed light on the Bahá'í perspective regarding the responsibilities associated with rank. The manner in which she carried out her functions differs markedly from many contemporary models. Absent is any sense of superiority, exclusiveness, or self-promotion. On the contrary, Shoghi Effendi states that Bahíyyih Khánum possessed "an unaffected simplicity of manners; an extreme sociability which made her accessible to all," and "a quiet and unassuming disposition that served to enhance a thousandfold the prestige of her exalted rank." Furthermore, she manifested "a tenderness of heart that obliterated every distinction of creed, class and colour."[54]

Personal humility and modesty were outstanding characteristics of the Greatest Holy Leaf. Illustrative of this is her response to Shoghi Effendi's appointment of her to give leadership to the Faith. She writes, "During his absence ... this prisoner is appointed to administer the affairs of the Faith, in consultation with the members of the Holy Household."[55]

Throughout her life Bahíyyih Khánum was, in the words of Shoghi Effendi, "forgetful of her own self." In her personal chronicles she recounts the details of the life of her father and the exploits of 'Abdu'l-Bahá. She rarely inserts herself into the historical record, and even more rarely does she share her personal reactions to the events that she not only witnessed but in which she actively participated.[56]

No task was too menial or too unimportant for her to undertake. She seized the opportunities for service that came her way. Her guiding principle was to give the highest priority to meeting the needs of the Faith. She exemplified a consummate blend of humility and will. Shoghi Effendi testifies, "Stranger and friend alike were captured by her loving-kindness, her spiritual nature, her unceasing care for them and tender ways; enamoured of her great indulgence toward them, and how she favoured them and cherished them. The mind could only marvel at that subtle and ethereal being, at the majesty and greatness of her, and the heavenly modesty, and the forbearance and long suffering. Even in the thick of the worst ordeals, she would smile like an opening rose, and no matter how dark and calamitous the times, like a bright candle she would shed her light."[57]

The members of the family, the pilgrims, and all who had the opportunity to meet her were attracted to her presence. As reported by one of the Bahá'í pilgrims, Bahíyyih <u>Kh</u>ánum's "strong yet gentle quality of authority made her naturally the head of the household group that circled about 'Abdu'l-Bahá." Another pilgrim left the following record of her impressions of the Greatest Holy Leaf and the lessons she drew from her example. She writes,

> Her balance, sense of fineness and fitness and practical judgment she displayed in creating order and grace in the household, and all the elements that make for well-being she blended in an ambience of harmony. Her strong will was never used to override and her decided opinions were never pressed upon another. Her ways were gentle. Others might break the shell with a blow; it was for her to unsheath the kernel with infinite care and skill. In her you met with no exactions, no biddance: she beckoned, smiling, and would have no one come heavy-footed or bent to her will. So quietly did she make her influence felt that you were scarcely conscious of its working. [58]

The Greatest Holy Leaf's approach illustrates her skill in bringing to bear a sense of organization, order, and a unifying spirit.

Throughout her life the Greatest Holy Leaf was a peacemaker and a force for unity and understanding. Her approach to friend and enemy of the Faith, to high and low, was constructive, sensitive, respectful, and invariably patient. Indeed, it is interesting to consider the importance she gave to her interactions with others. Shoghi Effendi indicates that the Greatest Holy Leaf "assiduously cultivated" "social relationships" for the sole purpose of shielding both Bahá'u'lláh and 'Abdu'l-Bahá. She did not retreat from conflict, nor did she hesitate to call attention to the Bahá'í standard and to set limits when necessary. The unity she fostered was based on spiritual and administrative principles rather than on compromise, thereby creating conditions for the establishment of "a culture of peace," for social cohesion, and progress.[59]

The following passage from a letter written on behalf of Shoghi Effendi provides insight into the nature of Bahíyyih Khánum's relationships with others and illustrates some of the particular traits that characterized her interactions:

> She who was left in trust by Bahá'u'lláh was the symbol of His infinite compassion, the day star in the heaven of His bounty and grace. That sanctified spirit revealed the loving-kindness of Him who was the Beauty of the All-Glorious, and was the welling spring of the favours and bestowals of Him Who was the Lord, the Most High. She was the comforter of anyone who grieved, the solace of any with a broken heart. She, that Remnant of Bahá, was a loving mother to the orphan, and for the hapless and bewildered it was she who would find a way. Her holy life lit up the world; her heavenly qualities and ways were a standard for people all over the earth. Like a cloud of grace, she

showered down gifts, and her bestowals, like the morning winds, refreshed the soul.[60]

The Greatest Holy Leaf's relationship with others was sensitive and very nurturing. At the time of 'Abdu'l-Bahá's passing, she showed her understanding of the believers' sorrows and anxieties. In addition, she consoled the Bahá'ís and encouraged them to be steadfast in their service to the Cause. She empathized with them as they endeavored to understand the new provisions of the Covenant and the necessity of following the embryonic institutions of the Faith. Showering her loving attention on the believers, she advised and trained them and then rejoiced in their accomplishments.

The Greatest Holy Leaf's relationship to the young Guardian, Shoghi Effendi, was very tender and worthy of close examination. The extent to which Shoghi Effendi drew upon his great-aunt's encouragement and strength is evident in his affirmations that he was "reared by the hands of her loving kindness" and that his "frail being" was "leavened with her love, refreshed by her companionship, [and] sustained by her eternal spirit." Shoghi Effendi states that in the dark period following 'Abdu'l-Bahá's passing, he was "in the embrace of her love," and that "with incomparable pity and tenderness" the Greatest Holy Leaf "persuaded, guided, and urged" him "on to the requirements of servitude."[61]

The letters Shoghi Effendi wrote at the time of the passing of the Greatest Holy Leaf are replete with expressions of loving affection and gratitude for the support she gave him. It is also clear that Shoghi Effendi was greatly inspired by her example of sacrifice and service. In one of his letters he writes, "When, in the morning and the evening, I call her beloved face to mind, and let her smiles, that nourished the spirit, pass again before my eyes, and I think over all her bounty to me, all her unnumbered kindnesses, and remember that astonishing meekness she showed in her sufferings—then the flames of yearning love are kindled yet again. . . ."[62]

From the foregoing, it is apparent that the Greatest Holy Leaf manifested a number of maternal characteristics in her relationships with others. Indeed, Shoghi Effendi describes her as "a real mother to every one of us, a comforter in our pains and anxieties, and a friend in our moments of utter loneliness and despair." Elaborating on her nurturing qualities, Shoghi Effendi calls attention to the "maternal care and love" that Bahíyyih Khánum exemplified. He characterizes it as a "consuming love which is born of God and which alone can galvanize the souls of men." It is evident, therefore, that the kind of "maternal care and love" she manifested transcends the usual notions of a mother-child relationship. It represents, instead, a broad and more inclusive conception that applies equally to both women and men.[63]

Finally, when Bahíyyih Khánum passed away, and the Guardian depicted the wave of grief that swept through the Bahá'í community in both the East and the West, he indicated that not only had the Bahá'ís lost a beloved and respected friend, but that they were, he said, "lamenting like orphans left destitute." This graphic phrase captures the uniqueness of the Greatest Holy Leaf's relationship with others and the depth of their response to her person.[64]

The life and example of the Greatest Holy Leaf not only provides a unique perspective on the issue of rank and its role in society, but also on the manner in which the responsibilities associated with rank might be discharged so as to foster social cohesion and individual initiative. She actively supported and collaborated with the governing institutions, and she modeled a leadership style that exemplified nurturance, trust, and encouragement. She inspired and motivated others by appealing to spiritual principles and the standards set out in the writings of the Bahá'í Faith. She earned the respect of the believers and nonbelievers alike because of the outstanding quality of her contribution to the unity and unfoldment of the Bahá'í community.

Dealing with Change

Accelerating change is one of the pervasive characteristics of the modern world today. The forces of modernization have a direct impact on the individual and on all facets of human society. While some changes are readily embraced, changes in values and patterns of behavior tend to arouse the active resistance of those who are committed to preserving the status quo. In such instances, change is seen as a threat to personal, religious, ethnic, or national identity, and as the cause of social tension and disunity. One of the challenges of contemporary society, therefore, is the need to envision and then create a dynamic social order that can accommodate both change and constancy within the overall limits of preserving the unity and identity of the community. Associated with this challenge is the identification of the coping strategies used by individuals who not only manage personal change in a constructive manner but who also foster the processes of social evolution.

In this section we will examine the Bahá'í perspective on change and offer the example of the strategies the Greatest Holy Leaf used in steering the Bahá'í community through its period of transition from the Heroic Age to the Formative Age of the Faith.

An Ever-Advancing Civilization

The great religions of the world have traditionally been sources of vision and values and primary agents of socialization. The spiritual principles and values they inculcate not only form the basis of a unifying world view but also serve to motivate individuals and social institutions to act on these principles and to use them as a standard against which to weigh practical actions. Religion can, therefore, make a significant contribution to the process of change. The purpose of religion is to give rise to true liberty of the human spirit, so that each individual can be free to develop his or her capabilities. This liberation is the basis for the expression of the powers of creativity and innovation. The result must necessarily be change in all aspects of human life, the acquisition of new knowledge, the development of sciences and means of education, the flourishing of artistic expression and cultural forms, advances in trade and communications, and the creation of new forms of social organization.

In the following passage 'Abdu'l-Bahá emphasizes the vital role of religion in forging social cohesion and fostering the development of civilization. He writes,

> Universal benefits derive from the grace of the Divine religions, for they lead their true followers to sincerity of intent, to high purpose, to purity and spotless honor, to surpassing kindness and compassion, to the keeping of their covenants when they have covenanted, to concern for the rights of others, to liberality, to justice in every aspect of life, to humanity and philanthropy, to valor and to unflagging efforts in the service of mankind. It is religion, to sum up, which produces all human virtues, and it is these virtues which are the bright candles of civilization.[65]

History, including the contemporary record, shows that religion has also been antagonistic to change and has proven to be a resolute and determined opponent to the forces of change. One might well inquire why this should be the case, that so powerful a change agent, designed to promote the upliftment of humanity, should betray its fundamental purpose and become a reactionary obstacle to change.

The reasons are many. Principal among them is the apprehension of the ecclesiastical authorities that change will lead to an undermining of their position, through the expression of democratic aspirations, the quest for equality of the sexes, and the desire for new organizational structures to meet the needs of a modern society. Social change also renders some of the precepts of the religion inappropriate in the new circumstances. New issues arise on which the religion is silent, with the result that consensus cannot be obtained from the body of adherents. Advances in scientific knowledge also provide refutation to the dogmatic statements of the ecclesiastical authorities about such matters as the size and nature of the universe, the age of the earth, the disintegration of physical remains after death, the sources of illness and disease, evolution, and the diversity of races and peoples.

The Bahá'í Faith presents an entirely different model. It is a religion that promotes change and regards all human beings as having the true purpose of participating in advancing civilization. 'Abdu'l-Bahá spells out the wisdom of change, observing that "the times never remain the same, for change is a necessary quality and an essential attribute of this world, and of time and place."[66]

Bahá'u'lláh's writings view the progress of human history in terms of the evolution, through stages of infancy and adolescence to adulthood, of increasing levels of human capacity and maturity. This evolution toward maturity has its counterpart in the increasingly complex organization of human society, which, starting with the family in primitive times, has evolved successively into the tribe, the city-state, and the nation. The culmination of this process is the unification of the whole world, which will signalize the "coming of age of the entire human race" and mark the "last and highest stage in the . . . evolution of man's collective life on this planet."[67]

The Bahá'í writings go beyond mere theory. The provisions of the Bahá'í Covenant and the institutions it established—the clear and unambiguous appointment of successors, the designation of authorized interpreters of the writings of Bahá'u'lláh, and the election of the Universal House of Justice, an institution charged with legislating on matters not expressly covered in the sacred writings, or which are obscure and causing division—serve as an impetus to the stimulation of creative thought and the promotion of change. Shoghi Effendi characterizes the central institution of the Administrative Order as having as one of its purposes to "adapt loyally and intelligently the Faith to the requirements of progressive society." He further describes the Bahá'í teachings as functioning to create a worldwide community that is able "even as a living organism, to expand and adapt itself to the needs and requirements of an ever-changing society."[68]

The Bahá'í social order accommodates change while preserving the basic unity and identity of the community. On the one hand, the spiritual principles, laws, and teachings of the Faith and the pattern of the Administrative Order constitute the basis for the maintenance of order. On the other hand, progress, which is characterized as one of the "ordinances of God," is an important value and underlies the Bahá'í worldview.[69]

The Bahá'í Faith strongly encourages all of its members to explore the meaning of its authoritative teachings and to offer to others their insights and understanding. The Universal House of Justice states that "such individual interpretation is considered the fruit of man's rational power and conducive to a better understanding of the teachings, provided that no disputes or arguments arise among the friends and the individual himself understands and makes it clear that his views are merely his own." However, it warns the Bahá'ís against the dangers of dogmatic statements on issues that will only become clear in the course of time, perhaps with advances in scientific understanding or in the light of human experience and social development. The Universal House of Justice writes, the believers must recognize the importance of intellectual honesty and humility. In past dispensations many errors arose because the believers in God's Revelation were overanxious to encompass the Divine Message within the framework of their limited understanding, to define doctrines where definition was beyond their power, to explain mysteries which only the wisdom and experience of a later age would make comprehensible, to argue that something was true because it appeared desirable and necessary. Such compromises with essential truth, such intellectual pride, we must scrupulously avoid.[70]

In relation to the nature of Bahá'í law, while certain fundamental principles remain unchanged, subsidiary laws may be modified according to the exigencies of time and local conditions. Similarly, spiritual principles are designed to produce stability and promote change by inducing an attitude that facilitates the discovery of practical solutions to social problems. In addition, although the pattern of the Administrative Order is specified by the Covenant, the organic nature of its institutions and the organic nature of the Bahá'í community itself ensure flexibility both in the way the Administrative Order evolves and the manner in which its provisions are implemented. The Bahá'í Faith, therefore, provides for evolutionary change that can be implemented at a rate determined by the Universal House of Justice in accord with the stage of development and the conditions that prevail within the Bahá'í community.

Creating a Culture of Growth

The Bahá'í conception of evolutionary change gives rise to process thinking and to the creation of a culture of growth. The writings of the Faith spell out a number of factors associated with organic growth, including the importance of vision, the necessity of a long-term perspective, recognition of the value of progress, identification of the requirements for change, and the development of human and administrative resources.

As to the importance of vision and the value of adopting a long-term perspective on the events of life, Bahá'u'lláh states that vision acts as "the agent and guide for true knowledge," and He affirms that "in the estimation of men of wisdom keenness of understanding is due to keenness of vision." In another tablet He counsels, "At the outset of every endeavour, it is incumbent to look to the end of it." Furthermore, the writings of 'Abdu'l-Bahá provide a number of examples of the strategic value of process thinking to evolutionary change. In the following passage, for instance, he stresses the importance of not underestimating the significance of the small beginning of a process. He illustrates his point by reference to the impact of the exploits of the disciples of Christ. 'Abdu'l-Bahá writes,

Look ye not upon the present, fix your gaze upon the times to come. In the beginning, how small is the seed, yet in the end it is a mighty tree. Look ye not upon the seed, look ye upon the tree, and its blossoms, and its leaves and its fruits. Consider the days of Christ, when none but a small band followed Him; then observe what a mighty tree that seed became, behold ye its fruitage. And now shall come to pass even greater things than these, for this is the summons of the Lord of Hosts, this is the trumpet-call of the living Lord, this is the anthem of world peace, this is the standard of righteousness and trust and understanding raised up among all the variegated peoples of the globe; this is the splendor of the Sun of Truth, this is the holiness of the spirit of God Himself. This most powerful of dispensations will encompass all the earth, and beneath its banner will all peoples gather and be sheltered together. Know then the vital import of this tiny seed that the true Husbandman hath, with the hands of His mercy, sown in the ploughed fields of the Lord, and watered with the rain of bestowals and bounties and is now nurturing in the heat and light of the Daystar of Truth.[71]

'Abdu'l-Bahá calls attention to the importance of recognizing the potential benefits of progress and to the opportunities presented by the present in relation to the past. He writes,

> The superiority of the present in relation to the past consists in this, that the present can take over and adopt as a model many things which have been tried and tested and the great benefits of which have been demonstrated in the past, and that it can make its own new discoveries and by these augment its valuable inheritance. It is clear, then, that the accomplishment and experience of the past are known and available to the present, while the discoveries peculiar to the present were unknown to the past. This presupposes that the later generation is made up of persons of ability; otherwise, how many a later generation has lacked even so much as a drop out of the boundless ocean of knowledge that was its forbears'.[72]

As to those who are inclined to resist change, ignore the forces of modernity, and cling to the traditions of the past, 'Abdu'l-Bahá issues the following challenge: "Reflect a little: let us suppose that, through the power of God, certain individuals are placed on earth; these obviously stand in need of many things, to provide for their human dignity, their happiness and ease. Now is it more practicable for them to acquire these things from their contemporaries, or should they, in each successive generation, borrow nothing, but instead independently create one or another of the instrumentalities which are necessary to human existence?"[73]

The Bahá'í perspective on evolutionary change calls for the adoption of a learning mode of operation in which individual initiative and collective will are important ingredients. In this regard, it is interesting to examine 'Abdu'l-Bahá's advice to the people of his homeland, contained in *The Secret of Divine Civilization,* the book Shoghi Effendi describes as the Master's "outstanding contribution to the future reorganization of the world." He attests that "What she [Persia] urgently requires . . . is deep reflection, resolute action, training, inspiration and encouragement. Her people must make a massive effort, and their pride must be aroused." 'Abdu'l-Bahá's guidance might well be taken to constitute a succinct definition of some of the basic requirements for the achievement of enduring social change and the emergence of a progressive order. The emphases on reflection, training, unified action, and the assessment of progress are all critical to promoting a culture of growth.[74]

In the following sections we will consider the contribution of the Greatest Holy Leaf in steering the Bahá'í Faith through its transition from the Heroic Age to the Formative Age, and we will examine the unique personal qualities that she manifested in the face of change and in fostering the culture of growth.

The Greatest Holy Leaf—The Link between Two Ages

A striking feature of the life of the Greatest Holy Leaf is her ability to adapt to change. In early childhood her life of comfort and ease was suddenly changed to one of hardship and poverty, enabling her to experience "the bitterness of destitution and want." She was banished from her native land and accompanied her father in His exiles. She experienced imprisonment and war and suffered the loss of those members of the family who were most dear to her. Over the span of her life, she witnessed the introduction of the Bahá'í Covenant, changes in the leadership of the Bahá'í community, attacks on the Faith by the disaffected, and ultimately the transformation of the fortunes of the Cause of Bahá'u'lláh with the rise of the Administrative Order and the expansion of the Faith throughout the world.[75]

Her approach to change was active, principled, and goal directed, rather than a passive acceptance of what came her way, or an inflexible attempt to cling to the past, much less an expression of expediency. It is clear that Bahíyyih Khánum had a realistic understanding of the condition in which she found herself, an appreciation of how circumstances had changed, and a grasp of the kind of response that was demanded by the exigencies of the new situation.

Bahíyyih Khánum played a vital role in the initial stage of the Formative Age of the Bahá'í Faith, an age associated with the rise and establishment of the Bahá'í Administrative Order. It was through her deep understanding of the Will and Testament of 'Abdu'l-Bahá, her undeviating adherence to its provisions, her complete and loving support for the designated Guardian, Shoghi Effendi, and the efforts she exerted to educate the believers concerning the significance of the Covenant, that the Greatest Holy Leaf helped to prepare the Bahá'í world for its transition from the Heroic Age to the Formative Age of the Faith.

The Greatest Holy Leaf, the precious "Remnant of that Heroic Age," serves as the tangible link between the past, present, and future of the Bahá'í Faith—the link between one cycle of social evolution and the next. Her vision encompassed the future as well as the past. She succeeded in imparting a sense of continuity based on the familiar guidance provided in the writings of Bahá'u'lláh and 'Abdu'l-Bahá, and she helped the believers to understand the continuing relevance of this guidance to the needs of the present. She also projected an understanding, based on the letters of the Guardian, of the particular needs and opportunities associated with the present-day functioning of the Bahá'í community.[76]

Shoghi Effendi, in a letter written on his behalf, characterized the distinctive qualities required of the believers and the needs of the transitional age in the following terms:

> Every day has certain needs. In those early days the Cause needed Martyrs, and people who would stand all sorts of torture and persecution in expressing their faith and spreading the message sent by God. Those days are, however, gone. The Cause at present does not need martyrs who would die for the faith, but servants who desire to teach and establish the Cause throughout the world. To live to teach in the present day is like being martyred in those early days. It is the spirit that moves us that counts, not the act through which that spirit expresses itself; and that spirit is to serve the Cause of God with our heart and soul.[77]

In filling her role as a link between the Heroic Age and the Formative Age of the Faith, the Greatest Holy Leaf shared the suffering and persecution of the early believers and martyrs. She also epitomized the qualities necessary for the future evolution of the Faith. She manifested great resilience in the face of adversity, and she maintained the ability to recognize and seize the opportunities for service inherent in the present. Her commitment to the Cause of Bahá'u'lláh and the Covenant strengthened her will to endure and motivated her to dedicate her life to the protection and promotion of the Faith and to the establishment of its institutions. The ways in which she served depended on the specific needs of the Faith and the conditions that prevailed at a particular point in time.

The transition to the Formative Age of the Bahá'í Faith not only required the acceptance of the newly appointed Guardian as the head of the Faith but also called for an adjustment in thinking to accommodate the authority of elected Spiritual Assemblies. From a perusal of the letters written by the Greatest Holy Leaf, it is evident that she actively promoted the establishment and development of these embryonic institutions and used her consummate skills to bridge the transition and shape the awareness of the worldwide Bahá'í community. The guidance and encouragement she provided to the believers was derived from the letters written by Shoghi Effendi in the early days of his ministry. These seminal documents set the course for the Faith's development, highlighted its needs, and established priorities for action.

The Guardian's letters address such issues as the vital necessity of establishing both Local and National Spiritual Assemblies throughout the world, the means for the election of this important institution, its functions, and its relationship to the Universal House of Justice. The Guardian also explains the unique Bahá'í election process and the importance of consultation as the means by which Spiritual Assemblies arrive at their decisions. Shoghi Effendi also describes the spiritual, personal, and intellectual qualities to be manifested by those who are elected to Assembly membership. All of these themes are reiterated and lovingly explained in the letters written by Bahíyyih Khánum during the absences of the Guardian from the Holy Land.

The historical record discloses a clear unity of purpose and a close collaboration between the Guardian and the Greatest Holy Leaf. In the absence of the Guardian, she was the source of guidance and encouragement to the friends, and she exercised wise and mature leadership. She steadied the course of the Faith during this period of transition. Through the letters she wrote to the Bahá'ís and the embryonic Spiritual Assemblies in the East and the West, the Greatest Holy Leaf rallied the Bahá'í community. She instilled a spirit of confidence in the believers and, with patience and insight, educated them in the provisions of 'Abdu'l-Bahá's will and testament. She fostered acceptance of, and support for, the newly appointed Guardian and set in motion the implementation of the policies he set in place. She also helped the believers to gain a deeper understanding of the importance of establishing Spiritual Assemblies.

Fostering a Culture of Change

In assisting the Bahá'í community to negotiate the transition from the Heroic Age of the Faith to the Formative Age, the Greatest Holy Leaf exemplified qualities that resonate with the requirements specified by 'Abdu'l-Bahá for social transformation. Her clear understanding of the mission of the Bahá'í Faith and its teachings, as well as the provisions of the Covenant and seminal letters of Shoghi Effendi, provided motivation and direction for her actions throughout the course of her life. She understood the significance of the unchanging foundational principles and the flexibilities that existed. The Greatest Holy Leaf also continually renewed her knowledge of the guidance contained in the teachings and remained ever cognizant of the fact that changing conditions require new solutions and approaches.

Furthermore, the Greatest Holy Leaf called the believers' attention to the new circumstances and opportunities for service that existed because of the evolution of the Faith, and she encouraged them to review their practices in light of past experience and of the new situation that prevailed. To assist them in this process, she implemented, through her letters, a degree of training concerning the functioning of Spiritual Assemblies. She also urged the Bahá'ís to engage in the kinds of service required by the exigencies of the times, and she called attention to the fact that the confirmations of the Holy Spirit surround those who arise to serve the Cause. In this way the Greatest Holy Leaf enhanced the capacity of the believers and their embryonic Assemblies to devise systematic plans of action, to execute them with confidence, and to learn from experience—skills that are crucial to furthering the ever-advancing civilization envisaged by Bahá'u'lláh.

Her Enduring Legacy

An examination of the life of the Greatest Holy Leaf provides ample evidence of her outstanding contributions to the unfoldment of the Bahá'í Faith. Beyond that, the ideals and values she manifested have continuing relevance to contemporary society. Her confident and resilient response to suffering and hardship, her acceptance of administrative responsibility and exemplary leadership behavior, and her capacity to deal constructively with change are not only worthy of emulation, but are skills critical to influencing the direction of social evolution.

Shoghi Effendi underlines the dynamic nature of the enduring legacy of Bahíyyih Khánum in the following extract from a letter written on his behalf. He observes that she "exemplified perhaps more that anyone the true spirit that animates" the teachings of Bahá'u'lláh, and he expresses the hope that the friends will be motivated and spiritually sustained as they acquire a deeper awareness and appreciation of her life. The letter states, "His sincere hope is that your love for our departed Greatest Holy Leaf will attain such depth and intensity as to enable you to follow on her footsteps and to carry out with increasing devotion and vigour all that she cherished so much during the entire course of her earthly life. The memory of her saintly life will undoubtedly sustain and feed your energies and will provide you with that spiritual potency of which we are all in such a great need."[78]

Appendix 🐝

Notes on Historical Sources

The challenge of researching the life and contribution of Bahíyyih Khánum is to find ways of circumventing the traditional lack of detailed historical information about the situation of women in Muslim countries in the nineteenth and early twentieth centuries. Adib Taherzadeh accounts for the seeming invisibility of women in the historical record by the fact that

> women in those days took no part in public affairs; their entire lives were spent at home in private life. To enquire into the life of a woman was considered unethical, even insulting. It was discourteous even to ask the name of someone's wife. She would usually be referred to as "the person of the house" or, if she had a son, as the "mother of so and so." Within such a society historians (always male) usually could not invade the privacy of women by delving into their lives. To do so would highly offend the men of the household.[1]

While the sources of information about the Greatest Holy Leaf are, indeed, scattered and sometimes sparse, it is significant to consider Shoghi Effendi's assertion that, contrary to the cultural constraints of the period, Bahá'u'lláh chose to withdraw "the veil of concealment" from His daughter and to make her "to be a true example" for all her kind to follow. By withdrawing "the veil of concealment" from Bahíyyih Khánum, Bahá'u'lláh opened the way for historians to study the life and contribution of the Greatest Holy Leaf. More generally, He legitimized the study of women, rescued them from invisibility, and recognized their role in society.[2]

While there are relatively few detailed sources of information about her specific activities, the compilation entitled *Bahíyyih Khánum: The Greatest Holy Leaf* (Haifa: Bahá'í World Centre, 1982) contains many passages about Bahíyyih Khánum excerpted from the writings of Bahá'u'lláh and 'Abdu'l-Bahá in the letters of Shoghi Effendi. These statements tend to describe her qualities of character and to allude to her activities at various stages in the formative years of the Bahá'í Faith. In particular, the tributes of the Greatest Holy Leaf written by Shoghi Effendi around the time of her death are fruitful sources of information about her and help to highlight her significance.

Shoghi Effendi acknowledges that many of the details of the life and services of Bahíyyih <u>Kh</u>ánum are "unrecorded" and "in the main unsuspected." Nevertheless, he also clearly envisages that the life of Bahíyyih <u>Kh</u>ánum will become the subject of historical analysis. To this end, he calls attention to a number of areas worthy of investigation and highlights some potential challenges. He states,

> Only future generations and pens abler than mine can, and will, pay a worthy tribute to the towering grandeur of her spiritual life, to the unique part she played throughout the tumultuous stages of Bahá'í history, to the expressions of unqualified praise that have streamed from the pen of both Bahá'u'lláh and 'Abdu'l-Bahá, the Centre of His Covenant, though unrecorded, and in the main unsuspected by the mass of her passionate admirers in East and West, the share she has had in influencing the course of some of the chief events in the annals of the Faith, the sufferings she bore, the sacrifices she made, the rare gifts of unfailing sympathy she so strikingly displayed—these, and many others stand so inextricably interwoven with the fabric of the Cause itself that no future historian of the Faith of Bahá'u'lláh can afford to ignore or minimize.[3]

Elsewhere, Shoghi Effendi singles out two important aspects of her contribution that require study. These are her unique "share in the advancement and consolidation of the world-wide Community," and the significant role she played "during the early days of the Revelation and especially after the ascension of 'Abdu'l-Bahá." The letters of Bahíyyih Khánum that are published in *Bahíyyih Khánum: The Greatest Holy Leaf* and are addressed to the Bahá'ís and Bahá'í institutions throughout the world, provide insight into the depth of her understanding of the spirit and the teachings of the Faith and to the administrative functions she performed, especially during the tenure of her headship of the Faith.[4]

With regard to the details of her life, the Greatest Holy Leaf has left a rich legacy in the form of two spoken chronicles. The first was narrated to Lady Blomfield, an early English Bahá'í who spent extended periods of time with the members of 'Abdu'l-Bahá's family. It is published in *The Chosen Highway* (Wilmette: Bahá'í Publishing Trust, 1966). The second chronicle was related to Madame de Canavarro, an American Buddhist who was a student of religion, during her visit to the Holy Land. It is published in Myron H. Phelps, *The Master in 'Akká* (Los Angeles: Kalimát Press, 1985). In both instances, the chronicle was related in the Persian language by Bahíyyih Khánum, then translated into English by a member of the household and recorded by the Western visitor, thus creating many opportunities for misunderstanding and the recording of erroneous information. Nevertheless, these chronicles provide fascinating glimpses into the events surrounding the exiles of the family of Bahá'u'lláh and into the life of 'Abdu'l-Bahá from the perspective of one of the participants.

Finally, there are a number of accounts of Bahá'ís, in general written by female believers from the West who came as pilgrims to the Holy Land. The first group of Western pilgrims came around the turn of the twentieth century. These accounts provide descriptions of Bahíyyih Khánum and her services mostly during the period of her old age. Among these, the biography of Shoghi Effendi titled *The Priceless Pearl* (Rutland Gate, London: Bahá'í Publishing Trust, 1969), written by his widow, Rúḥíyyih Khánum, contains particularly useful material.

Notes ☙

1 ❧ Bahíyyih <u>Kh</u>ánum, Scion of Bahá'u'lláh

1. For the history of that turbulent period, see, for example, Shoghi Effendi, *God Passes By*, and William S. Hatcher and J. Douglas Martin, *Bahá'í Faith*; extract from a letter written on behalf of Shoghi Effendi, in *Bahíyyih <u>Kh</u>ánum*, p. 89.

2. Shoghi Effendi, in ibid., p. 28.

3. Ibid., p. 21.

4. Ibid., p. 31.

5. Ibid., p. 54.

6. Bahá'u'lláh, in *Bahíyyih <u>Kh</u>ánum*, p. 3.

7. Shoghi Effendi, in ibid., pp. 63, 22.

8. Shoghi Effendi, in *Bahíyyih <u>Kh</u>ánum*, p. 62; Shoghi Effendi, dedication, *Dawn-Breakers*, Shoghi Effendi, in *Bahíyyih <u>Kh</u>ánum*, p. 30; extract from a letter written on behalf of Shoghi Effendi, in ibid., p. 76.

9. See, for example, *Oxford English Dictionary*, s. v. "archetype"; *New Encyclopaedia Britannica*, s. v. "archetype."

10. See, for example, Moojan Momen, *Phenomenon of Religion*, chapter 11, "Archetype, Myth and the Sacred."

11. See Adib Taherzadeh, *Child of the Covenant*, pp. 22–23.

2 ❧ Bahá'u'lláh's Precious Daughter

1. Shoghi Effendi, in *Bahíyyih <u>Kh</u>ánum*, p. 58.

2. Recollections of the Greatest Holy Leaf, reported in Myron H. Phelps, *Master in 'Akká*, pp. 90–91.

3. Bahá'u'lláh, in *Bahíyyih <u>Kh</u>ánum*, pp. v, 4.

4. Ibid., pp. 3, 4.

5. Shoghi Effendi, in ibid., pp. 32, 26.

6. Ibid., p. 32.

7. Ibid., pp. 33, 26.

8. The spoken chronicle of Bahíyyih <u>Kh</u>ánum, in Lady Blomfield, *Chosen Highway*, pp. 41–42.

9. Ibid., p. 42.

10. Ibid., pp. 42–43.

11. Shoghi Effendi, *Promised Day Is Come*, ¶22.

12. Bahá'u'lláh, quoted in Shoghi Effendi, *God Passes By*, p. 109.

13. Shoghi Effendi, *God Passes By*, p. 107.

14. Shoghi Effendi, in *Bahíyyih <u>Kh</u>ánum*, p. 26; the spoken chronicle of Bahíyyih <u>Kh</u>ánum, in Lady Blomfield, *Chosen Highway*, pp. 45–46.

15. The spoken chronicle of Bahíyyih Khánum, in Lady Blomfield, *Chosen Highway,* p. 47.

16. Ibid.

17. Shoghi Effendi, in *Bahíyyih Khánum,* pp. 26–27, 33.

18. The spoken chronicle of Bahíyyih Khánum, in Lady Blomfield, *Chosen Highway,* p. 51.

19. Shoghi Effendi, in *Bahíyyih Khánum,* p. 27.

20. From the spoken chronicle of Túbá Khánum, in Lady Blomfield, *Chosen Highway,* p. 93.

21. Shoghi Effendi, in *Bahíyyih Khánum,* p. 33.

22. Shoghi Effendi, *God Passes By,* pp. 155–56.

23. Ibid., p. 157.

24. Ibid., p. 161; Bahá'u'lláh, quoted in ibid., p. 161; Bahá'u'lláh, *Summons of the Lord of Hosts,* Súriy-i-Mulúk, ¶75.

25. Nabíl, quoted in Shoghi Effendi, *God Passes By,* p. 161; account of one of the exiles, quoted in ibid.

26. The Greatest Holy Leaf, quoted in Myron Phelps, *Master in 'Akká,* pp. 47–48.

27. Shoghi Effendi, in *Bahíyyih Khánum,* p. 34.

28. Shoghi Effendi, *God Passes By,* p. 162.

29. Bahá'u'lláh, quoted in ibid., p. 163; Shoghi Effendi, *God Passes By,* p. 167; Bahá'u'lláh, quoted in ibid., p. 163.

30. Shoghi Effendi, *God Passes By,* pp. 163–64, 170.

31. Bahíyyih Khánum, quoted in Myron Phelps, *Master in 'Akká,* pp. 48–50; the spoken chronicle of Bahíyyih Khánum, in Lady Blomfield, *Chosen Highway,* p. 60.

32. The spoken chronicle of Bahíyyih Khánum, in Lady Blomfield, *Chosen Highway,* p. 63.

33. Ibid., p. 61.

34. Shoghi Effendi, in *Bahíyyih Khánum,* p. 33, 27.

35. Ibid., pp. 27–28.

36. Shoghi Effendi, *God Passes By,* p. 179; the spoken chronicle of Bahíyyih Khánum, in Lady Blomfield, *Chosen Highway,* p. 62; Bahá'u'lláh, *Summons of the Lord of Hosts,* Lawḥ-i-Ra'ís, ¶26.

37. Bahá'u'lláh, *Summons of the Lord of Hosts,* Lawḥ-i-Ra'ís, ¶2–3.

38. Shoghi Effendi, *God Passes By,* p. 181.

39. Ibid., p. 182.

40. Bahá'u'lláh, *Summons of the Lord of Hosts,* Lawḥ-i-Ra'ís, ¶5.

41. Shoghi Effendi, in *Bahíyyih Khánum,* p. 34.

42. Shoghi Effendi, *God Passes By,* p. 185.

43. Ibid., p. 185; Bahá'u'lláh, *Summons of the Lord of Hosts,* Lawḥ-i-Ra'ís, ¶6; Bahá'u'lláh, quoted in Shoghi Effendi, *God Passes By,* p. 185; Bahá'u'lláh, *Summons of the Lord of Hosts,* Súriy-i-Haykal, ¶267.

44. The spoken chronicle of Bahíyyih Khánum, in Lady Blomfield, *Chosen Highway,* p. 66.

45. Bahá'u'lláh, *Summons of the Lord of Hosts,* Lawḥ-i-Ra'ís, ¶4.

46. See recollections of the Greatest Holy Leaf, in Myron Phelps, *Master in 'Akká,* pp. 78, 80–81.

47. See the spoken chronicle of Bahíyyih Khánum, in Lady Blomfield, *Chosen Highway,* p. 68; see Ṭúbá Khánum, in ibid., p. 93.

48. The spoken chronicle of Bahíyyih Khánum, in ibid., p. 68.

49. Shoghi Effendi, *God Passes By,* p. 188.

50. For details, see ibid., pp. 189–90.

51. Ibid., p. 191; Bahá'u'lláh, in ibid., p. 196.

52. Ibid., p. 205.

53. Ibid., p. 221.

54. Shoghi Effendi, in *Bahíyyih Khánum,* p. 34.

55. Ibid., pp. 34–35.

56. Ibid., p. 35.

57. Shoghi Effendi, *God Passes By,* pp. 221–22.

58. Ibid., p.221.

59. See the spoken chronicle of Ṭúbá Khánum, in Lady Blomfield, *Chosen Highway,* pp. 109–10.

60. Bahíyyih Khánum, in *Bahíyyih Khánum,* p. 97.

61. Ibid., p. 99.

62. 'Abdu'l-Bahá, in ibid., pp. 14–15.

63. Shoghi Effendi, in ibid., p. 36.

64. Ibid., p. 28.

65. Ibid., p. 37, 36.

3 ✝ 'Abdu'l-Bahá's Brilliant Sister

1. 'Abdu'l-Bahá, in *Bahíyyih Khánum,* pp. 7, 10, 17.

2. Shoghi Effendi, in ibid., p. 28.

3. Shoghi Effendi, *God Passes By,* pp. 238, 244–45.

4. Ibid., p. 243.

5. Ibid., pp. 245–46.

6. Ibid., pp. 246–47.

7. Ibid., p. 247. For a detailed discussion, refer to Adib Taherzadeh, *Covenant of Bahá'u'lláh,* part 2.

8. Shoghi Effendi, in *Bahíyyih Khánum,* p. 37.

9. Shoghi Effendi, *God Passes By,* p. 248.

10. Ibid., p. 247.

11. Shoghi Effendi, in *Bahíyyih Khánum,* p. 37.

12. Bahíyyih Khánum, in ibid., p. 101.

13. Shoghi Effendi, *God Passes By*, p. 252.

14. Ibid., pp. 252–53.

15. Ibid., pp. 257–58.

16. Ibid., p. 259.

17. Shoghi Effendi, in *Bahíyyih Khánum*, pp. 59–60.

18. May Maxwell, *An Early Pilgrimage*, p. 18.

19. Ibid., p. 19.

20. Ella Goodall Cooper, "Bahiyyih Khanum—An Appreciation," *Star of the West* 23, no. 7 (1932): 202.

21. Phoebe Hearst, letter dated 19 November 1899 to Mr. Isaiah H. Bradford, in *Bahá'í World* 7: 801; Phoebe Hearst, letter dated 5 December 1899 to O. M. Babcock, in ibid.: 802.

22. May Maxwell, *An Early Pilgrimage*, pp. 42–43.

23. Cooper, "Bahiyyih Khanum—An Appreciation," p. 204.

24. Bahíyyih Khánum, in *Bahíyyih Khánum*, p. 104.

25. Shoghi Effendi, *God Passes By*, pp. 261–62.

26. Ibid., p. 263.

27. Ibid., pp. 265, 266.

28. Ibid., p. 267.

29. Ibid.

30. Shoghi Effendi, in *Bahíyyih Khánum*, p. 28; Marzieh Gail, *Summon up Remembrance*, pp. 277–78.

31. For details, see Helen Goodall and Ella Goodall Cooper, *Daily Lessons Received at 'Akká*, pp. 42–43.

32. Shoghi Effendi, *God Passes By*, p. 268.

33. Ibid., pp. 268–69.

34. Ibid., p. 269.

35. Helen Goodall and Ella Goodall Cooper, *Daily Lessons Received at 'Akká*, pp. 9–10.

36. For details see H. M. Balyuzi, *'Abdu'l-Bahá*, p. 118.

37. Shoghi Effendi, *God Passes By*, pp. 270–71.

38. Ibid., p. 271.

39. Ibid., p. 272.

40. Shoghi Effendi, in *Bahíyyih Khánum*, pp. 37–38.

41. Ibid., p. 38.

42. Shoghi Effendi, *God Passes By*, pp. 274, 275.

43. Zeenat Baghdadi, quoted in 'Alí Nakhjaváни, "The Greatest Holy Leaf: A Reminiscence," *Bahá'í World* 18, (1979–83): 60.

44. Shoghi Effendi, *God Passes By*, p. 276.

45. Ibid., p. 279; Shoghi Effendi, in *Bahíyyih Khánum*, pp. 39, 28.

46. *Webster's Third International Dictionary of the English Language Unabridged*, s.v. "vicegerent."

47. Bahíyyih Nakhjaváни, "The Life and Service of the Greatest Holy Leaf," in *Bahá'í World* 18 (1979–83): 71.

48. 'Abdu'l-Bahá, in *Bahíyyih Khánum,* p. 13.

49. For details of 'Abdu'l-Bahá's travels in Europe and North America, see Shoghi Effendi, *God Passes By,* chapter 19.

50. 'Abdu'l-Bahá, in *Bahíyyih Khánum,* pp. 17–18.

51. Shoghi Effendi, *God Passes By,* pp. 281–82.

52. Shoghi Effendi, in *Bahíyyih Khánum,* p. 39.

53. 'Abdu'l-Bahá, in ibid., pp. 11–12.

54. Shoghi Effendi, *God Passes By,* p. 281; Shoghi Effendi, in *Bahíyyih Khánum,* pp. 39–40.

55. See Mírzá Ahmad Sohrab, *'Abdu'l-Bahá in Egypt,* pp. 141, 182, 330.

56. Rúhá Asdaq, *One Life One Memory,* pp. 25–26.

57. 'Abdu'l-Bahá, quoted by Dr. Músá Khudádúst, in ibid., p. 26.

58. Shoghi Effendi, in *Bahíyyih Khánum,* pp. 34–35.

59. Cooper, "Bahiyyih Khanum—An Appreciation," pp. 202–03.

60. Shoghi Effendi, in *Bahíyyih Khánum,* p. 38.

61. Cooper, "Bahiyyih Khanum—An Appreciation," p. 203.

62. 'Alí Nakhjavání, in "The Greatest Holy Leaf: A Reminiscence," p. 60.

63. Marie A. Watson, *My Pilgrimage to the Land of Desire,* p. 8.

64. Cooper, "Bahiyyih Khanum—An Appreciation," p. 203; see also Alí Nakhjavání, "The Greatest Holy Leaf: A Reminiscence," p. 63.

65. Marie A. Watson, *My Pilgrimage to the Land of Desire,* pp. 8–9.

66. Ibid., p. 9.

67. Cooper, "Bahiyyih Khanum—An Appreciation," p. 204.

68. Mary Hanford Ford, *Oriental Rose,* pp. 162–63.

69. Marjory Morton, "Bahíyyih Khánum," *Bahá'í World* 5 (1932–1934): 181.

70. Ibid., p. 185.

71. Ibid., p. 181.

72. Bahíyyih Khánum, in *Bahíyyih Khánum,* p. 110.

73. Ibid., p. 111.

74. Shoghi Effendi, *God Passes By,* p. 304.

75. Lady Blomfield, *Chosen Highway,* pp. 210, 214.

76. Shoghi Effendi, *God Passes By,* p. 306.

77. Shoghi Effendi, in *Bahíyyih Khánum,* p. 41.

78. Ibid., p. 40.

79. Ibid., pp. 40–41.

80. Mrs. Corinne True, letter dated 16 November 1919 to the editors, in *Star of the West* 10, no. 17 (1920): 312; Genevieve L. Coy, "A Week in 'Abdu'l-Bahá's Home," *Star of the West* 12, no. 12 (1921): 197.

81. Shoghi Effendi, *God Passes By,* p. 306.

82. Ibid., p. 307.

83. Ibid., pp. 306, 307.

84. Shoghi Effendi, in *Bahíyyih Khánum,* p. 28.

85. 'Abdu'l-Bahá, in ibid., pp. 7–8, 18.

4 ❧ The Remnant of Bahá

1. Shoghi Effendi, in *Bahíyyih Khánum*, pp. 60, 23.

2. Shoghi Effendi, in ibid., pp. 41–42; extract from a letter written on behalf of Shoghi Effendi, in ibid., p. 71.

3. See Ethel Rosenberg, letter dated 8 December 1921 to Beloved friends in England, in *Star of the West* 12, no. 19 (1922): 300.

4. Shoghi Effendi, *God Passes By*, pp. 310, 311.

5. See Abbas Adib, letter dated 4 January 1922 to Dr. Zia M. Bagdadi, in *Star of the West* 12, no. 19 (1922): 302; Shoghi Effendi, *God Passes By*, p. 311.

6. Mrs. Louise Bosch, letter dated 5 December 1921 to Ella G. Cooper, in *Star of the West* 12, no. 18, (1922): 278.

7. Bahíyyih Khánum, in *Bahíyyih Khánum*, pp. 174–75.

8. Shoghi Effendi, in ibid., p. 41.

9. Nathan Rutstein, *He Loved and Served*, pp. 94–95.

10. Bahíyyih Khánum, in *Bahíyyih Khánum*, p. 114; Shoghi Effendi, *God Passes By*, p. 311.

11. See 'Alí Nakhjavání, "The Greatest Holy Leaf: A Reminiscence," p. 60; Rúhíyyih Rabbani, *Priceless Pearl*, p. 44.

12. Shoghi Effendi, *God Passes By*, pp. 312–13.

13. Louise Bosch, letter dated 9 December 1921 to Ella G. Cooper, in *Star of the West* 12, no. 18 (1922): 282–83.

14. Johanna Hauff, letter dated 3 December 1921 to her parents, in ibid., p. 299; Ethel Rosenberg, letter dated 8 December 1921 to Beloved friends in England, in ibid., p. 301.

15. Marzieh Gail, ed., "'Abdu'l-Bahá: Portrayals from East and West, materials from the papers of Ali-Kuli Khan and the conversations of John and Louise Bosch," *World Order* 6: no. 1 (1971): 41.

16. Shoghi Effendi, *God Passes By*, p. 313.

17. Lady Blomfield (and Shoghi Effendi), "The Passing of 'Abdu'l-Bahá, Excerpts from Compilation prepared in January 1922," in *Bahá'í Year Book*, 1 (April 1925–April 1926): 29.

18. Abbas Adib, letter dated 4 January 1922 to Dr. Zia M. Bagdadi, in *Star of the West* 12, no. 19 (1922): 302–03; Adib Taherzadeh, *Covenant of Bahá'u'lláh*, pp. 276–77.

19. Bahíyyih Khánum, in *Bahíyyih Khánum*, pp. 114, 121.

20. Adib Taherzadeh, *Covenant of Bahá'u'lláh*, p. 276.

21. Bahíyyih Khánum, in *Bahíyyih Khánum*, p. 114.

22. Ibid., p. 114.

23. Monover Khanum, letter dated 22 December 1921 to Ruth Wales Randall, in *Star of the West* 12, no. 18 (1922): 275–76; Louise Bosch, letter dated 5 December 1921, in ibid., pp. 276–79.

24. Adib Taherzadeh, *Covenant of Bahá'u'lláh*, p. 284.

25. Ibid., p. 285; Rúḥíyyih Rabbani, *Priceless Pearl*, p. 42.
26. Rúḥíyyih Rabbani, *Priceless Pearl*, pp. 42–43.
27. Ibid., p. 46
28. Nathan Rutstein, *He Loved and Served*, pp. 103–04.
29. Rúḥíyyih Rabbani, *Priceless Pearl*, p. 47.
30. Bahíyyih Ḵẖánum, in ibid., p. 47; Bahíyyih Ḵẖánum, in *Bahíyyih Ḵẖánum*, p. 114.
31. Rúḥíyyih Rabbani, *Priceless Pearl*, pp. 53–54.
32. Ibid., p. 56.
33. Ibid., pp. 56, 63.
34. Ibid., p. 62.
35. Ibid., p. 48.
36. Shoghi Effendi, in *Bahíyyih Ḵẖánum*, p. 29.
37. Shoghi Effendi, in ibid., p. 21.
38. Rúḥíyyih Rabbani, *Priceless Pearl*, p. 57; Adib Taherzadeh, *Covenant of Bahá'u'lláh*, p. 293.

5 ❧ Her Role during Shoghi Effendi's Absences

1. Shoghi Effendi, in *Bahíyyih Ḵẖánum*, p. 21; Ruḥíyyih Rabbani, *Priceless Pearl*, p. 72.
2. Shoghi Effendi, in *Bahíyyih Ḵẖánum*, p. 21; extracts from a letter dated 5 April 1922 from Shoghi Effendi to Colonel Symes, representative of the Palestine Authorities, cited in Rúḥíyyih Rabbani, *Priceless Pearl*, p. 276.
3. Bahíyyih Ḵẖánum, in *Bahíyyih Ḵẖánum*, pp. 114–15. See also Bahíyyih Ḵẖánum, letter dated Shaban 1340 (April 1922) to the servants of the Blessed Beauty and the dear friends of His Holiness Abdu'l-Baha, in *Star of the West* 13, no. 4 (1922): 81–83. Note: The revised English translation found in *Bahíyyih Ḵẖánum* varies slightly from the one published in *Star of the West*.
4. Bahíyyih Ḵẖánum, undated letter to Our very dear friends in America, in *Star of the West* 13, no. 4 (1922): 88.
5. Bahíyyih Ḵẖánum, in *Bahíyyih Ḵẖánum*, p. 149.
6. Bahíyyih Ḵẖánum, in ibid., pp. 158–59.
7. 'Abdu'l-Bahá, quoted by Bahíyyih Ḵẖánum, in ibid., pp. 123–24.
8. Bahíyyih Ḵẖánum, in ibid., p. 124.
9. Ibid., pp. 142–43.
10. Ibid., pp. 180–81.
11. Ibid., pp. 186–87.
12. Ibid., p. 187.
13. Ibid., p. 148.
14. Ibid., pp. 163, 147–48.

15. Ibid., p. 163.

16. Shoghi Effendi, *God Passes By*, p. 328.

17. Ibid.

18. Ibid., p. 329.

19. Bahíyyih Khánum, in *Bahíyyih Khánum*, pp. 133–34.

20. Ibid., pp. 160–61.

21. Ibid., p. 122.

22. Ibid., p. 170.

23. Ibid., pp. 141, 217.

24. Ibid., pp. 159, 161–62.

25. 'Abdu'l-Bahá, *Will and Testament of 'Abdu'l-Bahá*, p. 25; Bahíyyih Khánum, in *Bahíyyih Khánum*, p. 179.

26. Bahíyyih Khánum, in *Bahíyyih Khánum*, pp. 203–04.

27. Ibid., pp. 204–05.

28. Ibid., p. 205.

29. Shoghi Effendi, quoted in ibid., pp. 206–08.

30. Bahíyyih Khánum, in ibid., p. 208.

31. Ruhíyyih Rabbani, *Priceless Pearl*, p. 146.

32. For details, see Bahíyyih Khánum, in *Bahíyyih Khánum*, pp. 125–39.

33. Bahíyyih Khánum, in ibid., pp. 164–165.

34. Nathan Rutstein, *He Loved and Served*, pp. 108–09.

35. Bahíyyih Khánum, letter dated 11 July 1922 to the Spiritual Assembly of the Bahá'ís of Tehran, in *Star of the West* 13, no. 11 (1923): 314.

36. Ibid.

37. Ibid., p. 314.

38. Bahíyyih Khánum, in *Bahíyyih Khánum*, pp. 220–21.

39. For some of the early letters of Shoghi Effendi, see *Bahá'í Administration*.

40. Shoghi Effendi, extract from a letter dated 16 January 1923 to the beloved of the Lord and the handmaids of the merciful throughout the United States and Canada, in *Star of the West* 14, no. 1 (1923): 26.

41. Shoghi Effendi, *Bahá'í Administration*, pp. 57–60; extract from a letter dated 11 June 1924 written on behalf of Bahíyyih Khánum to Mr. Simpson, President of the National Spiritual Assembly of England, in *Unfolding Destiny*, p. 25.

42. Bahíyyih Khánum, in *Bahíyyih Khánum*, 192–93.

43. Ibid., p. 171.

44. Ibid., p. 188.

45. Ibid., p. 222.

46. Ibid., p. 180

47. Ruhíyyih Rabbani, *Priceless Pearl*, pp. 57–58.

48. Shoghi Effendi, *Bahá'í Administration*, p. 63.

49. Bahíyyih Khánum, in *Bahíyyih Khánum*, pp. 116, 223.

50. Ibid., pp. 211, 213–14.

51. Ibid., pp. 221–22.

52. Ibid., p. 191.

53. Ibid., pp. 143–44.

54. Ibid., pp. 196–97.

55. Ibid., pp. 190–91.

56. Haifa Spiritual Assembly, letter dated March 1923, in *Star of the West* 14, no. 3 (1923): 90, 89.

57. Ibid., p. 90.

58. Letter dated April 1923, written on behalf of the Haifa Spiritual Assembly, in *Star of the West* 14, no. 5 (1923): 152–53; Alfred Hyde Dunn, extract from a letter quoted in ibid., p. 153.

59. See *Star of the West* 14, no. 6 (1923): 184–85.

60. Haifa Spiritual Assembly, letter dated 24 November–13 December 1923, in *Star of the West* 14, no. 12 (1924): 372.

61. Ibid., p. 374.

62. Bahíyyih Khánum, in *Bahíyyih Khánum,* p. 119.

63. Bahíyyih Khánum, in ibid., pp. 119–20.

64. Ibid., p. 120.

65. See Ruhíyyih Rabbani, *Priceless Pearl,* p. 71.

66. Bahíyyih Khánum, in *Bahíyyih Khánum,* pp. 165, 166.

67. Ibid., p. 167.

68. Ibid., pp. 168–69.

69. Ibid., p. 169.

70. Ibid., pp. 212–13.

71. For details, see Shoghi Effendi, *Bahá'í Administration,* pp. 137–39.

72. Bahíyyih Khánum, in *Bahíyyih Khánum,* pp. 216–17.

73. Ibid., pp. 218–19.

74. Shoghi Effendi, *Bahá'í Administration,* p. 194.

75. Ibid., pp. 66–67.

6 ॐ The Glorious Companion of Shoghi Effendi

1. Extract from a letter written on behalf of Shoghi Effendi, in *Bahíyyih Khánum,* p. 77; Shoghi Effendi, in ibid., p. 29.

2. Shoghi Effendi, in ibid., p. 29.

3. Ibid., p. 21.

4. Ibid., pp. 29, 31.

5. Ibid., pp. 54, 42, 53.

6. Ibid., pp. 44.

7. Ibid., pp. 44, 54–55.

8. Extract from a letter written on behalf of Shoghi Effendi, in ibid., pp. 75,

83, 76–77.

9. Ibid., p. 81.

10. Rúḥíyyih Rabbani, *Priceless Pearl,* pp. 148, 144.

11. Ibid., p. 146; extract from a letter written on behalf of Shoghi Effendi, in *Baḥíyyih Khánum,* p. 86.

12. 'Alí Nakhjavání, "The Greatest Holy Leaf: A Reminiscence," p. 64.

13. Rúḥíyyih Rabbani, *Priceless Pearl,* pp. 146, 147.

14. Ibid., p. 147.

15. Extract from a letter written on behalf of Shoghi Effendi, in *Baḥíyyih Khánum,* p. 78.

16. Shoghi Effendi, quoted in Rúḥíyyih Rabbani, *Priceless Pearl,* p. 146; Shoghi Effendi, *Messages to the Antipodes,* p. 53.

17. Shoghi Effendi, *Bahá'í Administration,* p. 70.

18. Shoghi Effendi, *Messages of Shoghi Effendi to the Indian Subcontinent,* pp. 69, 70.

19. Shoghi Effendi, *God Passes By,* pp. 387, 389.

20. Ibid., p. 390.

21. See, for example, Shoghi Effendi, *God Passes By,* pp. 389–95; Rúḥíyyih Rabbani, *Priceless Pearl,* pp. 112–17; Della L. Marcus, *Her Eternal Crown*; Shoghi Effendi, *God Passes By,* p. 390.

22. Shoghi Effendi, quoted in Della Marcus, *Her Eternal Crown,* p. 169.

23. Ibid., p. 114.

24. Shoghi Effendi, *God Passes By,* p. 392; Rúḥíyyih Rabbani, *Priceless Pearl,* pp. 115–16.

25. Shoghi Effendi, in *Baḥíyyih Khánum,* pp. 52, 59.

26. Shoghi Effendi, *God Passes By,* p. 350.

27. Ibid., p. 349; Bruce W. Whitmore, *Dawning Place.*

28. Bruce W. Whitmore, *Dawning Place,* p. 139.

29. Shoghi Effendi, in *Bahá'í Administration,* p. 181.

30. Shoghi Effendi, quoted in Bruce W. Whitmore, *Dawning Place,* p. 157.

31. Shoghi Effendi, *World Order of Bahá'u'lláh,* pp. 67–68.

32. *Bahá'í News,* no. 66 (1932): 2.

33. Extract from a letter written on behalf of Shoghi Effendi, in *Baḥíyyih Khánum,* p. 68.

34. Shoghi Effendi, in ibid., p. 49.

35. Bahíyyih Khánum, in ibid., pp. 224–25.

36. Ibid., p. 225.

37. Ibid., p. 226.

38. Extract from a letter written on behalf of Shoghi Effendi, in ibid., p. 88.

39. Ibid., p. 90.

40. Keith Ransom-Kehler, "Excerpts from My Diary," in *Star of the West* 17, no. 8 (1926): 258–59.

41. Gertrude Richardson Brigham, "A Modern Pilgrimage to Bahá'í Shrines," in *Star of the West* 18, no. 9 (1925): 280.

42. Ibid., p. 280.

43. Ibid., p. 282.

44. ʻAlí Nakhjavání, "The Greatest Holy Leaf: A Reminiscence," p. 63.

45. A. Q. Faizi, quoted in ʻAlí Nakhjavání, "The Greatest Holy Leaf: A Reminiscence," p. 62.

46. Ibid., p. 62.

47. Marjory Morton, "Bahíyyih Khánum," in *Baháʼí World* 5 (1932–34): 184.

48. "Excerpts from Diary of Mrs. Keith Ransom-Kehler," in *Baháʼí World* 5 (1932–34): 187.

49. Ibid.

7 ❧ The Hill of God Is Stirred

1. Shoghi Effendi, in *Bahíyyih Khánum,* p. 54; extract from a letter written on behalf of Shoghi Effendi, in ibid., pp. 85–86, 90–91; Marjory Morton, "Bahíyyih Khánum," p. 185.

2. Extract from a letter written on behalf of Shoghi Effendi, in *Bahíyyih Khánum,* p. 80; Shoghi Effendi, in ibid., p. 62; extract from a letter written on behalf of Shoghi Effendi, in ibid., p. 67; Shoghi Effendi, in ibid., p. 31.

3. Shoghi Effendi, in ibid., pp. 23–24.

4. Ibid., pp. 22–23.

5. Ibid., p. 23.

6. Shoghi Effendi, *Baháʼí Administration,* pp. 187–96. See also Shoghi Effendi, in *Bahíyyih Khánum,* pp. 31–45.

7. Shoghi Effendi, in *Bahíyyih Khánum,* p. 60; extract from a letter written on behalf of Shoghi Effendi, in ibid., pp. 70–71.

8. Shoghi Effendi, in ibid., p. 22.

9. ʻAlí Nakhjavání, "The Greatest Holy Leaf: A Reminiscence," p. 64.

10. Ibid., pp. 64–65.

11. Ibid., p. 65.

12. Ibid.

13. Rúhíyyih Rabbani, *Priceless Pearl,* pp. 146–47.

14. Shoghi Effendi, in *Bahíyyih Khánum,* p. 22; extract from a letter written on behalf of Shoghi Effendi, in ibid., pp. 84–85; Shoghi Effendi, in ibid., p. 30.

15. Extract from a letter written on behalf of Shoghi Effendi, in *Bahíyyih Khánum,* pp. 72–73, 85, 88–89.

16. Shoghi Effendi, in *Bahíyyih Khánum,* pp. 62, 58, 59.

17. Ibid., pp. 57–58.

18. *Baháʼí World* 5 (1932–34): 22–23, 85–86, 114–15.

19. Shoghi Effendi, in *Bahíyyih Khánum,* pp. 52, 59.

20. *Baháʼí World* 5 (1932–34): 85–86.

21. Shoghi Effendi, in *Bahíyyih Khánum,* p. 58.

22. *Baháʼí World* 5 (1932–34): 114–15.

23. Extracts from a letter written by A. Samimi and a letter written by A. H. Naimi, quoted in Bertha Hyde Kirkpatrick, "A Western Visitor in the Land of Bahá'u'lláh," *Star of the West* 23, no. 10 (1933): 318–19.

24. Ibid., p. 319.

25. *Bahá'í World* 5 (1932–34): 130, 132.

26. Shoghi Effendi, in *Bahíyyih Khánum*, pp. 24–25.

27. Extract from a letter written on behalf of Shoghi Effendi, in *Bahíyyih Khánum*, pp. 85, 87–88, 89.

28. Extract from a letter written on behalf of Shoghi Effendi, in ibid., p. 81; Shoghi Effendi, in ibid., p. 48.

29. Ibid., pp. 51–52.

30. Extract from a letter written on behalf of Shoghi Effendi, in ibid., pp. 82, 80.

31. Shoghi Effendi, in ibid., p. 57.

32. Extract from a letter written on behalf of Shoghi Effendi, in ibid., p. 92.

33. Shoghi Effendi, *God Passes By*, pp. 315–16.

34. Ibid., p. 347; Shoghi Effendi, in *Bahíyyih Khánum*, p. 61.

35. Shoghi Effendi, *This Decisive Hour*, no. 64.6.

36. Shoghi Effendi, *God Passes By*, p. 348.

37. Shoghi Effendi, *This Decisive Hour*, no. 64.7.

38. Shoghi Effendi, in *Bahíyyih Khánum*, p. 63.

39. Rúḥíyyih Khánum, "The Completion of the International Archives," in *Bahá'í World* 13 (1954–63): 433.

40. *Messages from the Universal House of Justice 1963–1986*, no. 115.1; 'Alí Nakhjavání, "The Greatest Holy Leaf: A Reminiscence," p. 59.

41. *Messages from the Universal House of Justice, 1963–1986*, no. 354.1.

42. Report of "The Fifth International Convention for the Election of the Universal House of Justice, Riḍván 1983," in *Bahá'í World* 18 (1979–83): 461.

43. Bahíyyih Khánum, in *Bahíyyih Khánum*, pp. 181, 183.

44. Rúḥíyyih Rabbani, *Priceless Pearl*, p. 146.

45. The Universal House of Justice, letter dated 24 May 2001 to the Believers Gathered for the Events Marking the Completion of the Projects on Mount Carmel.

46. Shoghi Effendi, *This Decisive Hour*, no. 64.1.

8 ❧ Archetype of the People of Bahá

1. Shoghi Effendi, in *Bahíyyih Khánum*, p. 30.

2. See, for example, Moojan Momen, *Phenomenon of Religion*, Chapter 11; Beverly Moon, "Archetypes," in Mircea Eliade, ed., *Encyclopedia of Religion* (New York: Macmillan Publishing, 1987) 1: 379–82.

3. Shoghi Effendi, in *Bahíyyih Khánum*, p. 56.

4. Ibid., pp. 42–43.

5. 'Abdu'l-Bahá, *Selections from the Writings of 'Abdu'l-Bahá,* no. 156.9; 'Abdu'l-Bahá, *Paris Talks,* no. 57.1.

6. Ibid., no. 57.1; Bahá'u'lláh, cited in Shoghi Effendi, *Advent of Divine Justice,* p. 33.

7. Bahá'u'lláh, *Gleanings,* pp. 42–43.

8. See, for example, Diane L. Coutu, "How Resilience Works," *Harvard Business Review* (May 2002): 46–55; Kennon M. Sheldon and Laura King, "Why Positive Psychology is Necessary," *American Psychologist* 56, no. 3 (2001): 216–17; Barbara L. Fredrickson, "The Role of Positive Emotions in Positive Psychology: The Broaden-and-Build Theory of Positive Emotions," ibid.: 218–26; Sandra L. Schneider, "In Search of Realistic Optimism," ibid.: 250–62.

9. Diane L. Coutu, "How Resilience Works," pp. 50–52.

10. Ibid., p. 50.

11. Barbara L. Fredrickson, "The Role of Positive Emotions in Positive Psychology," pp. 218–26.

12. Diane L. Coutu, "How Resilience Works," p. 48; Shoghi Effendi, in *Bahíyyih Khánum,* p. 30.

13. Extract from a letter written on behalf of Shoghi Effendi, in *Bahíyyih Khánum,* p. 73; Shoghi Effendi, in ibid., p. 25; extract from a letter written on behalf of Shoghi Effendi, in ibid., p. 83.

14. Extract from a letter written on behalf of Shoghi Effendi, in ibid., pp. 75–76.

15. Ibid., p. 76.

16. Abdu'l-Missagh Ghadirian, "Psychological and Spiritual Dimensions of Persecution and Suffering," *Journal of Bahá'í Studies* 6, no. 3: 19.

17. Extract from a letter written on behalf of Shoghi Effendi, in *Bahíyyih Khánum,* pp. 70–71.

18. Shoghi Effendi, in ibid., p. 35.

19. Extract from letter written on behalf of Shoghi Effendi, in ibid., p. 77.

20. Ibid., p. 77.

21. Ibid., pp. 90–91, 89, 91.

22. Shoghi Effendi, *World Order of Bahá'u'lláh,* p. 5.

23. Ibid., p. 145.

24. Ibid., pp. 152–53.

25. Ibid., pp. 153–54.

26. 'Abdu'l-Bahá, *Selections from the Writings of 'Abdu'l-Bahá,* no. 43.1.

27. Ibid., no. 142.1.

28. Bahíyyih Khánum, in *Bahíyyih Khánum,* pp. 141, 160–61.

29. Ibid., p. 191.

30. Shoghi Effendi, *Bahá'í Administration,* p. 88; 'Abdu'l-Bahá, cited in ibid., p. 22.

31. Ibid., p. 22.

32. Shoghi Effendi, in *Bahíyyih Khánum,* pp. 59–60.

33. Hugh Miall, *Peacemakers,* Chapter 4.

34. Peter Wallensteen, ed., *Peace Research,* Chapter 6.

35. *Messages from the Universal House of Justice, 1963–1986,* no. 206.3; see 'Abdu'l-Bahá, *Secret of Divine Civilization,* pp. 20–22.

36. Bahá'u'lláh, cited in *Messages from the Universal House of Justice, 1963–1986,* no. 206.3a–3b.

37. Bahá'u'lláh, *Tablets of Bahá'u'lláh,* pp. 38, 96–97.

38. Shoghi Effendi, *Messages to the Bahá'í World,* p. 127; *Messages from the Universal House of Justice, 1963–1986,* no. 206.2.

39. Bahá'u'lláh, *Tablets of Bahá'u'lláh,* p. 222; extract from an unpublished letter dated 26 January 1939 written on behalf of Shoghi Effendi to an individual. Used with permission of the Universal House of Justice, from a letter dated October 13, 1998. See http://bahai-library.com/uhj/pronouns.etc.html.

40. Shoghi Effendi, *God Passes By,* p. 408; Shoghi Effendi, *This Decisive Hour,* no. 64.7.

41. Extract from a letter written on behalf of Shoghi Effendi, quoted in *Messages from the Universal House of Justice, 1963–1986,* nos. 111.12, 206.3; Bahá'u'lláh, cited in ibid., no. 206.3b.

42. *Messages from the Universal House of Justice, 1963–86,* no. 206.4.

43. Ibid., no. 206.5.

44. Bahá'u'lláh, *Tablets of Bahá'u'lláh,* p. 186.

45. Ibid., p. 138; 'Abdu'l-Bahá, *Secret of Divine Civilization,* pp. 71, 23–24.

46. Bahá'u'lláh, *Tablets of Bahá'u'lláh,* p. 88; 'Abdu'l-Bahá, *Secret of Divine Civilization,* p. 19.

47. 'Abdu'l-Bahá, *Secret of Divine Civilization,* pp. 2, 103, 96–97.

48. Committee for the Psychological Study of Peace (IUPsyS), "Cultures of Peace: Social-Psychological Foundations," based on a UNESCO-commissioned background paper, p. 2.

49. Jim Collins, "Level 5 Leadership: The Triumph of Humility and Fierce Resolve," in *Harvard Business Review* (January 2001): 66–76.

50. Ibid., p. 73.

51. Bahá'u'lláh, in *Bahíyyih Khánum,* p. 3.

52. Shoghi Effendi, in ibid., pp. 34–35.

53. Ibid., pp. 28, 30.

54. Ibid., pp. 42–43.

55. Bahíyyih Khánum, in ibid., p. 115.

56. Shoghi Effendi, in ibid., p. 38.

57. Extract from a letter written on behalf of Shoghi Effendi, in ibid., p. 79.

58. Ella Goodall Cooper, "Bahiyyih Khanum—An Appreciation," pp. 202–03; Marjorie Morton, "Bahíyyih Khánum," in *Bahá'í World* 5 (1936): 181.

59. Shoghi Effendi, in *Bahíyyih Khánum,* pp. 34–35; IUPsyS, "Cultures of Peace: Social-Psychological Foundations," p. 2.

60. Extract from a letter written on behalf of Shoghi Effendi, in *Bahíyyih Khánum,* pp. 78–79.

61. Shoghi Effendi, in ibid., pp. 26, 29.

62. Ibid., p. 53.

63. Extract from a letter written on behalf of Shoghi Effendi, in ibid., pp. 68, 69.

64. Shoghi Effendi, in ibid., p. 24.

65. 'Abdu'l-Bahá, *Secret of Divine Civilization*, p. 98.

66. 'Abdu'l-Bahá, quoted in *Messages from the Universal House of Justice, 1963–1986*, no. 35.7a.

67. Shoghi Effendi, *World Order of Bahá'u'lláh*, p. 163.

68. Ibid., pp. 20, 23.

69. Bahá'u'lláh, *Tablets of Bahá'u'lláh*, p. 130.

70. *Messages from the Universal House of Justice, 1963–1986*, nos. 35.13, 35.11.

71. Bahá'u'lláh, *Tablets of Bahá'u'lláh*, pp. 35, 168; 'Abdu'l-Bahá, *Selections from the Writings of 'Abdu'l-Bahá*, no. 40.3.

72. 'Abdu'l-Bahá, *Secret of Divine Civilization*, p. 114.

73. Ibid.

74. Shoghi Effendi, *World Order of Bahá'u'lláh*, p. 37; 'Abdu'l-Bahá, *Secret of Divine Civilization*, p. 10.

75. Shoghi Effendi, in *Bahíyyih Khánum*, p. 26.

76. Extract from a letter written on behalf of Shoghi Effendi, in ibid., p. 74.

77. Letter written on behalf of Shoghi Effendi, in *Bahá'í News*, no. 68 (November 1932): 3.

78. Extract from a letter written on behalf of Shoghi Effendi, in *Bahíyyih Khánum*, p. 92.

Appendix

1. Adib Taherzadeh, *Child of the Covenant*, p. 22.

2. Shoghi Effendi, in *Bahíyyih Khánum*, p. 54.

3. Ibid., p. 32.

4. Ibid., p. 41; letter written on behalf of Shoghi Effendi, in ibid., p. 71.

Glossary

'Abdu'l-Bahá. *Servant of Bahá:* the title assumed by 'Abbás Effendi (1844–1921), eldest son and appointed successor of Bahá'u'lláh, the Founder of the Bahá'í Faith. After Bahá'u'lláh's death in 1892, 'Abdu'l-Bahá became head of the Bahá'í Faith. He is known by a number of titles including the Center of the Covenant, the Mystery of God, the Master, and the Perfect Exemplar of Bahá'u'lláh's teachings.

'Abdu'l-Ḥamíd II. (1842–1918) Sultan of the Ottoman Empire from 1876 to 1909. He was responsible for the renewal of 'Abdu'l-Bahá's incarceration in Acre. Public discontent with his despotic rule and resentment against European intervention in the Balkans led to the military revolution of the Young Turks in 1908. 'Abdu'l Ḥamíd was subsequently deposed in 1909.

Acre or **'Akká.** A four-thousand-year-old seaport located on the coast of what is now Israel. In the mid-nineteenth century Acre was a penal colony of the Ottoman Empire. In 1868 Bahá'u'lláh and His family and companions were banished to Acre by Sulṭán 'Abdu'l-'Azíz. Because of the privations suffered within its walls Bahá'u'lláh named Acre "the Most Great Prison."

Administrative Order. The international system for administering the affairs of the Bahá'í community. It is unique in religious history in that clear instructions concerning succession of authority and the form of organization are set out in writing by Bahá'u'lláh, the Founder of the Faith. The principal institutions of the Bahá'í Administrative Order are the Guardianship and the Universal House of Justice. The Administrative Order consists of democratically elected Local and National Spiritual Assemblies which direct the affairs of the Bahá'í community, uphold Bahá'í laws and standards, and take responsibility for the education, guidance, and protection of the community. In addition, it includes the institutions of the Hands of the Cause of God, the International Teaching Center, and the Continental Board of Counselors and their Auxiliary Boards and assistants, whose members are appointed. The appointed members of these institutions perform a counseling and advisory function and have particular responsibility for the protection and expansion of the Bahá'í Faith. See also **Continental Board of Counselors, Guardianship, International Teaching Center, Local Spiritual Assembly, National Spiritual Assembly, Spiritual Assemblies,** and **Universal House of Justice.**

Adrianople. Present-day Edirne, a city in European Turkey, to which Bahá'u'lláh and His family were exiled in 1863, and where they resided for five years.

Ages. The Bahá'í Dispensation is divided into three Ages: the Heroic Age, the Formative Age, and the Golden Age—which correspond to stages in the development and growth of the Bahá'í Faith. The Heroic Age or Apostolic Age began in 1844 with the Declaration of the Báb and spanned the ministries of the Báb (1844–53), Bahá'u'lláh (1853–92), and 'Abdu'l-Bahá (1892–1921). The Formative Age began in 1921 when Shoghi Effendi became the Guardian of the Bahá'í Faith. This second and current age is identified with the rise and establishment of the Bahá'í Administrative Order. It is to be followed by the third and final age, the Golden Age, which is destined to witness the establishment of the Bahá'í World Commonwealth. See also **Báb, the; Dispensation; Bahá'í World Commonwealth.**

Apostolic Age. See **Ages.**

Áqáy-i-Kalím. See **Mírzá Músá.**

Arc, the. A curved path laid out by Shoghi Effendi on Mount Carmel, stretching across the Bahá'í properties near the Shrine of the Báb and centered on the graves of distinguished members of Bahá'u'lláh's family. The seats of the major international administrative institutions of the Bahá'í Faith are constructed along this arc.

Archbreaker of the Covenant. Mírzá Muhammad-'Alí, a son of Bahá'u'lláh and younger half-brother of 'Abdu'l-Bahá who attempted to subvert the provisions of Bahá'u'lláh's written will and to seize leadership of the Bahá'í community after the passing of Bahá'u'lláh. See also **Covenant-breaker.**

Ásíyih Khánum, also known as *Navváb* (an honorific implying "Grace" or "Highness"); *the Most Exalted Leaf:* She was the mother of 'Abdu'l-Bahá, Bahíyyih Khánum, and Mírzá Mihdí. She married Bahá'u'lláh in 1835, accompanied Him in His exiles, and died in 1886.

Báb, the. *The Gate:* title assumed by Siyyid 'Alí-Muhammad (1819–1850), the Prophet-Founder of the Bábí Faith, and the Herald and Forerunner of Bahá'u'lláh.

Bábí. Follower of the Báb.

Bahá'í World Center. The world spiritual and administrative centers of the Bahá'í Faith, located in the twin cities of Acre and Haifa, Israel. See also **Administrative Order.**

Bahá'í World Commonwealth. The future commonwealth of the nations of the world envisaged in the Bahá'í writings. It will include a federal system of governance, to which all national governments will be accountable, a system of international communication; an international auxiliary language; a world script and literature; a uniform and universal system of currency, weights, and measures; and an integrated economic system with coordinated markets and regulated channels of distribution. See also **World Order of Bahá'u'lláh.**

Bahá'u'lláh. *The Glory of God:* title of Mírzá Ḥusayn-'Alí (1817–1892), Prophet-Founder of the Bahá'í Faith. Bahá'ís refer to Him with a variety of titles, including the Promised One of All Ages, the Blessed Beauty, the Blessed Perfection, the Ancient Beauty. Bahá'u'lláh's writings are considered by Bahá'ís to be direct revelation from God.

Bahjí. *Delight, gladness, joy:* the name of the property north of Acre where Bahá'u'lláh lived from 1880 until His ascension in 1892, and where His shrine is situated.

Book of the Covenant. A translation of *Kitáb-i-'Ahd* or *Kitáb-i-'Ahdí,* meaning "the Book of the, or My, Covenant": Bahá'u'lláh's last will and testament, written in His own hand, it designates 'Abdu'l-Bahá as His successor and the Center of His Covenant and provides for the continuation of divine authority over the affairs of the Bahá'í Faith in the future.

Branch or **branches.** A description referring to the male members of Bahá'u'lláh's family.

British mandate. Authorization given to Great Britain by the League of Nations to govern parts of the former territories of the Ottoman Empire after World War I. These territories included Iraq and Palestine.

Caliphate. In the Sunní branch of Islam, a successor to the Prophet Muḥammad and spiritual leader.

Center of the Covenant. A title of 'Abdu'l-Bahá referring to His appointment by Bahá'u'lláh as the successor to whom all must turn after Bahá'u'lláh's passing. See also **Covenant.**

Central Figures. Term used to refer collectively to Bahá'u'lláh, the Báb, and 'Abdu'l-Bahá. See also **Bahá'u'lláh; Báb, the;** and **'Abdu'l-Bahá.**

Constantinople. Present-day Istanbul, the former capital of the Ottoman Empire to which Bahá'u'lláh was banished in 1863.

Continental Boards of Counselors. An institution of the Bahá'í Administrative Order established by the Universal House of Justice in 1968. Its members are appointed to five-year terms by the Universal House of Justice and serve in five zones—Africa, the Americas, Asia, Australasia, and Europe. Its duties are concerned with the expansion and development of the Bahá'í Faith and the direction of the work of the Auxiliary Board members.

Covenant. A reference to the provisions made in the Bahá'í writings concerning the succession of authority in the Bahá'í Faith after the passing of Bahá'u'lláh and the structure of the Bahá'í Administrative Order. Bahá'u'lláh's Covenant with His followers designates 'Abdu'l-Bahá as the Center of the Covenant and confers upon him the authority to interpret Bahá'u'lláh's writings. The Covenant also formally established the institutions of the Guardianship and the Universal House of Justice as the twin successors of Bahá'u'lláh and 'Abdu'l-Bahá.

Covenant-breaker. A Bahá'í term used to describe a Bahá'í who attempts to disrupt the unity of the Bahá'í Faith by publicly denying the line of succession (i.e., Bahá'u'lláh, 'Abdu'l-Bahá, Shoghi Effendi, and the Universal House of Justice), or who rebels against the head of the Faith and actively works to undermine the Covenant. Bahá'ís who persist in these activities may be removed from membership in the Bahá'í Faith. This is a very rare occurrence. See also **Covenant.**

Dispensation. The period of time during which the laws and teachings of a Prophet or Manifestation of God have spiritual authority. A dispensation begins with the Manifestation's declaration of His mission and ends with the advent of the next Manifestation of God.

Díyár-Bakr. A commercial city on the banks of the Tigris River in Turkey.

Elijah. Hebrew prophet who taught that there is only one God.

Farmán. An order, command, or royal decree.

Formative Age. See **Ages.**

Gallipoli. A seaport that lies west-southwest of present-day Istanbul.

Getsinger, Lua. (1871–1916) Born Louisa A. Moore; an outstanding early American Bahá'í who traveled widely in the United States, Europe, and India to teach others about the Bahá'í Faith. She was among the first Western pilgrims to visit 'Abdu'l-Bahá in Acre in 1898. For an account of her life and service to the Faith, see Velda Piff Metelmann, *Lua Getsinger: Herald of the Covenant* (Oxford: George Ronald, 1997).

Golden Age. See **Ages.**

Guardian of the Cause of God and **Guardianship.** The institution, anticipated by Bahá'u'lláh in the *Kitáb-i-Aqdas* and created by 'Abdu'l-Bahá in his Will and Testament, to which Shoghi Effendi was appointed. He held this office from 1921 until his death in 1957. The Guardian's chief functions were to interpret the writings of Bahá'u'lláh, the Báb, and 'Abdu'l-Bahá and to guide the development of the Bahá'í community. See also **Shoghi Effendi.**

Haifa. Seaport located in present-day Israel where the Bahá'í World Center is located.

Handmaid or **handmaiden.** A poetic term used in the Bahá'í writings to refer to a female member of the Bahá'í community.

Hands of the Cause of God. Eminent Bahá'ís appointed by Bahá'u'lláh and later by Shoghi Effendi to stimulate the propagation and ensure the protection of the Bahá'í Faith. See also **Continental Boards of Counselors, International Teaching Center.**

Heroic Age. See **Ages.**

House of Worship. See **Mashríqu'l-Adhkár.**

International Teaching Center. An institution established by the Universal House of Justice in 1973. Its Counselor members are appointed to a five-year term. The duties of the International Teaching Center include coordinating and stimulating the activities of the Continental Boards of Counselors, serving as the liaison between them and the Universal House of Justice, keeping fully informed of the condition of the Bahá'í Faith throughout the world, and stimulating the development of social and economic life both within and outside the Bahá'í community. See also **Continental Boards of Counselors** and **Hands of the Cause of God.**

'Ishqábád. (also Ashkhabad) Capital of present-day Turkmenistan, site of the first Bahá'í Mashríqu'l-Adhkár. See also **Mashríqu'l-Adhkár.**

Kitáb-i-Aqdas. *The Most Holy Book (Kitáb* means "book"; *Aqdas* means "Most Holy"): revealed in Acre in 1873, it is the chief repository of Bahá'u'lláh's laws and is considered by Bahá'ís to be the charter of a future world civilization.

Leaf or **Leaves,** a poetic term used in the Bahá'í writings to refer to female members of the Bahá'í community.

Local Spiritual Assembly. The local administrative body of the Bahá'í community ordained in the writings of Bahá'u'lláh. Its nine members are elected annually from among the adult membership of the community and serve for one year. The Assembly oversees the affairs of the community. Its decisions are made after consultation. See **Spiritual Assemblies.**

Maidservant or **maidservants.** A designation applied to a female Bahá'í signifying recognition of her commitment to conform her life to the precepts of the religion.

Manifestation of God. The term used to describe a Prophet or Messenger of God Who is the Founder of a religious dispensation. The Manifestations are not God descended to earth, but They reflect God's attributes, just as a mirror reflects the sun but is not the sun itself. See also **Dispensation.**

Mashríqu'l-Adhkár. *The Dawning-place of the Praise of God:* title designating a Bahá'í House of Worship or Temple. Open to the public for devotional meetings, Bahá'í Houses of Worship have been constructed in Wilmette, near Chicago, Illinois; Kampala, Uganda; Ingleside, near Sydney, Australia; Langenhain, near Frankfurt am Main, Germany; Panama City, Panama; Apia, Western Samoa; and New Delhi, India. Plans for construction of one in Santiago, Chile, are underway. The first Bahá'í House of Worship, built in 1902 in 'Ishqábád, Turkmenistan, was damaged by an earthquake in 1948 and, following heavy rains, had to be razed in 1963.

Master, the. A title of 'Abdu'l-Bahá.

Maxwell, May. (1870–1940) A distinguished early American Bahá'í who was among the first group of Western pilgrims to visit 'Abdu'l-Bahá in Acre in 1898/ 99. For a brief account of her life and service to the Bahá'í Faith, see *The Bahá'í World* 8: 631–42.

Mírzá Mihdí. (1848–70) A son of Bahá'u'lláh to whom He gave the title *The Purest Branch:* He served as his Father's amanuensis. He died in 1870 at the age of twenty-two after falling to his death in the Most Great Prison in 'Akká.

Mírzá Muḥammad-'Alí. See **Archbreaker of the Covenant.**

Mírzá Músá. (d. 1887) Also known as Áqáy-i-Kalím. A younger brother of Bahá'u'lláh who recognized the station of the Báb and of Bahá'u'lláh and faithfully served Bahá'u'lláh throughout His exiles. He often met with government officials and religious leaders on Bahá'u'lláh's behalf until 'Abdu'l-Bahá assumed that function.

Mírzá Yaḥyá. (c. 1831/2–1912) A younger half-brother of Bahá'u'lláh, also known as Ṣubḥí-i-Azal (the Morn of Eternity). He broke away from Bahá'u'lláh, claiming to be the Báb's successor. His spurious challenge was unsuccessful, and he was exiled to Cyprus by the Ottoman authorities at the time Bahá'u'lláh and His companions were sent to Acre. He died in Cyprus in 1912.

Mount Carmel. The mountain in Haifa, Israel, spoken of by Isaiah as the "mountain of God." Today, the site of the Shrine of the Báb and the administrative buildings of the Bahá'í World Center.

Muftí. A professional jurist responsible for the interpretation of Islamic law.

Muḥammad. (A.D. 570–632) The Prophet and Founder of Islam. Bahá'ís regard Muḥammad as a Manifestation of God and His book, the Qur'án, as holy scripture.

Munírih Khánum. (d. 1938) The wife of 'Abdu'l-Bahá; also known as the Holy Mother.

Nabíl. Literally *noble, learned:* surname of Mullá Muḥammad-i-Zarandí, who wrote the detailed history of the Bábí Faith titled *The Dawn-Breakers.*

National Spiritual Assembly. The elected national administrative body of the Bahá'í Faith, ordained in the Bahá'í writings. The members, elected at a National Convention from among the Bahá'ís in the country, serve for one year. The National Assembly is responsible for overseeing the work of the Bahá'í Faith in its area of jurisdiction. See **Spiritual Assemblies.**

Navváb. See Ásíyih Khánum.

Naw-Rúz. Literally *New Day:* the Bahá'í New Year's Day, the date of the vernal equinox, which normally falls on 21 March.

Nineteen Day Feast. A Bahá'í institution inaugurated by the Báb and confirmed by Bahá'u'lláh in the Kitáb-i-Aqdas. It is held on the first day of every Bahá'í month, each consisting of nineteen days and bearing the name of one of the attributes of God. The Nineteen Day Feast is the heart of Bahá'í community life at the local level and consists of devotional, consultative, and social elements. See also **Kitáb-i-Aqdas.**

Ottoman Empire. An empire with its capital in Constantinople (modern-day Istanbul). The empire lasted from the decline of the Byzantine Empire in the fourteenth century until the establishment of Turkey as a republic in 1922. Two of its leaders, Sulṭán 'Abdu'l-'Azíz and Sulṭán 'Abdu'l-Ḥamíd II, were responsible for the imprisonment and banishment of Bahá'u'lláh and 'Abdu'l-Bahá in Constantinople, Adrianople, and Acre. Both leaders were eventually deposed.

Prime mover of sedition. Refers to Mírzá Muḥammad-'Alí. See also **Archbreaker of the Covenant.**

Purest Branch. See **Mírzá Mihdí.**

Queen Marie of Romania. (1875–1938) Queen of Romania from 1914 to 1927 and the first monarch to embrace the teachings of the Bahá'í Faith. She learned of the Bahá'í Faith from **Martha Root.** Her association with the Bahá'í Faith is described in Della A. Marcus, *Her Eternal Crown, Queen Marie of Romania and the Bahá'í Faith* (Oxford: George Ronald, 2000).

Qiblih. *"That which one faces; prayer-direction; point of adoration":* the focus to which the faithful turn in prayer. The Qiblih for Bahá'ís is the Most Holy Tomb of Bahá'u'lláh at Bahjí.

Ransom-Kehler, Keith. (d. 1933) A distinguished American Bahá'í who traveled to Persia to represent the National Spiritual Assembly of the Bahá'ís of the United States and Canada with a petition requesting the removal of a ban on the entry and circulation of Bahá'í literature. She died in Isfahan on 23 October 1933. A brief account of her life is in *The Bahá'í World* 5: 389–410.

Revelation. The laws, teachings and message of God transmitted through His Manifestations to humanity.

Root, Martha. (1872–1939) An American Bahá'í known for her unique exertions in the field of international teaching, which carried her around the globe four times over a period of some twenty years. She spoke of the Bahá'í Faith to kings, queens, high-ranking government and religious officials, professors, leaders of thought, and other prominent people. An account of her life is presented in M.R. Garis, *Martha Root, Lioness at the Threshold* (Wilmette: Bahá'í Publishing Trust, 1983).

Rúḥíyyih Khánum. (1910–2000) Born Mary Maxwell, also called Rúḥíyyih Rabbání; daughter of May Bolles Maxwell and Sutherland Maxwell of Montreal, and wife of Shoghi Effendi Rabbání, the Guardian of the Bahá'í Faith. *Rúḥíyyih* (meaning "spiritual") is a name given to her by Shoghi Effendi on their marriage. *Khánum* is a Persian title meaning "Lady," "Madame," or "Mrs."

Servant. A designation usually applied to a male Bahá'í signifying recognition of his commitment to conform his life to the precepts of the religion.

Sháh Bahrám. Title of the world savior foretold in Zoroastrian prophecy Who will triumph over evil and bring peace to the earth.

Shíráz. The city in Iran where the Báb declared His mission in 1844. See also **Báb, the.**

Shoghi Effendi. The title by which Shoghi Rabbání (1897–1957), great-grandson of Bahá'u'lláh and eldest grandson of 'Abdu'l-Bahá, is known to Bahá'ís. (*Shoghi* is an Arabic name meaning "the one who longs"; *Effendi* is a Turkish honorific signifying "sir" or "master.") He was appointed Guardian of the Bahá'í Faith by 'Abdu'l-Bahá in his Will and Testament and assumed the office after 'Abdu'l-Bahá's death in 1921.

Síyáh-Chál. *Black Pit:* the subterranean dungeon in Tehran in which Bahá'u'lláh was imprisoned from August through December 1852. Here, He received the first intimations of His world mission.

Spiritual Assemblies. The name of elected Bahá'í administrative institutions that operate at the local and national levels of society. They are responsible for coordinating and directing the affairs of the Bahá'í community in their areas of jurisdiction. See also **Local Spiritual Assembly, National Spiritual Assembly.**

Star of the West. The first Western Bahá'í magazine, published in North America from 1910 to April 1924.

Ṣubḥ-i-Azal. See **Mírzá Yaḥyá.**

Tablet. Refers to letters written by Bahá'u'lláh, the Báb, or 'Abdu'l-Bahá.

Tabríz. City in present-day Iran where the Báb was martyred. See also **Báb, the.**

Templers. Members of the Society of the Temple, founded in the mid-1800s in Germany. They believed that Christ's return was imminent and settled in the Holy Land in anticipation of the event. The first and largest of their settlements was in Haifa at the foot of Mount Carmel, where they built their homes.

Tripolitania. A former Ottoman colony that is now part of present-day Libya.

True, Corinne. An early American Bahá'í and Hand of the Cause of God who greatly assisted in the completion of the Bahá'í House of Worship in Wilmette, Illinois. Her services are described in Nathan Rutstein, *Corinne True, Faithful Handmaid of 'Abdu'l-Bahá* (Oxford: George Ronald, 1987).

Universal House of Justice. The Head of the Bahá'í Faith after the passing of the Guardian, Shoghi Effendi, the Universal House of Justice is the supreme international governing and legislative body of the Bahá'í Faith. Established in 1963, the Universal House of Justice is elected every five years by members of the National Spiritual Assemblies who assemble at an international Bahá'í convention. The Universal House of Justice directs and guides the administrative activities of the worldwide Bahá'í community. It is the institution ordained by Bahá'u'lláh as the agency invested with authority to legislate on matters not covered in His writings.

Will and Testament of 'Abdu'l-Bahá. A document, in the handwriting of 'Abdu'l-Bahá, that establishes the institution of the Guardianship and appoints Shoghi Effendi as Guardian. It provides for the election of the Universal House of Justice and for the appointment of the Hands of the Cause of God, and it prescribes the functions of these two institutions. It also creates the institution of the National Spiritual Assembly.

World Order of Bahá'u'lláh. A critical element of the Bahá'í teachings is the concept of a new World Order, which, in coming centuries, is destined to embrace the whole of mankind, to be a force for peace and justice, and to provide the basis for the emergence of a world civilization. Its details are set out in the writings of Bahá'u'lláh and 'Abdu'l-Bahá and the letters of Shoghi Effendi, and its current Bahá'í Administrative Order is viewed as the nucleus and pattern of the evolving world order. See also **Administrative Order.**

Young Turk Revolution. A revolutionary movement against the authoritarian regime of Ottoman Sultan 'Abdu'l-Ḥamíd II, which resulted in the establishment of a constitutional government in 1908 and the subsequent release of all political and religious prisoners—including 'Abdu'l-Bahá. In 1909 Sulṭán 'Abdu'l-Ḥamíd was deposed.

A Selected Bibliography ❧

Works of Bahá'u'lláh

Gleanings from the Writings of Bahá'u'lláh. 1st pocket-size ed. Translated by Shoghi Effendi. Wilmette, IL: Bahá'í Publishing Trust, 1983.

The Summons of the Lord of Hosts: Tablets of Bahá'u'lláh. Haifa, Israel: Bahá'í World Centre, 2002.

Tablets of Bahá'u'lláh revealed after the Kitáb-i-Aqdas. Compiled by the Research Department of the Universal House of Justice and translated by Habib Taherzadeh with the assistance of a Committee at the Bahá'í World Centre. 1st pocket-size ed. Wilmette, IL: Bahá'í Publishing Trust, 1988.

Works of 'Abdu'l-Bahá

The Secret of Divine Civilization. Translated from the Persian by Marzieh Gail in consultation with Ali-Kuli Khan. 1st pocket-size ed. Wilmette, IL: Bahá'í Publishing Trust, 1990.

Selections from the Writings of 'Abdu'l-Bahá. Compiled by the Research Department of the Universal House of Justice. Translated by a Committee at the Bahá'í World Center and by Marzieh Gail. 1st pocket-size ed. Wilmette, IL: Bahá'í Publishing Trust, 1996.

Will and Testament of 'Abdu'l-Bahá. Wilmette, IL: Bahá'í Publishing Trust, 1944.

Works of Shoghi Effendi

The Advent of Divine Justice. 1st pocket-size ed. Wilmette, IL: Bahá'í Publishing Trust, 1990.

Bahá'í Administration: Selected Messages, 1922–1932. 7th ed. Wilmette, IL: Bahá'í Publishing Trust, 1974.

God Passes By. New ed. Wilmette, IL: Bahá'í Publishing Trust, 1974.

Messages to the Antipodes: Communications from Shoghi Effendi to the Bahá'í Communities of Australasia. Ed. Graham Hassall. Mona Vale, Australia: Bahá'í Publications Australia, 1997.

Messages to the Bahá'í World, 1950–1957. Rev. ed. Wilmette, IL: Bahá'í Publishing Trust, 1971.

Messages of Shoghi Effendi to the Indian Subcontinent, 1923–1957. Rev. and enlarged ed. Compiled and edited by Írán Fúrútan Muhájir. New Delhi: Bahá'í Publishing Trust, 1995.

The Promised Day Is Come. 3rd ed. Wilmette, IL: Bahá'í Publishing Trust, 1980.

This Decisive Hour: Messages from Shoghi Effendi to the North American Bahá'ís, 1932–1946. Wilmette, IL: Bahá'í Publishing Trust, 2002.

The Unfolding Destiny of the British Bahá'í Community: The Messages from the Guardian of the Bahá'í Faith to the Bahá'ís of the British Isles. London: Bahá'í Publishing Trust, 1981.
The World Order of Bahá'u'lláh: Selected Letters. 1st pocket-size ed. Wilmette, IL: Bahá'í Publishing Trust, 1991.

Works of the Universal House of Justice

Messages from the Universal House of Justice, 1963–1986: The Third Epoch of the Formative Age. Compiled by Geoffrey W. Marks. Wilmette, IL.: Bahá'í Publishing Trust, 1996.

Other Works

Aṣdaq, Rúḥá, with the assistance of Lameah Khodadoost. *One Life, One Memory: In the Presence of 'Abdu'l-Bahá, Haifa, January 1914.* Oxford: George Ronald, 1999.

Bahá'u'lláh, 'Abdu'l-Bahá, Shoghi Effendi, and Bahíyyih Khánum. *Bahíyyih Khánum: The Greatest Holy Leaf.* Compiled by the Research Department at the Bahá'í World Centre. Haifa: Bahá'í World Centre, 1982.

Balyuzi, H. M. *'Abdu'l-Bahá: The Centre of the Covenant of Bahá'u'lláh.* London: George Ronald, 1971.

Blomfield, Lady (Sitárih Khánum). *The Chosen Highway.* Wilmette, IL.: Bahá'í Publishing Trust, n.d.; repr. 1975.

Committee for the Psychological Study of Peace (IUPsyS). "Cultures of Peace: Social-Psychological Foundations." Based on a UNESCO-commissioned background paper.

Ford, Mary Hanford. *The Oriental Rose, or The Teachings of Abdul Baha Which Trace the Chart of "The Shining Pathway."* Chicago: Bahai Publishing Society, 1910.

Fredrickson, Barbara L. "The Role of Positive Emotions in Positive Psychology: The Broaden-and-Build Theory of Positive Emotions." *American Psychologist* 56, no. 3 (2001): 218–26.

Gail, Marzieh. *Summon Up Remembrance.* Oxford: George Ronald, 1987.

Ghadirian, Abdu'l-Missagh. "Psychological and Spiritual Dimensions of Persecution and Suffering." *Journal of Bahá'í Studies* 6, no. 3: 19.

Goodall, Helen S., and Ella Goodall Cooper. *Daily Lessons Received at 'Akká, January 1908.* Rev. ed. Wilmette, IL: Bahá'í Publishing Trust, 1979.

Hatcher, William S., and J. Douglas Martin. *The Bahá'í Faith: The Emerging Global Religion.* New edition. Wilmette, IL: Bahá'í Publishing, 2002.

Marcus, Della L. *Her Eternal Crown: Queen Marie of Romania and the Bahá'í Faith.* Foreword by Ian C. Semple. Oxford: George Ronald, 2000.

Maxwell, May. *An Early Pilgrimage.* 2d rev. ed. London: George Ronald, 1969.

Metelmann, Velda Piff. *Lua Getsinger: Herald of the Covenant.* Oxford: George Ronald, 1997.

Miall, Hugh. *Peacemakers: Peaceful Settlement of Disputes since 1945.* London: Macmillan, Oxford Research Group, 1992.

Momen, Moojan. *Phenomenon of Religion: A Thematic Approach.* Oxford: Oneworld, 1999.

Nábil-i-Aʻẓam [Muḥammad-i-Zarandí]. *The Dawn-Breakers: Nabíl's Narrative of the Early Days of the Bahá'í Revelation.* Translated and edited by Shoghi Effendi. Wilmette, IL: Bahá'í Publishing Trust, 1932.

Phelps, Myron H. *The Master in ʻAkká.* Revised and annotated, with a new foreword from Marzieh Gail. Los Angeles: Kalimát Press, 1985.

Rabbaní, Rúḥíyyih. *The Priceless Pearl.* London: Bahá'í Publishing Trust, 1969.

Rutstein, Nathan, with Edna M. True. *Corinne True: Faithful Handmaid of ʻAbdu'l-Bahá.* Oxford: George Ronald, 1987.

———. *He Loved and Served: The Story of Curtis Kelsey.* Oxford: George Ronald, 1982.

Sohrab, Mírzá Ahmad. *ʻAbdu'l-Bahá in Egypt.* New York: J. H. Sears and Company, Inc., for the New History Foundation, 1929.

Taherzadeh, Adib. *Child of the Covenant: A study Guide to the Will and Testament of ʻAbdu'l-Bahá.* Oxford: George Ronald, 2000.

———. *The Covenant of Bahá'u'lláh.* Oxford: George Ronald, 1992.

Wallensteen, Peter, ed. *Peace Research: Achievements and Challenges.* Boulder & London: Westview Press, 1988.

Watson, Marie A. *My Pilgrimage to the Land of Desire.* New York: Bahá'í Publishing Committee, 1932.

Whitmore, Bruce W. *The Dawning Place: The Building of a Temple, the Forging of the North American Bahá'í Community.* Wilmette, IL: Bahá'í Publishing Trust, 1984.

A Basic Bahá'í Reading List ❧

The following list provides a sampling of works conveying the spiritual truths, social principles, and history of the Bahá'í Faith.

Introductory Works

Bahá'í International Community, Office of Public Information, New York. *Bahá'u'lláh.* Wilmette, IL: Bahá'í Publishing Trust, 1991.

Bowers, Kenneth E. *God Speaks Again: An Introduction to the Bahá'í Faith.* Wilmette, IL: Bahá'í Publishing, 2004.

Hatcher, William S., and J. Douglas Martin. *The Bahá'í Faith: The Emerging Global Religion.* Wilmette, IL: Bahá'í Publishing, 2002.

Smith, Peter. *A Concise Encyclopedia of the Bahá'í Faith.* Oxford: Oneworld Publications, 2000.

Selected Writings of Bahá'u'lláh

Gleanings from the Writings of Bahá'u'lláh. 1st ps ed. Translated by Shoghi Effendi. Wilmette, IL: Bahá'í Publishing Trust, 1983.

The Hidden Words. Translated by Shoghi Effendi. Wilmette, IL: Bahá'í Publishing, 2002.

The Kitáb-i-Aqdas: The Most Holy Book. Wilmette, IL: Bahá'í Publishing Trust, 1993.

The Kitáb-i-Íqán: The Book of Certitude. Translated by Shoghi Effendi. Wilmette, IL: Bahá'í Publishing, 2003.

Tablets of Bahá'u'lláh revealed after the Kitáb-i-Aqdas. Compiled by the Research Department of the Universal House of Justice. Translated by Habib Taherzadeh. 1st ps ed. Wilmette, IL: Bahá'í Publishing Trust, 1998.

Selected Writings of 'Abdu'l-Bahá

Paris Talks: Addresses given by 'Abdu'l-Bahá in Paris in 1911. 12th ed. London: Bahá'í Publishing Trust, 1995.

The Promulgation of Universal Peace: Talks Delivered by 'Abdu'l-Bahá during His Visit to the United States and Canada in 1912. Compiled by Howard MacNutt. 2nd ed. Wilmette, IL: Bahá'í Publishing Trust, 1982.

The Secret of Divine Civilization. 1st ps ed. Translated by Marzieh Gail and Ali-Kuli Khán. Wilmette, IL: Bahá'í Publishing Trust, 1990.

Selections from the Writings of 'Abdu'l-Bahá. Compiled by the Research Department of the Universal House of Justice. Translated by a Committee at the Bahá'í World Center and Marzieh Gail. Wilmette, IL: Bahá'í Publishing Trust, 1997.

Some Answered Questions. Compiled and translated by Laura Clifford Barney. 1st ps ed. Wilmette, IL: Bahá'í Publishing Trust, 1984.

Selected Writings of Shoghi Effendi

God Passes By. New ed. Wilmette, IL: Bahá'í Publishing Trust, 1974.

The Promised Day Is Come. 3rd ed. Wilmette, IL: Bahá'í Publishing Trust, 1980.

The World Order of Bahá'u'lláh: Selected Letters. 1st ps ed. Wilmette, IL: Bahá'í Publishing Trust, 1991.

Selected Writings of the Universal House of Justice

The Constitution of the Universal House of Justice. Haifa: Bahá'í World Centre, 1972.

Messages from the Universal House of Justice, 1963–1986: The Third Epoch of the Formative Age. Compiled by Geoffry W. Marks. Wilmette, IL: Bahá'í Publishing Trust, 1996.

The Promise of World Peace: To the Peoples of the World. Wilmette, IL: Bahá'í Publishing Trust, 1985.

History

Balyuzi, H. M. *'Abdu'l-Bahá: The Centre of the Covenant of Bahá'u'lláh.* London: George Ronald, 1971.

———. *Bahá'u'lláh: The King of Glory.* Oxford: George Ronald, 1980.

———. *The Báb: The Herald of the Day of Days.* Oxford: George Ronald, 1973.

Nábil-i-A'zam [Muhammad-i-Zarandí]. *The Dawn-Breakers: Nabíl's Narrative of the Early Days of the Bahá'í Revelation.* Translated and edited by Shoghi Effendi. Wilmette, IL: Bahá'í Publishing Trust, 1932.

Rabbaní, Rúhíyyih. *The Priceless Pearl.* London: Bahá'í Publishing Trust, 1969.

Index ❦

Note: The initials "BK" used in sub-entries stand for Bahíyyih Khánum.

For more information about the Bahá'í Faith,
or to contact the Bahá'ís near you, visit
www.us.bahai.org
or call
1-800-22-UNITE

Bahá'í Publishing and the Bahá'í Faith

Bahá'í Publishing produces books based on the teachings of the Bahá'í Faith. Founded nearly 160 years ago, the Bahá'í Faith has spread to some 235 nations and territories and is now accepted by more than five million people. The word "Bahá'í" means "follower of Bahá'u'lláh." Bahá'u'lláh, the Founder of the Bahá'í Faith, asserted that He is the Messenger of God for all of humanity in this day. The cornerstone of His teachings is the establishment of the spiritual unity of humankind, which will be achieved by personal transformation and the application of clearly identified spiritual principles. Bahá'ís also believe that there is but one religion and that all the Messengers of God—among them Abraham, Zoroaster, Moses, Krishna, Buddha, Jesus, and Muḥammad—have progressively revealed its nature. Together, the world's great religions are expressions of a single, unfolding divine plan. Human beings, not God's Messengers, are the source of religious divisions, prejudices, and hatreds.

The Bahá'í Faith is not a sect or denomination of another religion, nor is it a cult or a social movement. Rather, it is a globally recognized independent world religion founded on new books of scripture revealed by Bahá'u'lláh.

Bahá'í Publishing is an imprint of the National Spiritual Assembly of the Bahá'ís of the United States.

Other Books Available from Bahá'í Publishing

The Hidden Words

by Bahá'u'lláh

A collection of lyrical, gem-like verses of scripture that convey time-less spiritual wisdom "clothed in the garment of brevity," the Hidden Words is one of the most important and cherished scriptural works of the Bahá'í Faith.

Revealed by Bahá'u'lláh, the founder of the religion, the verses are a perfect guidebook to walking a spiritual path and drawing closer to God. They address themes such as turning to God, humility, detachment, and love, to name but a few. These verses are among Bahá'u'lláh's earliest and best-known works, having been translated into more than seventy languages and read by millions worldwide. This edition will offer many American readers their first introduction to the vast collection of Bahá'í scripture.

The Kitáb-i-Íqán: The Book of Certitude

by Bahá'u'lláh

The Book of Certitude is one of the most important scriptural works in all of religious history. In it Bahá'u'lláh gives a sweeping overview of religious truth, explaining the underlying unity of the world's religions, describing the universality of the revelations humankind has received from the Prophets of God, illuminating their fundamental teachings, and elucidating allegorical passages from the New Testament and the Koran that have given rise to misunderstandings among religious leaders, practitioners, and the public. Revealed in the span of two days and two nights, the work is, in the words of its translator, Shoghi Effendi, "the most important book written on the spiritual significance" of the Bahá'í Faith.

Advancement of Women:
A Bahá'í Perspective
by Janet A. Khan and Peter J. Khan

Advancement of Women presents the Bahá'í Faith's global perspective on the equality of the sexes, including:

- The meaning of equality
- The education of women and the need for their participation in the world at large
- The profound effects of equality on the family and family relationships
- The intimate relationship between equality of the sexes and global peace
- Chastity, modesty, sexual harassment, and rape

The equality of women and men is one of the basic tenets of the Bahá'í Faith, and much is said on the subject in Bahá'í writings. Until now, however, no single volume created for a general audience has provided comprehensive coverage of the Bahá'í teachings on this topic. In this broad survey, husband-and-wife team Janet and Peter Khan address even those aspects of equality of the sexes that are usually ignored or glossed over in the existing literature.

Tactfully treating a subject that often provokes argumentation, contention, polarization of attitudes, and accusations, the authors elevate the discussion to a new level that challenges all while offending none.

The Bahá'í Faith:
The Emerging Global Religion
by William S. Hatcher and J. Douglas Martin

Explore the history, teachings, structure, and community life of the worldwide Bahá'í community—what may well be the most diverse organized body of people on earth—through this revised and updated comprehensive introduction (2002).

Named by the *Encylopaedia Britannica* as a book that has made "significant contributions to knowledge and understanding" of religious thought, *The Bahá'í Faith* covers the most recent developments in a Faith that, in just over 150 years, has grown to become the second most widespread of the independent world religions.

An excellent introduction. [*The Bahá'í Faith*] offers a clear analysis of the religious and ethical values on which Bahá'ism is based (such as all-embracing peace, world harmony, the important role of women, to mention only a few)."—Annemarie Schimmel, past president, International Association for the History of Religions

"Provide[s] non-Bahá'í readers with an excellent introduction to the history, beliefs, and sociopolitical structure of a religion that originated in Persia in the mid-1800s and has since blossomed into an international organization with . . . adherents from almost every country on earth."—*Montreal Gazette*

The Challenge of Bahá'u'lláh: Does God Still Speak to Humanity Today?

by Gary L. Matthews

One person examines the astonishing claims made by the prophet who founded the Bahá'í religion.

Author Gary Matthews documents why he believes that the Revelation of Bahá'u'lláh is divine in origin, representing a unique summons of unequaled importance to humanity. The book contains discussions of Bahá'í prophecies concerning historical events and scientific discoveries. Among the events and discoveries discussed are the fall of the Ottoman Empire, the worldwide erosion of ecclesiastical authority, the Holocaust, and the development of nuclear weapons. A new and updated edition. The previous edition (George Ronald, ISBN 0-85398-360-7) was a limited release and not offered to the U.S. trade/consumer market.

Close Connections:
The Bridge between Spiritual and Physical Reality

by John S. Hatcher

Examines the bonds between physical and spiritual reality and their implications for science.

Close Connections will appeal to anyone interested in spirituality and its link to everyday life. For more than twenty-five years John Hatcher has studied the nature and purpose of physical reality by exploring the theological and philosophical implications of the authoritative Bahá'í texts. His latest book explains how the gap between physical and spiritual reality is routinely crossed and describes the profound implications that result from the interplay of both worlds.

God Speaks Again:
An Introduction to the Bahá'í Faith

by Kenneth E. Bowers

The Bahá'í Faith is a recognized independent world religion attracting increasing attention—and a growing number of followers—in the U.S. and around the globe as people from all walks of life search for practical spiritual direction and confident hope for the future. *God Speaks Again* tells the story of this thoroughly inclusive religion and describes how the history and teachings of the Bahá'í Faith center around the inspiring person of its Prophet and Founder, Bahá'u'lláh (1817–1892), Whom Bahá'ís around the world regard as the Messenger of God for this day. The cornerstone of Bahá'u'lláh's teachings is the establishment of the unity of humankind, which Bahá'ís believe will be achieved by the application of clearly identified spiritual principles revealed by Bahá'u'lláh. Bahá'ís also believe that there is but one religion, and that all the Messengers of God—among them Abraham, Zoroaster, Moses, Krishna, Buddha, Jesus, and Muḥammad—have progressively revealed its nature. Together, the world's great religions are expressions of a single, unfolding Divine plan. Human beings, not God's Messengers, are the source of religious divisions, prejudices, and hatreds.

It's Not Your Fault: How Healing Relationships Change Your Brain & Can Help You Overcome a Painful Past

by Patricia Romano McGraw

Simply put, you can't think your way to happiness if you're suffering the effects of trauma or abuse. Yet every day, millions receive this message from a multi-billion-dollar self-help industry. As a result, many think it's their fault when their efforts to heal themselves fail. Far too many sincere, intelligent, and highly motivated people who have followed popular advice for self-healing still feel depressed, anxious, unloved, and unlovable. Why is this? If popular pathways for self-healing don't work, what does? How can those who suffer begin to find relief, function better, and feel genuinely optimistic, relaxed, loved, and lovable? This engaging and highly readable book, based on the author's professional experience in treating those who suffer from the devastating effects of emotional trauma, offers hope for those who suffer and those who care about them. McGraw describes how trauma affects the brain and, therefore, one's ability to carry out "good advice"; explains the subtle and largely hidden processes of attunement and attachment that take place between parents and children, examining their impact on all future relationships; tells what is needed for healing to occur; discusses the profound health benefits of spirituality and a relationship with God in assisting and accelerating the healing process; and suggests how members of the helping professions can begin to tap the deepest, most authentic parts of themselves to touch the hearts of those they seek to help.

Marriage beyond Black and White:
An Interracial Family Portrait
by David Douglas and Barbara Douglas

A powerful story about the marriage of a Black man and a White woman, *Marriage beyond Black and White* offers a poignant and sometimes painful look at what it was like to be an interracial couple in the United States from the early 1940s to the mid-1990s. Breaking one of the strongest taboos in American society at the time, Barbara Wilson Tinker and Carlyle Douglas met, fell in love, married, and began raising a family. At the time of their wedding, interracial marriage was outlawed in twenty-seven states and was regarded as an anathema in the rest.

Barbara began writing their story to record both the triumphs and hardships of interracial marriage. Her son David completed the family chronicle. The result will uplift and inspire any reader whose life is touched by injustice, offering an invaluable perspective on the roles of faith and spiritual transformation in combating prejudice and racism.

Prophet's Daughter:
The Life and Legacy of Bahíyyih Khánum,
Outstanding Heroine of the Bahá'í Faith
by Janet A. Khan

The first full-length biography of a member of Bahá'u'lláh's family, an important woman in world religious history.

A biography of a largely unknown yet important woman in world religious history—the eldest daughter of Bahá'u'lláh, founder of the Bahá'í religion—who faithfully served her family and the early followers of a then completely new faith through nearly seven decades of extreme hardship. During the mid-nineteenth and early twentieth centuries, when women in the Middle East were largely invisible, deprived of education, and without status in their communities, she was an active participant in the religion's turbulent early years and contributed significantly to its emergence as an independent world religion. The example of her life, and her remarkable personal qualities, have special relevance to issues confronting society today.

The Reality of Man

compiled by Terry J. Cassiday, Christopher J. Martin, and Bahhaj Taherzadeh

An important new collection of Bahá'í writings on the spiritual nature of human beings.

This compilation provides a sample of the Bahá'í religion's vast teachings on the nature of man. Topics include God's love for humanity; the purpose of life; our spiritual reality; the nature of the soul; how human beings develop spiritually; and immortality and life hereafter. The writings are from Bahá'u'lláh and His appointed successor, 'Abdu'l-Bahá.

"Men at all times and under all conditions stand in need of one to exhort them, guide them and to instruct and teach them. Therefore He hath sent forth His Messengers, His Prophets, and chosen ones that they might acquaint the people with the divine purpose underlying the revelation of Books and the raising up of messengers, and that everyone may become aware of the trust of God, which is latent in the reality of every soul." —Bahá'u'lláh

"The mission of the Prophets, the revelation of the Holy Books, the manifestation of the heavenly teachers and the purpose of divine philosophy all center in the training of the human realities so that they may become clear and pure as mirrors and reflect the light and love of [God]. . . . Otherwise, by simple development along material lines man is not perfected. At most, the physical aspect of man, his natural or material conditions, may become stabilized and improved, but he will remain deprived of the spiritual or divine bestowal. He is then like a body without a spirit, a lamp without the light. . . ." — 'Abdu'l-Bahá

Refresh and Gladden My Spirit: Prayers and Meditations from Bahá'í Scripture

Introduction by Pamela Brode

Discover the Bahá'í approach to prayer with this uplifting collection of prayers and short, inspirational extracts from Bahá'í scripture. More than 120 prayers in *Refresh and Gladden My Spirit* offer solace and inspiration on themes including spiritual growth, nearness to God, comfort, contentment, happiness, difficult times, healing, material needs, praise and gratitude, and strength, to name only a few. An introduction by Pamela Brode examines the powerful effects of prayer and meditation in daily life, outlines the Bahá'í approach to prayer, and considers questions such as "What is prayer?" "Why pray?" "Are our prayers answered?" and "Does prayer benefit the world?"

Release the Sun

by William Sears

Millennial fervor gripped many people around the world in the early nineteenth century. While Christians anticipated the return of Jesus Christ, a wave of expectation swept through Islam that the "Lord of the Age" would soon appear. In Persia, this reached a dramatic climax on May 23, 1844, when a twenty-five-year-old merchant from Shíráz named Siyyid 'Alí-Muḥammad, later titled "the Báb," announced that he was the bearer of a divine Revelation destined to transform the spiritual life of the human race. Furthermore, he claimed that he was but the herald of another Messenger, who would soon bring a far greater Revelation that would usher in an age of universal peace. Against a backdrop of wide-scale moral decay in Persian society, this declaration aroused hope and excitement among all classes. The Báb quickly attracted tens of thousands of followers, including influential members of the clergy—and the brutal hand of a fearful government bent on destroying this movement that threatened to rock the established order.

Release the Sun tells the extraordinary story of the Báb, the Prophet-Herald of the Bahá'í Faith. Drawing on contemporary accounts, William Sears vividly describes one of the most significant but little-known periods in religious history since the rise of Christianity and Islam.

Seeking Faith: Is Religion Really What You Think It Is?

by Nathan Rutstein

What's your concept of religion? A 2001 Gallup Poll on religion in America found that while nearly two out of three Americans claim to be a member of a church or synagogue, more than half of those polled believe that religion is losing its influence on society. *Seeking Faith* examines today's concepts of religion and the various reasons why people are searching in new directions for hope and spiritual guidance. Author Nathan Rutstein explores the need for a sense of purpose, direction, and meaning in life, and the need for spiritual solutions to global problems in the social, economic, environmental, and political realms. Rutstein also discusses the concept of the Spiritual Guide, or Divine Educator, and introduces the teachings of Bahá'u'lláh and the beliefs of the Bahá'í Faith.

A Wayfarer's Guide to Bringing the Sacred Home

by Joseph Sheppherd

What's the spiritual connection between self, family, and community? Why is it so important that we understand and cultivate these key relationships? *A Wayfarer's Guide to Bringing the Sacred Home* offers a Bahá'í perspective on issues that shape our lives and the lives of those around us: the vital role of spirituality in personal transformation, the divine nature of child-rearing and unity in the family, and the importance of overcoming barriers to building strong communities—each offering joy, hope, and confidence to a challenged world. Inspiring extracts and prayers from Bahá'í scripture are included. This is an enlightening read for anyone seeking to bring spirituality into their daily lives.

Visit your favorite bookstore today to find or request these titles from Bahá'í Publishing.